ISLAND OF SHAME

ISLAND OF SHAME

The Secret History of
the U.S. Military Base
on Diego Garcia

David Vine

PRINCETON UNIVERSITY PRESS

PRINCETON ■ OXFORD

Copyright 2009 © by Princeton University Press
Published by Princeton University Press, 41 William Street,
Princeton, New Jersey 08540
In the United Kingdom: Princeton University Press, 6 Oxford Street,
Woodstock, Oxfordshire OX20 1TW

LIBRARY OF CONGRESS CATALOGING-IN-PUBLICATION DATA
Vine, David, 1974–
Island of shame : the secret history of the U.S. military base on Diego Garcia / David Vine.
p. cm.
Includes bibliographical references and index.
ISBN 978-0-691-13869-5 (hbk. : alk. paper) 1. United States. Naval Communications
Station, Diego Garcia—History. 2. Military bases, American—British Indian Ocean
Territory—Diego Garcia. 3. Chagossians—History. 4. Population transfers—Chagossians.
5. Refugees—Mauritius. 6. Refugees—British Indian Ocean Territory. 7. British Indian
Ocean Territory—History. 8. Diego Garcia (British Indian Ocean Territory)—History.
I. Title.
VA68.D53V66 2008
355.70969'7—dc22   2008027868

British Library Cataloging-in-Publication Data is available

This book has been composed in Adobe Garamond

The author will donate all royalties from the sale of this book to the Chagossians.

Printed on acid-free paper. ∞

press.princeton.edu

Printed in the United States of America

3 5 7 9 10 8 6 4 2

"No person shall be . . . deprived of life, liberty, or property, without due process; nor shall private property be taken for public use, without just compensation."

—*Fifth Amendment to the United States Constitution, 1791*

"No one shall be subjected to arbitrary arrest, detention or exile. . . . No one shall be subjected to arbitrary interference with his privacy, family [or] home. . . . No one shall be arbitrarily deprived of his property. . . . Everyone has the right to freedom of movement and residence within the borders of each State."

—*Articles 9, 12, 17, 13, Universal Declaration of Human Rights, 1948*

"We, the inhabitants of Chagos Islands—Diego Garcia, Peros Banhos, Salomon—have been uprooted from those islands. . . . Our ancestors were slaves on those islands, but we know that we are the heirs of those islands. Although we were poor there, we were not dying of hunger. We were living free."

—*Petition to the governments of the United Kingdom and the United States, 1975*

CONTENTS

ILLUSTRATIONS AND TABLES

ILLUSTRATIONS

TABLES

I write this foreword with pride and humility. Pride, because I was present when David Vine first had the inspiration to take on the task of research and writing that led to the book you are holding. The year was 2001. I was part of a team of lawyers from Great Britain, Mauritius, and the United States who were seeking justice for the Chagossian people. I had just returned from visiting the camps in which they are housed in Mauritius. It seemed to me that if we were to explain the Chagossian story of betrayal, struggle, and hope, it would be essential to understand their history, culture, and present condition. A series of telephone conversations led me to Dr. Shirley Lindenbaum, a cultural anthropologist of international renown. She suggested that David Vine would be a perfect candidate for this job. David, Dr. Lindenbaum, and two of my colleagues met in New York, and David launched the work that was to consume him for seven years. From this minor role in the beginning, I take pride.

As for humility: This book and the work it represents have succeeded beyond my greatest hopes. David Vine is one of those rare scholars who combines all the qualities that one must have to write in this field. We are witnessing, on a global scale, the subordination and forced disappearance of hundreds of indigenous populations. We read of the more sensational and violent episodes of these conflicts, but so many others escape our notice. An indigenous population is not "entitled," under what passes for international law, to automatic protection from dislocation. Its status as a cohesive group must first be established. When it is proposed to impose upon it, one must ask what aspects of its culture and history are to be seen as essential or important.

In this process of determining what is just and what is not, the people about whom one is speaking need a voice. They need the help of someone who will understand their lives as deeply as possible and portray their situation honestly and in terms that will withstand debate. David Vine has, in this book, shown us that he combines the scholar's rigor with the student's sympathetic understanding.

I have been a lawyer and law teacher for more than forty years. Given the nature of complex litigation, and particularly human rights litigation, we need to call upon experts in various fields to help us present claims for justice. We know that our adversaries will bring their own experts, and each expert's conclusions will be subject to testing in the crucible of cross-examination. From the beginning, David Vine has identified and followed all the principles of academic rigor that make this study credible as well as persuasive.

David Vine's scholarship is also informed by his systematic and disciplined worldview. He sees the Chagossian people in the context of global struggle. He provides us with a context that makes their story compelling—and relevant. Choices about people's fates and futures are not simply matters of preference, as to which one view is as good as another. Today, we understand that verifiable arguments about the human condition can, and must, be based on close observation of the social forces that people confront as they seek the basic rights that the international community has now defined as essential. David Vine has made an indispensable contribution to this process.

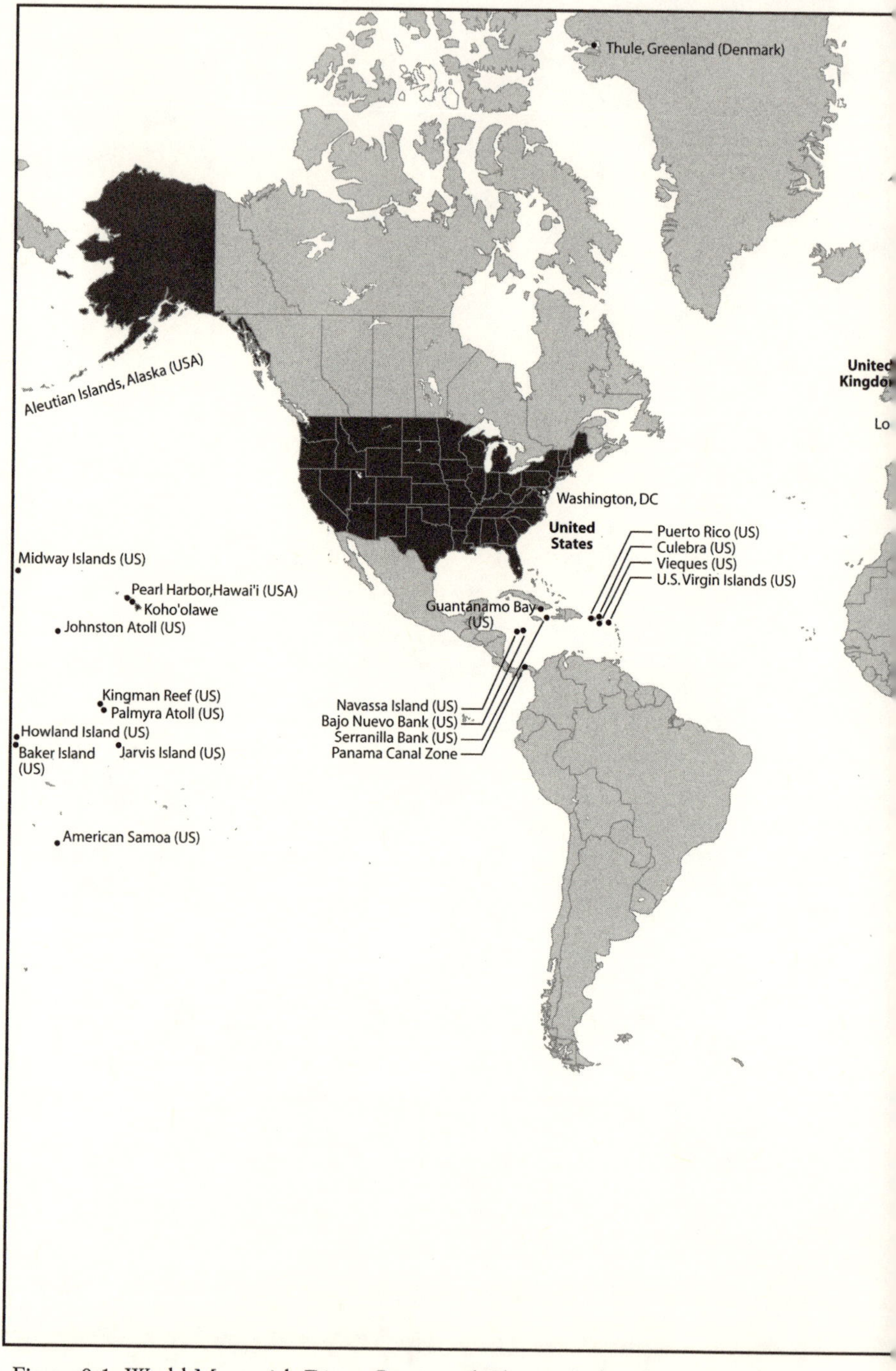

Thule, Greenland (Denmark)

United
Kingdom

Lo

Aleutian Islands, Alaska (USA)

Washington, DC

United
States

Puerto Rico (US)
Culebra (US)
Vieques (US)
U.S. Virgin Islands (US)

Midway Islands (US)

Pearl Harbor, Hawai'i (USA)
Koho'olawe
Johnston Atoll (US)

Guantánamo Bay
(US)

Kingman Reef (US)
Palmyra Atoll (US)
Howland Island (US)
Baker Island   Jarvis Island (US)
(US)

Navassa Island (US)
Bajo Nuevo Bank (US)
Serranilla Bank (US)
Panama Canal Zone

American Samoa (US)

Figure 0.1 World Map, with Diego Garcia and Chagos Archipelago near center; Mauritius and Seychelles insets; the United States of America including all officially claimed territories.

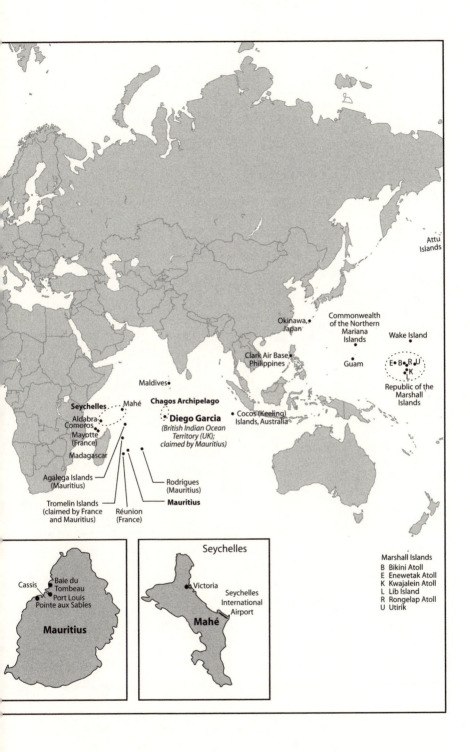

Attu
Islands

Commonwealth
of the Northern
Mariana
Islands

Okinawa,
Japan

Wake Island

Clark Air Base,
Philippines

Guam

E● B● R●U
●
K

Republic of the
Marshall
Islands

Maldives●

Seychelles ● ● ● Mahé

Chagos Archipelago

●● **Diego Garcia**
*(British Indian Ocean
Territory (UK);
claimed by Mauritius)*

● Cocos (Keeling)
Islands, Australia

Aldabra ●
Comoros ●
Mayotte
(France)

Madagascar

Agalega Islands
(Mauritius)

Rodrigues
(Mauritius)

Mauritius

Tromelin Islands
(claimed by France
and Mauritius)

Réunion
(France)

Marshall Islands
B Bikini Atoll
E Enewetak Atoll
K Kwajalein Atoll
L Lib Island
R Rongelap Atoll
U Utirik

Cassis ●
● Baie du
Tombeau
● Port Louis
Pointe aux Sables

Mauritius

Seychelles

● Victoria

Seychelles
International
Airport

Mahé

ABBREVIATIONS AND INITIALISMS

CIA   Central Intelligence Agency
CNO   Chief of Naval Operations
CRG   Chagos Refugees Group
DOD   Department of Defense
FOIA   Freedom of Information Act
GOM   Government of Mauritius
HMG   Her Majesty's Government [Government of the United Kingdom]
IMF   International Monetary Fund
ISA   Office of International Security Affairs, Department of Defense
JCS   Joint Chiefs of Staff
NASA   National Aeronautics and Space Administration
NSC   National Security Council
Rs   Rupees [currency of Mauritius and the Seychelles]
USG   U.S. Government
USO   United Service Organization

Quotations that appear in this book without citation come from interviews and conversations conducted during my research. Translations from French, Mauritian Kreol, and Seselwa (Seychelles Kreol) are my own. The names and some basic identifying features of Chagossians in the book (other than members of the Bancoult family and representatives of the Chagos Refugees Group) have been changed in accordance with anonymity agreements made during the research.

ISLAND OF SHAME

Rita felt like she'd been sliced open and all the blood spilled from her body.

"What happened to you? What happened to you?" her children cried as they came running to her side.

"What happened?" her husband inquired.

"Did someone attack you?" they asked.

"I heard everything they said," Rita recounted, "but my voice couldn't open my mouth to say what happened." For an hour she said nothing, her heart swollen with emotion.

Finally she blurted out: "We will never again return to our home! Our home has been closed!" As Rita told me almost forty years later, the man said to her: "Your island has been sold. You will never go there again."

Marie Rita Elysée Bancoult is one of the people of the Chagos Archipelago, a group of about 64 small coral islands near the isolated center of the Indian Ocean, halfway between Africa and Indonesia, 1,000 miles south of the nearest continental landmass, India. Known as Chagossians, none live in Chagos today. Most live 1,200 miles away on the western Indian Ocean islands of Mauritius and the Seychelles. Like others, 80-year-old Rita lives far from Mauritius's renowned tourist beaches and luxury hotels. Rita, or Aunt Rita as she is known, lives in one of the island's poorest neighborhoods, known for its industrial plants and brothels, in a small aging three-room house made of concrete block.

Rita and other Chagossians cannot return to their homeland because between 1968 and 1973, in a plot carefully hidden from the world, the United States and Great Britain exiled all 1,500–2,000 islanders to create a major U.S. military base on the Chagossians' island Diego Garcia. Initially, government agents told those like Rita who were away seeking medical treatment or vacationing in Mauritius that their islands had been closed and they could not go home. Next, British officials began restricting supplies to the islands and more Chagossians left as food and medicines dwindled. Finally, on the orders of the U.S. military, U.K. officials forced the remaining islanders to board overcrowded cargo ships and left them on the docks in Mauritius and the Seychelles. Just before the last deportations, British agents and U.S. troops on Diego Garcia herded the Chagossians' pet dogs into sealed sheds and gassed and burned them in front of their traumatized owners awaiting deportation.

The people, the descendants of enslaved Africans and indentured south Indians brought to Chagos beginning in the eighteenth century, received no resettlement assistance and quickly became impoverished. Today the group numbers around 5,000. Most remain deeply impoverished. Meanwhile the base on Diego Garcia has become one of the most secretive and powerful U.S. military facilities in the world, helping to launch the invasions of Afghanistan and Iraq (twice), threatening Iran, China, Russia, and nations from southern Africa to southeast Asia, host to a secret CIA detention center for high-profile terrorist suspects, and home to thousands of U.S. military personnel and billions of dollars in deadly weaponry.

"You were born—"

"Peros Banhos," replied Rita Bancoult* before I could finish my question.

"In what year?"

"1928. . . . The thirtieth of June."

Rita grew up in Peros Banhos's capital and administrative center, *L'île du Coin*—Corner Island. *"Lamem mon ne, lamem mon reste,"* she added in the songlike, up-and-down cadence of Chagossians' Kreol: La-MEM moan NAY, la-MEM moan rest-AY. "The island where I was born is the island where I stayed."[1]

Corner Island and 31 neighboring islands in the Peros Banhos atoll form part of the Chagos Archipelago. Portuguese explorers named the largest and best-known island in the archipelago Diego Garcia, about 150 miles to the south. The archipelago's name appears to come from the Portuguese *chagas*—the wounds of Christ.[2]

"And your parents?" I asked. "What island were your parents born on?"

"My parents were born there too," Rita explained. "My grandmother—the mother of my father—was born in Six Islands—*Six Îles*. My father was also born in Six Islands. My grandfather was born there too. My grandmother on my mother's side was born in Peros Banhos."

Rita does not know where her other ancestors were born, one of the injuries still borne by people with enslaved forebears. However, she remembers her grandmother, Olivette Pauline, saying that Olivette's grandmother—Rita's great-great-grandmother—had been enslaved and had the name "Masambo" or "Mazambo." Rita thinks she was a *Malgas*—a person from Madagascar.

---

* Rita's last name has since changed to Isou, but for reasons of clarity I will refer to her throughout by the name Bancoult.

Rita and her family are some of Chagos's indigenous people.[3] Chagossians lived in Diego Garcia and the rest of the previously uninhabited archipelago since the time of the American Revolution when Franco-Mauritians created coconut plantations on the islands and began importing enslaved and, later, indentured laborers from Africa and India.

Over the next two centuries, the diverse workforce developed into a distinct, emancipated society and a people known initially as the *Ilois*—the Islanders. Nearly everyone worked on the coconut plantations. Most worked in the production of copra—dried coconut flesh—and coconut oil made by pressing copra. The people built the archipelago's infrastructure and produced its wealth. As some maps still attest, the islands became known as the "Oil Islands"—meaning coconut oil, not the petroleum that would prove central to the archipelago's recent history. A distinct Chagos Kreol language emerged. The people built their own houses, inhabited land passed down from generation to generation, and kept vegetable gardens and farm animals. By the time Rita was a mother, there were nurseries and schools for her children. In 1961, Mauritian colonial governor Robert Scott remarked that the main village on Diego Garcia had the "look of a French coastal village miraculously transferred whole to this shore."[4]

While far from luxurious and still a plantation society, the islands provided a secure life, generally free of want, and featuring universal employment and numerous social benefits, including regular if small salaries in cash and food, land, free housing, education, pensions, burial services, and basic health care on islands described by many as idyllic.

"You had your house—you didn't have rent to pay," said Rita, a short, stocky woman with carefully French-braided white hair. "With my ration, I got ten and a half pounds of rice each week, I got ten and a half pounds of flour, I got my oil, I got my salt, I got my dhal, I got my beans—it was only butter beans and red beans that we needed to buy.

"And then I got my fresh fish, Saturday. I got my salted fish too, of at least four pounds, five pounds to take. But we didn't take it because we were able to catch fish ourselves. . . . We planted pumpkin, we planted greens. . . . Chickens, we had them. Pigs, the company fed them, and we got some. Chickens, ducks, we fed them ourselves.

"I had a dog named *Katorz*—Katorz, when the sea was at low tide, he would go into the sea. He caught fish in his mouth and he brought them back to me," recalled Rita 1,200 miles from her homeland.

"Life there paid little money, a very little," she said, "but it was the sweet life."

During the winter of 1922, eight-year-old Stuart Barber was sick and confined to bed at his family's home in New Haven, Connecticut. A solitary child long troubled by health problems, Stu, as he was known, found solace that winter in a cherished geography book. He was particularly fascinated by the world's remote islands and had a passion for collecting the stamps of far-flung island colonies. While the Falkland Islands off the coast of Argentina in the South Atlantic became his favorite, Stu noticed that the Indian Ocean was dotted with many islands claimed by Britain.[5]

Thirty-six years later, after having experienced a taste of island life as a naval intelligence officer in Hawai'i during World War II, Stu was drawing up lists of small, isolated colonial islands from every map, atlas, and nautical chart he could find. It was 1958. Thin and spectacled, Stu was a civilian back working for the Navy at the Pentagon.

The Navy ought to have a permanent facility, Stu suddenly realized, like the island bases acquired during the Pacific's "island hopping" campaign against Japan. The facility should be on "a small atoll, minimally populated, with a good anchorage." The Navy, he began to tell his superiors, should build a small airstrip, oil storage, and logistical facilities. The Navy would use it "to support minor peacetime deployments" and major wartime operations.[6]

Working in the Navy's long-range planning office, it occurred to Stu that over the next decades island naval bases would be essential tools for maintaining military dominance during the Cold War. In the era of decolonization, the non-Western world was growing increasingly unstable and would likely become the site of future combat. "Within the next 5 to 10 years," Stu wrote to the Navy brass, "virtually all of Africa, and certain Middle Eastern and Far Eastern territories presently under Western control will gain either complete independence or a high degree of autonomy," making them likely to "drift from Western influence."[7]

All the while, U.S. and other Western military bases were becoming dangerous targets of opposition both in the decolonizing world and from the Soviet Union and the United Nations. The inevitable result for the United States, Stu said, was "the withdrawal" of Western military forces and "the denial or restriction" of Western bases in these areas.[8]

But Stu had the answer to these threats. The solution, he saw, was what he called the "Strategic Island Concept." The plan would be to avoid traditional base sites located in populous mainland areas where they were vulnerable to local non-Western opposition. Instead, "only relatively small, lightly populated islands, separated from major population masses, could be safely held under full control of the West." Island bases were the key.

But if the United States was going to protect its "future freedom of military action," Stu realized, they would have to act quickly to "stockpile" island basing rights as soon as possible. Just as any sensible investor would "stockpile any material commodity which foreseeably will become unavailable in the future," Stu believed, the United States would have to quickly buy up small colonial islands around the world or otherwise ensure its Western allies maintained sovereignty over them. Otherwise the islands would be lost to decolonization forever.[9]

As the idea took shape in his head, Stu first thought of the Seychelles and its more than 100 islands before exploring other possibilities. Finally he found time to gather and "scan all the charts to see what useful islands there might be": There was Phuket, Cocos, Masirah, Farquhar, Aldabra, Desroches, Salomon, and Peros Banhos in and around the Indian Ocean alone. After finding all to be "inferior sites," Stu found "that beautiful atoll of Diego Garcia, right in the middle of the ocean."[10]

Stu saw that the small v-shaped island was blessed with a central location within striking distance of potential conflict zones, one of the world's great natural harbors in its protected lagoon, and enough land to build a large airstrip. But the Navy still needed to ensure it would get a base absent any messy "political complications." Any targeted island would have to be "free of impingement on any significant indigenous population or economic interest." Stu was pleased to note that Diego Garcia's population was "measured only in the hundreds."[11]

When in late 1967 a mule-drawn cart ran over the foot of Rita's three-year-old daughter Noellie, the nurse in Peros Banhos's eight-bed hospital told Rita that the foot needed an operation. She would have to take Noellie to the nearest full-service hospital, 1,200 miles away in Mauritius.

Going to Mauritius meant waiting for the next and only boat service—a four-times-a-year connection with the larger island. Which meant waiting two months. When the boat finally arrived, Rita packed a small box with some clothes and a pot to cook in, locked up the family's wood-framed, thatched-roof house, and left for Mauritius with Noellie, her husband, Julien Bancoult, and their five other children.

After four days on the open ocean, the family arrived in the Mauritian capital, Port Louis, and rushed Noellie to the nearest hospital. As Rita recalled, a doctor operated but saw immediately that the foot had gone untreated for "much too long." Gangrene had set in. Noellie died a month later.

Mourning her death, the family had to wait two months until the departure of the next boat for Chagos. With the departure date approaching, Rita walked to the office of the steamship company to arrange for the family's return. There the steamship company representative told her, "Your island has been sold. You will never go there again," leaving Rita to return to her family speechless and in tears.

When Julien finally heard his wife's news he collapsed backwards, his arms splayed wide, unable to utter a word. Prevented from returning home, Rita, Julien, and their five surviving children found themselves in a foreign land, separated from their home, their land, their animals, their possessions, their jobs, their community, and the graves of their ancestors. The Bancoults had been, as Chagossians came to say, *derasine*—deracinated, uprooted, torn from their natal lands.

"His sickness started to take hold of him," Rita explained. "He didn't understand" a thing she said.

Soon Julien suffered a stroke, his body growing rigid and increasingly paralyzed. "His hands didn't move, his feet didn't move. Everything was frozen," Rita said. Before the year was out, she would spend several weeks receiving treatment in a psychiatric hospital.

Five years after suffering the stroke, Julien died. Rita said the cause of death was *sagren*—profound sorrow.

"There *wasn't* sickness" like strokes or *sagren* in Peros Banhos, Rita explained. "There wasn't that sickness. Nor diabetes, nor any such illness. What drugs?" she asked rhetorically. "This is what my husband remembered and pictured in his mind. Me too, I remember these things that I've said about us, David. My heart grows heavy when I say these things, understand?"

After Julien's death, the Bancoults' son Alex lost his job as a dockworker. He later died at 38 addicted to drugs and alcohol. Their son Eddy died at 36 of a heroin overdose. Another son, Rénault, died suddenly at age eleven, for reasons still mysterious to the family, after selling water and begging for money at a local cemetery near their home.

"My life has been buried," Rita told me from the torn brown vinyl couch in her small sitting room. "What do I think about it?" she continued. "It's as if I was pulled from my paradise to put me in hell. Everything here you need to buy. I don't have the means to buy them. My children go without eating. How am I supposed to bear this life?"

"Welcome to the Footprint of Freedom," says the sign on Diego Garcia. Today, at any given time, 3,000 to 5,000 U.S. troops and civilian support staff live on the island. "Picture a tropical paradise lost in an endless expanse of cerulean ocean," described *Time* magazine reporter Massimo Calabresi when he became one of the first journalists in over twenty-five years to visit the secretive atoll. Calabresi earned the privilege traveling with President George W. Bush and Air Force One during a ninety-minute refueling stop between Iraq and Australia. "Glossy palm fronds twist in the temperate wind along immaculate, powder white beaches. Leathery sea turtles bob lazily offshore, and the light cacophony of birdsong accents the ambient sound of wind and waves," he reported. "Now add concrete. Lots and lots of concrete. . . . Think early-'70s industrial park."[12]

Confined to an auditorium during his stay (but presented with a souvenir t-shirt bearing "pictures of scantily clad women and mermaids" and the words "Fantasy Island, Diego Garcia"), Calabresi was prevented from touring the rest of the island. If he had, he would have found what, like most overseas U.S. bases, resembles a small American town, in this case magically transported to the middle of the Indian Ocean.

Leaving Diego Garcia International Airport, Calabresi might have stayed at the Chagos Inn; dined at Diego Burger or surfed the internet at Burgers-n-Bytes; enjoyed a game of golf at a nine-hole course; gone shopping or caught a movie; worked out at the gym or gone bowling; played baseball or basketball, tennis or racquetball; swam in one of several pools or sailed and fished at the local marina; then relaxed with some drinks at one of several clubs and bars. Between 1999 and 2007, the Navy paid a consortium of private firms called DG21 nearly half a billion dollars to keep its troops happy and to otherwise feed, clean, and maintain the base.

The United Kingdom officially controls Diego Garcia and the rest of Chagos as the British Indian Ocean Territory (BIOT). As we will later see, the British created the colony in 1965 using the Queen's archaic power of royal decree, separating the islands from colonial Mauritius (in violation of the UN's rules on decolonization) to help enable the expulsion. A secret 1966 agreement signed "under the cover of darkness" without congressional or parliamentary oversight gave the United States the right to build a base on Diego Garcia. While technically the base would be a joint U.S.-U.K. facility, the island would become a major U.S. base and, in many ways, *de facto* U.S. territory. All but a handful of the troops are from the United States. Private companies import cheaper labor from places like the Philippines, Sri Lanka, and Mauritius (though until 2006 no Chagossians were hired) to do the laundry, cook the food, and keep the base running. The few British soldiers and functionaries on the atoll spend most of their time raising the Union Jack, keeping an eye on substance abuse as the local police force, and offering authenticity at the local "Brit Club." Diego

Garcia may be the only place in what remains of the British Empire where cars drive on the right side of the road.

In the years since the last Chagossians were deported in 1973, the base has expanded dramatically. Sold to Congress as an "austere communications facility" (to assuage critics nervous that Diego Garcia represented the start of a military buildup in the Indian Ocean), Diego Garcia saw almost immediate action as a base for reconnaissance planes in the 1973 Arab-Israeli war. The base grew steadily throughout the 1970s and expanded even more rapidly after the 1979 revolution in Iran and the Soviet invasion of Afghanistan: Under Presidents Carter and Reagan, Diego Garcia saw the "most dramatic build-up of any location since the Vietnam War." By 1986, the U.S. military had invested $500 million on the island.[13] Most of the construction work was carried out by large private firms like long-time Navy contractor Brown & Root (later Halliburton's Kellogg Brown & Root).

Today Diego Garcia is home to an amazing array of weaponry and equipment. The lagoon hosts an armada of almost two dozen massive cargo ships "prepositioned" for wartime. Each is almost the size of the Empire State Building. Each is filled to the brim with specially protected tanks, helicopters, ammunition, and fuel ready to be sent off to equip tens of thousands of U.S. troops for up to 30 days of battle.

Closer to shore, the harbor can host an aircraft carrier taskforce, including navy surface vessels and nuclear submarines. The airport and its over two-mile-long runway host billions of dollars worth of B-1, B-2, and B-52 bombers, reconnaissance, cargo, and in-air refueling planes. The island is home to one of four worldwide stations running the Global Positioning System (GPS). There's a range of other high-tech intelligence and communications equipment, including NASA facilities (the runway is an emergency landing site for the Space Shuttle), an electro-optical deep space surveillance system, a satellite navigation monitoring antenna, an HF-UHF-SHF satellite transmission ground station, and (probably) a subsurface oceanic intelligence station. Nuclear weapons are likely stored on the base.[14]

Diego Garcia saw its first major wartime use during the first Gulf War. Just eight days after the U.S. military issued deployment orders in August 1990, eighteen prepositioned ships from Diego Garcia's lagoon arrived in Saudi Arabia. The ships immediately outfitted a 15,000-troop marine brigade with 123 M-60 battle tanks, 425 heavy weapons, 124 fixed-wing and rotary aircraft, and thirty days' worth of operational supplies for the annihilation of Iraq's military that was to come. Weaponry and supplies shipped from the United States took almost a month longer to arrive in Saudi Arabia, proving Diego Garcia's worth to many military leaders.[15]

Since September 11, 2001, the base has assumed even more importance for the military. About 7,000 miles closer to central Asia and the Persian Gulf than major bases in the United States, the island received around 2,000 additional Air Force personnel within weeks of the attacks on northern Virginia and New York. The Air Force built a new thirty-acre housing facility for the newcomers. They named it "Camp Justice."

Flying from the atoll, B-1 bombers, B-2 "stealth" bombers, and B-52 nuclear-capable bombers dropped more ordnance on Afghanistan than any other flying squadrons in the Afghan war.[16] B-52 bombers alone dropped more than 1.5 million pounds of munitions in carpet bombing that contributed to thousands of Afghan deaths.[17] Leading up to the invasion of Iraq, weaponry and supplies prepositioned in the lagoon were again among the first to arrive at staging areas near Iraq's borders. The (once) secret 2002 "Downing Street" memorandum showed that U.S. war planners considered basing access on Diego Garcia "critical" to the invasion.[18] Bombers from the island ultimately helped launch the Bush administration's war overthrowing the Hussein regime and leading to the subsequent deaths of hundreds of thousands of Iraqis and thousands of U.S. occupying troops.

In early 2007, as the Bush administration was upping its anti-Iran rhetoric and making signs that it was ready for more attempted conquest, the Defense Department awarded a $31.9 million contract to build a new submarine base on the island. The subs can launch Tomahawk cruise missiles and ferry Navy SEALs for amphibious missions behind enemy lines. At the same time, the military began shipping extra fuel supplies to the atoll for possible wartime use.

Long off-limits to reporters, the Red Cross, and all other international observers and far more secretive than Guantánamo Bay, many have identified the island as a clandestine CIA "black site" for high-profile detainees: Journalist Stephen Grey's book *Ghost Plane* documented the presence on the island of a CIA-chartered plane used for rendition flights. On two occasions former U.S. Army General Barry McCaffrey publicly named Diego Garcia as a detention facility. A Council of Europe report named the atoll, along with sites in Poland and Romania, as a secret prison.[19]

For more than six years U.S. and U.K. officials adamantly denied the allegations. In February 2008, British Foreign Secretary David Miliband announced to Parliament: "Contrary to earlier explicit assurances that Diego Garcia has not been used for rendition flights, recent U.S. investigations have now revealed two occasions, both in 2002, when this had in fact occurred."[20] A representative for Secretary of State Condoleezza Rice said Rice called Miliband to express regret over the "administrative error." The State

Department's chief legal adviser said CIA officials were "as confident as they can be" that no other detainees had been held on the island, and CIA Director Michael Hayden continues to deny the existence of a CIA prison on the island. This may be true: Some suspect the United States may hold large numbers of detainees on secret prison ships in Diego Garcia's lagoon or elsewhere in the waters of Chagos.[21]

"It's the single most important military facility we've got," respected Washington-area military expert John Pike told me. Pike, who runs the website GlobalSecurity.org, explained, "It's the base from which we control half of Africa and the southern side of Asia, the southern side of Eurasia." It's "the facility that at the end of the day gives us some say-so in the Persian Gulf region. If it didn't exist, it would have to be invented." The base is critical to controlling not just the oil-rich Gulf but the world, said Pike: "Even if the entire Eastern Hemisphere has drop-kicked us" from every other base on their territory, he explained, the military's goal is to be able "to run the planet from Guam and Diego Garcia by 2015."

Before I received an unexpected phone call one day late in the New York City summer of 2001, I'd only vaguely known from my memories of the first Gulf War that the United States had an obscure military base on an island called Diego Garcia. Like most others in the United States, I knew nothing of the Chagossians.

On the phone that day was Michael Tigar, a lawyer and American University law professor. Tigar, I later learned from my father (an attorney), was famously known for having had an offer of a 1966 Supreme Court clerkship revoked at the last moment by Justice William Brennan. The justice had apparently succumbed to right-wing groups angered by what they considered to be Tigar's radical sympathies from his days at the University of California, Berkeley. As the story goes, Brennan later said it was one of his greatest mistakes. Tigar went on to represent the likes of Angela Davis, Allen Ginsberg, the Washington Post, Texas Senator Kay Bailey Hutchison, and Oklahoma City bomber Terry Nichols. In 1999, Tigar ranked third in a vote for "Lawyer of the Century" by the California Lawyers for Criminal Justice, behind only Clarence Darrow and Thurgood Marshall. Recently he had sued Henry Kissinger and other former U.S. officials for supporting assassinations and other human rights abuses carried out by the government of Chilean dictator Augusto Pinochet.

As we talked that day, Tigar outlined the story of the Chagossians' expulsion. He described how for decades the islanders had engaged in

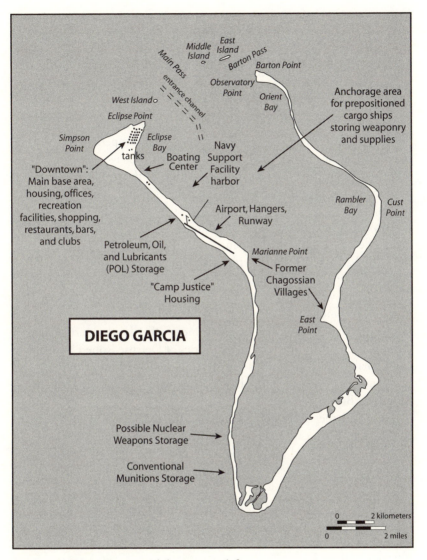

Figure 0.2 Diego Garcia, with base area at left.

a David-and-Goliath struggle to win the right to return to Chagos and proper compensation.

In 1978 and 1982 their protests won them small amounts of compensation from the British. Mostly, though, the money went to paying off debts accrued since the expulsion, improving their overall condition little. Lately, they had begun to make some more significant progress. In 1997, with the help of lawyers in London and Mauritius, an organization called the Chagos Refugees Group, or the CRG, had launched a suit against the British Crown charging that their exile violated U.K. law. One of Nelson Mandela's former lawyers in battling the apartheid regime, Sir Sydney Kentridge, signed on to the case. And to everyone's amazement, Tigar said, in November 2000, the British High Court ruled in their favor.

The only problem was the British legal system. The original judgment, Tigar explained, made no award of damages or compensation. And the islanders had no money to charter boats to visit Chagos let alone to resettle and reconstruct their shattered societies. So the people had just filed a second suit against the Crown for compensation and money to finance a return.

Through a relationship with Sivarkumen "Robin" Mardemooto, a former student of Tigar's who happened to be the islanders' Mauritian lawyer, the CRG had asked Tigar to explore launching another suit in the United States. Working with law students in his American University legal clinic, Tigar said he was preparing to file a class action lawsuit in Federal District Court. Among the defendants they would name in the suit would be the United States Government, government officials who participated in the expulsion, including former Secretaries of Defense Robert McNamara and Donald Rumsfeld (for his first stint, in the Ford administration), and companies that assisted in the base's construction, including Halliburton subsidiary Brown & Root.

Tigar said they were going to charge the defendants with harms including forced relocation, cruel, inhuman, and degrading treatment, and genocide. They would ask the Court to grant the right of return, award compensation, and order an end to employment discrimination that had barred Chagossians from working on the base as civilian personnel.

As I was still absorbing the tale, Tigar said his team was looking for an anthropology or sociology graduate student to conduct some research for the suit. Troubled by the story and amazed by the opportunity, I quickly agreed.

Over the next six-plus years, together with colleagues Philip Harvey and Wojciech Sokolowski from Rutgers University School of Law and Johns Hopkins University, I conducted three pieces of research: Analyzing if, given contemporary understandings of the "indigenous peoples" concept, the Chagossians should be considered one (I found that they should and that other indigenous groups recognize them as such); documenting how Chagossians' lives have been harmed as a result of their displacement; and calculating the compensation due as a result of some of those damages.[22]

While I was never paid for my work, ironically enough, big tobacco helped foot some of the bill: Tigar reimbursed my expenses out of a human rights litigation fund he had established at American University with attorney fees won in a Texas tobacco suit.[23]

Not long after starting the project, however, I saw there was another side of the story that I wanted to understand. In addition to exploring the impact of the expulsion on the Chagossians, I wanted to tell the story of the United States and the U.S. Government officials who ordered the removals and created the base: How and why, I wanted to know, did my country and its officials do this?[24]

Between 2001 and 2008, I conducted research with both the islanders and some of the now mostly retired U.S. officials. To understand something of the fabric and texture of Chagossians' lives in exile, I lived in their communities in Mauritius and the Seychelles for more than seven months over four trips between 2001 and 2004. This meant living in the homes of Chagossian families and participating actively in their daily lives. I did everything with the people from working, cooking, studying, cleaning, praying, and watching French-dubbed Brazilian telenovelas on Mauritian TV to attending weddings, baptisms, first communions, public meetings, birthday parties, and funerals. In addition to hundreds of informal conversations, I conducted more than thirty formal interviews in Mauritian Kreol, Seselwa (Seychelles Kreol), English, and French, and, with the help of dedicated Mauritian interviewers, completed a large survey of living conditions with more than 320 islanders. I complemented this work by going to the British Public Records Office and the national archives of Mauritius and the Seychelles to unearth thousands of pages of historical and documentary records about the history of Chagos, the expulsion, and its aftermath.[25]

Back in the United States, I moved from New York to my hometown of Washington, DC, to try to understand the officials responsible for the base and the expulsion. I had no interest in turning them into caricatures, and wanted to dedicate the same anthropological attention and empathy to them that I had focused on the islanders.[26] During more than seven months of concentrated research in 2004 and 2005, and continuing over the next two years, I interviewed more than thirty former and current U.S. Government officials, primarily from the departments of Defense and State and the Navy, as well as journalists, academics, military analysts, and others who were involved in the story or otherwise knowledgeable about the base.[27]

Unfortunately, I was unable to speak with some of the highest-ranking and most influential officials involved. Many, including White House official Robert Komer and Admirals Elmo Zumwalt and Arleigh Burke, were deceased. Two, Paul Nitze and Admiral Thomas Moorer, died early in my research before I could request an interview. Others, including Henry Kissinger, did not respond to repeated interview requests.

After repeatedly attempting to contact Robert McNamara, I was surprised to return to my office one day to find the following voicemail: "Professor Vine. This is Robert McNamara. I don't believe I can help you. At 91, my memory is very, very bad. And I recall almost nothing about Diego Garcia. Thank you."

When I hurriedly called him back and asked if he had any memory of conversations about people on the island, he responded, "None."

When I asked why the Department of Defense would have wanted to remove the Chagossians, he said, "At 91, my memory's bad."

I asked if he could recommend anyone else to speak with. "No," he replied. I asked if he could suggest any other leads. "None," he said. Fumbling around to think what else I could ask, I heard McNamara say quickly, "Thank you very much," and then the click of the connection going dead.

With these kinds of limitations, I balanced my interviews with an analysis of thousands of pages of government documents uncovered in the U.S. National Archives, the Navy archives, the Kennedy and Johnson presidential libraries, the British Public Records Office, and the files of the U.S. and British lawyers representing the Chagossians.[28] While the Navy's archives proved a critical resource, all the files from Stu Barber's office responsible for the original base idea had been destroyed.[29]

While many of the relevant surviving documents were still classified (after 30–40 years), Freedom of Information Act (FOIA) requests revealed some formerly secret information. However, government agencies withheld hundreds of documents, claiming various FOIA exemptions "in the interest of national defense or foreign relations." Tens of other documents were released to me "in part"; this often meant receiving page after page partially or entirely blank. Britain's "30 year rule" for the automatic release of most classified government documents, by contrast, revealed hundreds of pages of critical material, much of it originally uncovered by the Chagossians' U.K. legal team and a Mauritian investigative reporter and contributing to the 2000 victory.[30]

Like trying to describe an object you can't actually see, telling the story of Diego Garcia was further complicated by not being able to go to Diego Garcia. The 1976 U.S.-U.K. agreement for the base restricts access "to members of the forces of the United Kingdom and of the United States" and their official representatives and contractors.[31] A 1992 document explains, "the intent is to restrict visits in order . . . to prevent excessive access to military operations and activities."[32] Visits by journalists have been explicitly banned, making the island something of a "holy grail" for reporters (only technically claimed by the recent ninety-minute visit of President Bush's reporting pool, during which reporters were confined to an airport hangar). In the 1980s, a *Time* magazine chief offered a "fine case of Bordeaux to the first correspondent who filed a legitimate story from Diego Garcia."[33]

The U.S.-U.K. agreement does allow visits by approved "scientific parties wishing to carry out research." Indeed scientists, including experts on coral atolls and the Royal Navy Bird Watching Society, have regularly surveyed Diego Garcia and the other Chagos islands. Encouraged, I repeatedly requested permission from both U.S. and U.K. representatives to visit and conduct research on the islanders' former society. After months of trading letters with British officials in 2003 and 2004, I finally received word from Charles Hamilton, the British Indian Ocean Territory administrator, stating that "after careful consideration, we are unable to agree at the present time to a scientific visit involving a survey of the former homes of the Chagossians. I am sorry to have to send you such disappointing news."[34] All my other requests were denied or went unanswered. John Pike described the chance of a civilian visiting Diego Garcia as "about as likely as the sun coming up in the west."

Still, if I had had a yacht at my disposal, I could have joined hundreds of other "yachties" who regularly visit Peros Banhos, Salomon, and other islands in Chagos far from Diego Garcia. (Enterprising journalist Simon Winchester convinced one to take him to Chagos in 1985, even managing to get onto Diego Garcia when his Australian captain claimed her right to safe harbor under the law of the sea.[35]) Many yachties today enjoy the "island paradise" for months at a time. They simply pay a fee to the BIOT for the right to stay in the territory and enjoy beachside barbeques by the "impossibly blue" water, parties with BIOT officials, and free range over the islands and the Chagossians' crumbling homes. "Welcome to the B.I.O.T.," a sign reads. "Please keep the island clean and avoid damage to buildings. Enjoy your stay."[36]

Sadly, the Chagossians are far from alone in having been displaced by a military base. As we will see in the story ahead, the U.S. military has exhibited a pattern of forcibly displacing vulnerable peoples to build its military bases. In the past century, most of these cases have taken place outside the United States. Generally those displaced have, like the Chagossians, been small in number, under colonial control, and of non-"white," non-European ancestry. Some of the examples are relatively well known, like those displaced in the Bikini Atoll and Puerto Rico's Vieques Island. Others have, like the Chagossians, received less attention, including the Inughuit of Thule, Greenland, and the more than 3,000 Okinawans displaced to, of all places, Bolivia.

It is no coincidence that few know about these stories. Few in the United States know that the United States possesses some 1,000 military bases and installations outside the fifty states and Washington, DC, on the sovereign land of other nations. Let me repeat that number again because it's hard to take in: 1,000 bases. On other people's sovereign territory. 1,000 bases.

More than half a century after the end of World War II and the Korean War, the United States retains 287 bases in Germany, 130 in Japan, and 106 in South Korea. There are some 89 in Italy, 57 in the British Isles, 21 in Portugal, and nineteen in Turkey. Other bases are scattered around the globe in places like Aruba and Australia, Djibouti, Egypt, and Israel, Singapore and Thailand, Kyrgyzstan and Kuwait, Qatar, Bahrain, and the United Arab Emirates, Crete, Sicily, and Iceland, Romania and Bulgaria, Honduras, Colombia, and Guantánamo Bay, Cuba—just to name a few (see fig. 2.1). Some can still be found in Saudi Arabia and others have recently returned to the Philippines and Uzbekistan, where locals previously forced the closure of U.S. bases. In total, the U.S. military has troops in some 150 foreign nations. Around the world the Defense Department reports having more than 577,519 separate buildings, structures, and utilities at its bases, conservatively valuing its facilities at more than $712 billion.[37]

It's often hard to come up with accurate figures to capture the scope of the base network, because the Pentagon frequently omits secret and even well-known bases—like those in Iraq and Afghanistan—in its own accounting. In Iraq, as President Bush's second term came to an end, the military controlled at least 55 bases and probably well over 100. In trying to negotiate a long-term military agreement with the Iraqi Government, the Bush administration hoped to retain 58 long-term bases in the country as part of a "protracted" presence of at least 50,000 troops, following the South Korean model; originally U.S. officials pressed for more than 200 military facilities. In Afghanistan, the base collection includes sixteen air bases and may run to over eighty in total amid similar Pentagon plans for permanent installations.[38]

While Pentagon and other officials have been careful never to refer to bases in Iraq and Afghanistan as "permanent," the structures on the ground tell a different story: A 2007 National Public Radio story reported that Balad Air Base near Baghdad, one of five "mega bases" in Iraq, housed some 30,000 troops and 10,000 private contractors in facilities complete with fortified Pizza Hut, Burger King, and Subway outlets and two shopping centers each about the size of a Target or Wal-Mart. "The base is one giant construction project, with new roads, sidewalks, and structures going up across this 16-square-mile fortress in the center of Iraq, all with an eye toward the next few decades," Guy Raz explained. "Seen from the sky at night, the base resembles Las Vegas: While the surrounding Iraqi villages get about 10 hours of electricity a day, the lights never go out at Balad Air Base."[39]

If you are anything like me and grew up in the United States, you may have a hard time imagining another nation occupying a military base on your nation's territory—let alone living next to such "simulacrums of suburbia" found the world over.[40] In 2007, Ecuadorian President Rafael Correa offered some insight into this phenomenon when he told reporters that he would only renew the lease on the U.S. military base in Ecuador if the United States agreed to one condition: "They let us put a base in Miami—an Ecuadorian base."

"If there's no problem having foreign soldiers on a country's soil," Correa added, "surely they'll let us have an Ecuadorian base in the United States."

The idea of an Ecuadorian military base in Miami, of a foreign base anywhere in the United States, is unthinkable to most people in the United States. And yet this is exactly what thousands of people in countries around the world live with every day: Military forces from a foreign country living in their cities, building huge military complexes on their lands, occupying their nations. About 95 percent of these foreign bases belong to the United States. Today the United States likely possesses more bases than any nation or people in world history.[41] Not to be confined to the globe alone, the Pentagon is making plans to turn outer space into a base as part of the rapid militarization of space.[42]

Growing recognition about the U.S. overseas base network has mirrored a renewed acknowledgment among scholars and pundits, following the wars in Afghanistan and Iraq, that the United States is in fact an empire.[43] With even the establishment foreign policy journal *Foreign Affairs* declaring, "The debate on empire is back," conversation has centered less on *if* the United States is an empire and more on *what kind* of empire it has become.[44]

Too often, however, the debates on empire have ignored and turned away from the lives of those impacted by empire. Too often analysts turn to abstract discussions of so-called foreign policy realism or macro-level economic forces. Too often, analysts detach themselves from the effects of empire and the lives shaped and all too often damaged by the United States. Proponents of U.S. imperialism in particular willfully ignore the death and destruction caused by previous empires and the U.S. Empire** alike.[45]

In 1975, the *Washington Post* exposed the story of the Chagossians' expulsion for the first time in the Western press, describing the people as living in "abject poverty" as a result of what the *Post*'s editorial page called an "act of mass kidnapping."[46] When a single day of congressional hearings followed, the U.S. Government denied all responsibility for the islanders.[47] From that moment onward, the people of the United States have almost completely turned their backs on the Chagossians and forgotten them entirely.

Unearthing the full story of the Chagossians forces us to look deeply at what the United States has done, and at the lives of people shaped and destroyed by U.S. Empire. The Chagossians' story forces us to focus on the damage that U.S. power has inflicted around the world, providing new insight into the nature of the United States as an empire. The Chagossians' story forces us to face those people whom we as citizens of the United States often find it all too easy to ignore, too easy to close out of our consciousness. The Chagossians' story forces us to consider carefully how this country has treated other peoples from Iraq to Vietnam and in far too many other places around the globe.[48]

At the same time, we would be mistaken to treat the U.S. Empire simply as an abstract leviathan. Empires are run by real people. People made the decision to exile the Chagossians, to build a base on Diego Garcia. While empires are complex entities involving the consent and cooperation of millions and social forces larger than any single individual, we would be mistaken to ignore how a few powerful people come to make decisions that have such powerful effects on the lives of so many others thousands of miles away. For this reason, the story that follows is two-pronged and bifocaled: We will explore both sides of Diego Garcia, both sides of U.S. Empire, focusing equally on the lives of Chagossians like Rita Bancoult and the actions of U.S. Government officials like Stu Barber. In the end

---

** Throughout the book I use the term *U.S. Empire* rather than the more widely recognized *American Empire*. Although "U.S. Empire" may appear and sound awkward at first, it is linguistically more accurate than "American Empire" and represents an effort to reverse the erasure of the rest of the Americas entailed in U.S. citizens' frequent substitution of *America* for the *United States of America* (America consists of all of North and South America). The name of my current employer, American University, is just one example of this pattern: Located in the nation's capital, the school has long touted itself as a "national university" when its name should suggest a hemispheric university. The switch to the less familiar U.S. Empire also represents a linguistic attempt to make visible the fact that the United States is an empire, shaking people into awareness of its existence and its consequences.

we will reflect on how the dynamics of empire have come to bind together Bancoult and Barber, Chagossians and U.S. officials, and how every one of us is ultimately bound up with both.***[49]

To begin to understand and comprehend what the Chagossians have suffered as a result of their exile, we will need to start by looking at how the islanders' ancestors came to live and build a complex society in Chagos. We will then explore the secret history of how U.S. and U.K. officials planned, financed, and orchestrated the expulsion and the creation of the base, hiding their work from Congress and Parliament, members of the media and the world. Next we will look at what the Chagossians' lives have become in exile. While as outsiders it is impossible to fully comprehend what they have experienced, we must struggle to confront the pain they have faced. At the same time, we will see how their story is not one of suffering alone. From their daily struggles for survival to protests and hunger strikes in the streets of Mauritius to lawsuits that have taken them to some of the highest courts in Britain and the United States, we will see how the islanders have continually resisted their expulsion and the power of two empires. Finally, we will consider what we must do for the Chagossians and what we must do about the empire the United States has become.

The story of Diego Garcia has been kept secret for far too long. It must now be exposed.

*** Those interested in reading more about the book's approach as a bifocaled "ethnography of empire" should continue to the following endnote.

CHAPTER 1

THE ILOIS, THE ISLANDERS

"*Laba*" is all Rita had to say. Meaning, "out there." Chagossians in exile know immediately that *out there* means one thing: Chagos.

"*Laba* there are birds, there are turtles, and plenty of food," she said. "There's a leafy green vegetable . . . called cow's tongue. It's tasty to eat, really good. You can put it in a curry, you can make it into a pickled chutney.

"When I was still young, I was a little like a boy. In those times, we went looking" for ingredients for "curries on Saturday. So very early in the morning we went" to another island and came back with our food.

"By canoe?" I asked.

"By sailboat," Rita replied.

Peros Banhos "has thirty-two islands," she explained. "There's English Island, Monpatre Island, Chicken Island, Grand Bay, Little Bay, Diamond, Peter Island, Passage Island, Long Island, Mango Tree Island, Big Mango Tree Island. . . . There's Sea Cow Island," and many more. "I've visited them all. . . ."[1]

EMPIRES COMING AND GOING

"A great number of vessels might anchor there in safety," were the words of the first naval survey of Diego Garcia's lagoon. The appraisal came not from U.S. officials, but from the 1769 visit to the island by a French lieutenant named La Fontaine. Throughout the eighteenth century, England and France vied for control of the islands of the western Indian Ocean as strategic military bases to control shipping routes to India, where their respective East India companies were battling for supremacy over the spice trade.[2]

Having occupied Réunion Island (Île Bourbon) in 1642, the French replaced a failed Dutch settlement on Mauritius (renamed Île de France) in 1721. Later they settled Rodrigues and, by 1742, the Seychelles. As with its Caribbean colonies, France quickly shifted its focus from military to commercial interests.[3] French settlers built societies on the islands around enslaved labor and, particularly in Mauritius, the cultivation of sugar cane. At first, the French Company of the Indies tried to import enslaved people from the same West African sources supplying the Caribbean colonies. Later the company developed a new slaving trade to import labor from Madagascar and the area of Africa known then as Mozambique (a larger stretch of the southeast African coast than the current nation). Indian Ocean historian Larry Bowman writes that French settlement in Mauritius produced "a sharply differentiated society with extremes of wealth and poverty and an elite deeply committed to and dependent upon slavery."[4]

Chagos, including Peros Banhos and Diego Garcia, remained uninhabited throughout the seventeenth and early eighteenth centuries, serving only as a safe haven and provisioning stop for ships growing familiar with what were sometimes hazardous waters—in 1786, a hydrographer was the victim of a shipwreck. But as Anglo-French competition increased in Europe and spilled over into a fight for naval and thus economic control of the Indian Ocean, Chagos's central location made it an irresistible military and economic target.[5]

France first claimed Peros Banhos in 1744. A year later, the English surveyed Diego Garcia. Numerous French and English voyages followed to inspect other island groups in the archipelago, including Three Brothers, Egmont Atoll, and the Salomon Islands, before Lieutenant La Fontaine delivered his prophetic report.[6]

TWENTY-TWO

Like tens of millions of other Africans transported around the globe between the fifteenth and nineteenth centuries, Rita's ancestors and the ancestors of other Chagossians were brought against their will. Most were from Madagascar and Mozambique and were brought to Chagos in slavery to work on coconut plantations established by Franco-Mauritians.

The first permanent inhabitants of the Chagos Archipelago were likely 22 enslaved Africans. Although we do not know their names, some of today's Chagossians are likely their direct descendants. The 22 arrived

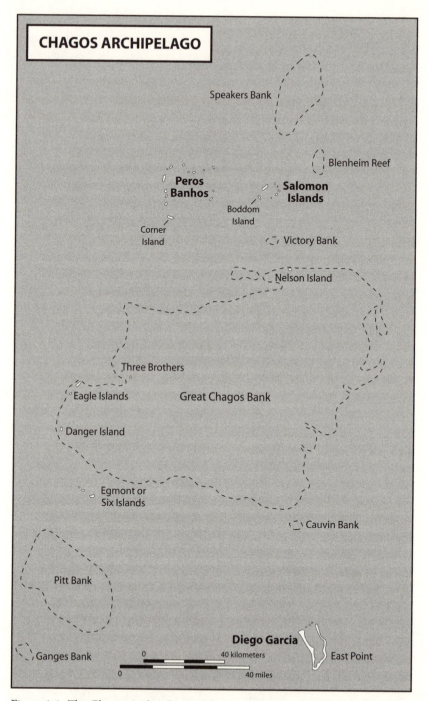

Figure 1.1 The Chagos Archipelago, with Peros Banhos and Salomon Islands at top center, Diego Garcia at bottom right.

around 1783, brought to the island by Pierre Marie Le Normand, an influential plantation owner born in Rennes but who left France for Mauritius at the age of 20.[7] Only half a century after the settlement of Mauritius, Le Normand petitioned its colonial government for a concession to settle Diego Garcia. On February 17, 1783, he received a "favourable reply" and "immediately prepared his voyage."[8]

Three years later, apparently unaware of Le Normand's arrival, the British East India Company sent a "secret committee" from Bombay to create a provisioning plantation on the atoll. Although they were surprised to find the French settlement, the British party didn't back down. On May 4, 1786, they took "full and ample Possession" of Diego Garcia and Chagos "in the name of our Most Gracious Sovereign George the third of Great Britain, France and Ireland King Defender of the faith etc. And of the said Honourable Company for their use and behoof."[9]

Unable to resist the newcomers, Le Normand left for Mauritius to report the British arrival. When France's Vicompte de Souillac learned of the landing, he sent a letter of protest to Bombay and the warship *Minerve* to reclaim the archipelago. To prevent an international incident liable to provoke war, the British Council in Bombay sent departure instructions to its landing party. When the *Minerve* arrived on Diego, its French crew found the British settlement abandoned and its grain and vegetable seeds washed into the sand.[10]

While France won this battle, governing Chagos along with the Seychelles as dependencies of Mauritius, its rule proved short-lived. By the turn of the nineteenth century and the Napoleonic Wars, French power in the Indian Ocean had crumbled. The British seized control of the Seychelles in 1794 and Mauritius in 1810. In the 1814 Treaty of Paris, France formally ceded Mauritius, including Chagos and Mauritius's other dependencies (as well as most of France's other island possessions worldwide), to Great Britain. Succeeding the Portuguese, Dutch, and French empires before it, the British would rule the Indian Ocean as a "British lake"[11] for a century and a half, until the emergence of a new global empire.

"IDEALLY SUITED"

Ernestine Marie Joseph Jacques (Diego Garcia). Joseph and Pauline Pona (Peros Banhos). Michel Levillain (Mozambique). Prudence Levillain (Madagascar). Lindor Courtois (India). Theophile Le Leger (Mauritius). Anastasie Legère (Three Brothers).[12] These are the slave names and birthplaces of some of the Chagossians' first ancestors.[13] While most arrived from Mauritius, some may have come via the Seychelles and on slaving ships from Madagascar and continental Africa as part of an illegal slave trade taking advantage of Chagos's isolation from colonial authority.[14]

Not long after Le Normand established his settlement, hundreds more enslaved laborers began arriving to build a fishing settlement and four more coconut plantations established by Franco-Mauritians Dauquet, Lapotaire, Didier, and the brothers Cayeux. By 1808 there were 100 enslaved people working under Lapotaire alone. By 1813, a similar number were working in Peros Banhos, as settlement spread throughout an archipelago judged to have "a climate ideally suited to the cultivation of coconuts."[15] Less than eight degrees from the equator, Chagos's environment is marked by "the absence of a distinct flowering season and the gigantic size of many native and cultivated trees." The islands are also free from the cyclones (hurricanes) that frequently devastate Mauritius and neighboring islands. Meaning that coconut palms produce bountiful quantities of nuts year round for potential harvest. Hundreds more enslaved Africans were soon establishing new plantations at Three Brothers, Eagle and Salomon Islands and at Six Islands.[16]

THE PLANTATION SYSTEM

Despite being under British colonial rule, Mauritius and its dependencies surprisingly retained their French laws, language, religion, and ways of life—including that of enslaving Africans. "Mauritius became formally British but remained very French," explains one historian.[17]

Slavery thus remained the defining feature of life in Chagos from Le Normand's initial settlement until the abolition of slavery in Mauritius and its dependencies in 1835. Enslaved labor built the archipelago's infrastructure, produced its wealth (mostly in coconut oil), and formed the overwhelming majority of inhabitants. Colonial statistics from 1826 illustrate the nature of the islands as absolute slave plantation societies relying on a small number of Franco-Mauritians and free people of African or mixed ancestry to rule much larger populations of enslaved Africans.

The considerable gender imbalance in the islands is also important to note. Although it had generally equalized by the mid-twentieth century, the imbalance may help explain the power and authority Chagossian women came to exercise, as we will see in the story ahead.

Plantation owners at the time described their enslaved workforce as "happy and content" and their treatment as being of "the greatest gentle-

TABLE 1.1
Chagos Population, 1826.

	Male	Female
Noirs/Enslaved Blacks	269	108
Blancs/Whites	8	1
Libres/Free Persons	13	9

SOURCE: Commissioners of Compensation, Copy of Abstract of Biennial Returns of Slaves at Seychelles for the Year 1830, Minor Dependencies for the Year 1832, Port Louis, Mauritius, May 14, 1835, PRO: T 71/643.

ness." The laborers surely disagreed, working "from sunrise to sunset for six days a week" under the supervision of overseers.[18] However, outside these grueling workdays, each enslaved person was allowed to maintain a *"petite plantation"*—a small garden—to raise crops and animals and to save small sums of money from their sale. Significantly, these garden plots marked the beginnings of formal Chagossian land tenure.[19]

Society in Chagos had little in common with the Maldivian islands and Sri Lanka several hundred miles away, sharing much more with societies thousands of miles away in the Americas from southern Brazil to the islands of the Caribbean and north to the Mason-Dixon line. What these disparate places (as well as Natal, Zanzibar, Fiji, Queensland, Mauritius, the Seychelles, Réunion, and others) shared was the plantation system.[20]

With the plantation system of agriculture well established in the sugar fields of Mauritius by the end of the eighteenth century, Franco-Mauritian entrepreneurs applied the same technology in Chagos. Like societies from Bahia to Barbados and Baltimore, Chagos had all the major features of the plantation world: a mostly enslaved labor force, an agriculture-based economy organized around large-scale capitalist plantations supplying specialized products to distant markets, political control emanating from a distant European nation, a population that was generally not self-sustaining and required frequent replenishment (usually by enslaved peoples and, later, indentured laborers), and elements of feudal labor control. Still, Chagos exhibited important particularities: Unlike most of the Americas, society was based on slavery and slavery alone. Similarly, there was no preexisting indigenous population to force into labor and to replace when they were killed off. And perhaps because of its late settlement, the plantations in Chagos never employed European indentured laborers, or *engagés*.[21]

Likewise, although Chagos was an agriculture-based economy organized around capitalist plantations supplying a specialized product—copra—to distant markets, the majority of the copra harvest was not produced for European markets but was instead for the Mauritian market. The islands were thus a dependent part of the Mauritian sugar cane economy, which was itself a dependent part of the French and, later, British economies. Put another way, Chagos was a colony of a colony, a dependency of a dependency: Chagos helped meet Mauritius's oil needs to keep its mono-crop sugar industry satisfying Europe's growing sweet tooth.

From the workers' perspective, the plantations were in some ways "as much a factory as a farm," employing the "factory-like organization of agricultural labor into large-scale, highly coordinated enterprises."[22] While some of the work was agricultural in nature, much of it required the repetitive manual processing of hundreds of coconuts a day by women, men, and children in what was essentially an outdoor factory area at the center of each plantation. Still, as in the Caribbean, most of the work was performed on a "task" basis, generally allowing laborers to control the pace and rhythm of their work. Plantation owners—who mostly lived far away in Mauritius—probably viewed the (relatively) less onerous task system as the best way to maintain discipline and prevent greatly feared slave revolts, given Chagos's isolation and the tiny number of Europeans.[23]

Authority over work regimens was carefully—and at times brutally—controlled, helping to shape a rigid color-based plantation hierarchy that mirrored the one in the French Caribbean. This was also undoubtedly related to owners' fears of revolt, which in Mauritius and the Seychelles made "domestic discipline," armed militias, and police the backbone of society.[24]

Plantation owners came from the *grand blanc*—literally, "big white"—ruling class and ran the settlements essentially as patriarchal private estates. "Responsibility for the administration of the settlements, before and after emancipation, was vested in the proprietors," explains former governor Scott. "For all practical purposes, however, it was normally delegated to the manager on the spot, the *administrateur*," who was usually a relative or member of the *petit blanc*—"little white"—class, running the plantation from the master's house, the *grand case*.[25]

Petit blanc or "mulatto" submanagers and other staff recruited to Chagos helped run the islands, and were rewarded with better salaries, housing, and other privileges rarely extended to laborers. The submanagers in turn delivered daily work orders and controlled the workers through a group of *commandeurs*—overseers—primarily of African descent who were given some privileges and, after emancipation, paid higher wages.

As on slave plantations elsewhere, owners and their subordinates generally ruled largely through fear.[26] Despite the constraints on their lives, some laborers achieved a degree of upward mobility by becoming artisans and performing other specialized tasks. The vast majority of the population were general laborers of African descent at the bottom of the work and status hierarchy in a system that, as in the U.S. South, became engrained in the social order.

CHANGE AND CONTINUITY

Slavery was finally abolished in Mauritius and its dependencies in 1835. After emancipation, a period of apprenticeship continued for about four years. The daily routine of plantation life during and after the apprenticeship period changed according to the dictates of each island's administrator. On some islands, like Diego Garcia, life and conditions changed little. On others, daily work tasks were reduced in accordance with stipulations ordered by officials in Mauritius.[27]

Following emancipation, plantation owners in Mauritius began recruiting large numbers of Indians to the sugar cane fields as a way to keep labor costs down and replace formerly enslaved laborers leaving the plantations en masse; by century's end, Indians constituted a majority in Mauritius. While plantation owners in Chagos also imported Indian indentured laborers, Indian immigration was relatively light and people of African descent remained in the majority.[28] So, too, Chagos did not experience the large-scale departure of formerly enslaved Africans (in fact, at least some of those previously enslaved on sugar plantations in Mauritius appear to have emigrated to work on Diego Garcia).[29]

This demographic stability, in such contrast to Mauritius, needs explanation: Ultimately it seems to point to a change in the quality of labor relations and the development of a society rooted in the islands. Newly freed Africans and the Indian indentured laborers who joined them massively outnumbered the plantation management of mostly European descent in a setting of enormous isolation. For management, this demographic imbalance and the lack of a militia or police force like the ones in Mauritius and the Seychelles made the threat of an uncontrollable labor revolt frighteningly real. Indeed the islands had a history of periodic labor protest. In one case in 1856, four workers who had been "kidnapped from Cochin" revolted and killed an abusive manager of Six Islands.[30] These facts combined with gradual improvements in salaries and workload (especially compared to the brutal work of cutting sugar cane) suggest that despite the continuation of the plantation system after emancipation, the general nature of labor relations probably improved noticeably in favor of the Chagossians. Even before the end of the apprentice period, a colonial investigator charged with supervising apprenticeship conditions found the work to be "of a much milder nature than that which is performed on the Sugar Plantations of Mauritius" and the workers to be "a more comfortable body of people" due "to so much of their own time being employed to their own advantage" (he also credited the archipelago's absence of both outsiders and liquor).[31] In general it appears that Chagossians gradually struck what for a plantation society was a relatively—and I stress the word *relatively*—good work bargain. Indeed more than a century later, in 1949, a visiting representative of the Mauritian Labour Office commented on the generally "patriarchal" relations between management and labor in Chagos, "dating back to what I imagine would be the slave days—by this I do not imply any oppression but rather a system of benevolent rule with privileges and no rights."[32]

A "CULTURE DES ÎLES"

By the middle of the nineteenth century, a succession of laws increasingly protected workers from the continuation of any slavery-like conditions. Around 1860, wages were the equivalent of 10 shillings a month, a dollop of rum, and a "twist of tobacco if times were good." Rations, which were treated as part of wages, totaled 11–14 pounds a week of what was usually rice. Two decades later, wages had increased to 16 shillings a month for male coconut laborers and 12 shillings a month for women. Some women working in domestic or supervisory jobs received more. Men working the coconut oil mills earned 18–20 shillings a month and had higher status than "rat-catchers, stablemen, gardeners, maize planters, toddy-makers and pig- and fowl-keepers." A step higher in the labor hierarchy, blacksmiths, carpenters, assistant carpenters, coopers, and junior commandeurs made 20–32 shillings.[33]

Management often paid bonuses in the form of tobacco, rum, toddy, and, for some, coconut oil. Housing was free, and at East Point the manager "introduced the system of allowing labourers to build their own houses, if they so opted, the management providing all the materials." The system apparently proved a success, creating "quite superior dwellings," with wood frames and thatched coconut palm leaves, and "a sense of proprietorship" for the islanders.[34] By 1880, the population had risen to around 760.

"As a general rule the men enjoy good health, and seem contented and happy, and work cheerfully," reported a visiting police magistrate. Fish was "abundant on nearly all the Islands, and on most of them also pumpkins, bananas, and a fruit called the 'papaye,' grow pretty freely."[35] Ripe coconuts were freely available upon request. Anyone could use boats and nets for fishing. Many kept gardens and generally management encouraged chicken and pig raising.

Although the exploitation and export of the coconut—in the form of copra, oil, whole coconuts, and even husks and residual *poonac* solids from the pressing of oil—dominated life in Chagos, the islands also produced and traded in honey, guano, timber, wooden ships, pigs, salt fish, maize and some vegetable crops, wooden toys, model boats, and brooms and brushes made from coconut palms. Guano—bird feces used as fertilizer—in particular became an increasingly important export for the Mauritian sugar fields in the twentieth century, reaching one-third of Diego's exports by 1957.[36]

For about six years in the 1880s, two companies attempted to turn Diego Garcia into a major coal refueling port for steamer lines crossing the Indian Ocean. About the same time, the British Navy became interested in obtaining a site on the island.[37] The Admiralty never followed through, and the companies soon closed as financial failures, having faced the "promiscuous plundering of coconuts" by visiting steamship passengers and revolt from a group of imported English, Greek, Italian, Somali, Chinese, and Mauritian laborers—which required the temporary establishment of a Mauritian police post.[38]

By the turn of the twentieth century, a distinct society was well established in Chagos. The population neared 1,000 and there were six villages on Diego Garcia alone, served by a hospital on each arm of the atoll. While conditions varied to some extent from island to island and from administrator to administrator within each island group, growing similarities became the rule. Chagos Kreol, a language related to the Kreols in Mauritius and the Seychelles, emerged among the islanders.[39] People born in Chagos became collectively known by the Kreol name *Ilois*.*[40] Most considered themselves Roman Catholic—a chapel was built at East Point in 1895, followed by a church and chapels on other islands—although religious and spiritual practices and beliefs of African, Malagasy, and Indian origins remain present

---

* Many today prefer the term *Chagossian*. In exile, the older name has often been used as a slur against the islanders.

Figure 1.2 View of East Point village, Diego Garcia, from the lagoon, 1968. Photo courtesy of Kirby Crawford.

to this day. A distinct *"culture des îles"*—culture of the islands—had developed, fostered by the islands' isolation. "It is a system peculiar to the Lesser Dependencies," Scott would later write, "and it may be fairly described as indigenous and spontaneous in its emergence."[41]

KUTO DEKOKE

Most mornings, Rita rose for work at 4 a.m. "At four o'clock in the morning, I got up. I made tea for the children, cleaned the house everywhere. At seven o'clock I went for the call to work."

Each morning, she said, the manager gave work orders to the commandeurs, who delivered them to other Chagossians. There were many jobs: cleaning the camp, cutting straw for the houses, harvesting the coconuts, drying the coconuts, work for the manager and his assistant, work at the hospital, child care. Most men worked picking coconuts, 500 or more a day, removing the fibrous husk with the help of a long, spearlike *pike dekoke* knife, planted in the ground. This left the small hard nut within the coconut, which others transported to the factory center. There, like most other women, Rita shelled the interior nut, digging the flesh out with a specialized coconut-shelling knife, the *kuto dekoke*.

"I put it on the ground. I hit it. It splits. I have my knife. I scoop it in quickly, and I dump it over there: the shell on one side, the coconut flesh on the other," Rita explained.

Often she would complete the day's task of shelling 1,200 coconuts by 10:00 or 10:30 in the morning—meaning a rate of about one nut every 10 seconds. The women sat in groups, children often at their sides, amid hills of coconuts, cracked emptied shells, and bright white coconut flesh. Their hands were a concentrated swirl of movement—picking the nut, hitting it once, scoop, scoop with the knife between the flesh and the shell, flesh flying in one direction, empty shell in another. And again, pick, hit, scoop, scoop, flesh, flesh, shell. And again, pick, hit, scoop, scoop, flesh, flesh, shell. And again.

"Then there are other people who take the flesh," Rita said, "to dry it" in the sun. "When it's dry, they gather it up and put it in the *kalorifer*," a heated shed fueled by burning coconut husks. There the flesh was fully dried, producing copra to make oil. Some of the copra was crushed on the spot in a donkey-powered oil mill. Most, Rita explained, went "to Mauritius—was sent all over."[42]

"THINGS WILL BE OVERTURNED"

On a seemingly ordinary Monday morning in August 1931, when Rita Bancoult was ten, Peros Banhos commandeur Oscar Hilaire gave his usual work orders to fifteen Chagossian men to go to Petit Baie island for a week to gather and husk 3,000 coconuts each. The fifteen refused the order.[43] Two days later they finally left for Petit Baie, but returned the same day, refusing to work any further. For the remainder of the week, the men went on strike and didn't report to work.

The following Saturday, nine islanders confronted the assistant manager, Monsieur Dagorne, about the size of a task of weeding he was giving some women. Two days later, a group again confronted Dagorne and demanded that he reduce the women's tasks. This time he complied.

A few hours later, according to a police magistrate's eventual report, one woman assaulted another "for having advised her fellow workers . . . to obey the orders of the staff and to refuse to obey those who wished to create a disorder on the estate." When the victim went to complain to the head manager, Jean Baptiste Adam, a crowd followed, yelling "threatening language" at Adam.[44]

The crowd then turned and hurried into the kalorifer. There they ripped from the wall a rod, the length of a French fathom, used to measure lengths of rope made by elderly, infirm women working from their homes and paid by the length. They rushed back to Monsieur Adam with the rod and protested that it was a "false measure."[45] Moments later they returned to the kalorifer and placed a new measure on the wall—this one about 8 French inches shorter.

The next morning, the same group showed up at the center of the plantation and told the women to stop shelling coconuts. The group threatened to stop all work if Monsieur Adam did not add an extra laborer to the workforce at the kalorifer. The manager agreed to the change. Later they forced him to reduce the women's weeding and cleaning tasks, and still, all but two of the women walked off the job. The men told the manager they would refuse to unload and load the next cargo ship to arrive at Peros unless he and Dagorne were on the ship when it returned to Mauritius.

The insurgency continued into September. "Adam had lost all authority over these men," the police magistrate later reported. After a Chagossian drowned to death while sailing from Corner Island to another islet to collect coconuts, his partner and a crowd of supporters entered the manager's office, barred the exits, and forced him to sign a document granting her a widow's pension. They also forced him to give her free coffee, candles, sugar, and other goods from the company store to observe the islanders' traditional mourning rites.[46]

Over the next two weeks, leaders of the insurgency twice made Dagorne buy them extra wine from the company store. One leader, Etienne Labiche, again protested the task assigned to some women. "You are going on again because I am remaining quiet," Labiche challenged the managers in Chagos Kreol, according to the police magistrate. "We shall see when the boat arrives. *Sa boule-la pour devirer.*" Things will be overturned. Within minutes of issuing the challenge, the islanders had left work for the day. Days later Labiche and some supporters forced Dagorne to reveal that he was living with a mistress. Adam suspended Dagorne on the spot for "scandalous conduct."[47]

Labor unrest continued into a second month, with Labiche, Willy Christophe, and others forcing the manager to lower the price of soap at the company store when they suspected price gouging and Adam was unable to show them a price invoice. During the protest a few approached the store's back door. The island's pharmacist pulled out a revolver and "threatened to blow out the brains of the first man who tried to enter the shop."[48]

When two weeks later the cargo ship *Diego* finally came within sight on its voyage from Mauritius, the blast of a conch shell reverberated through the air as a signal among the islanders. Manager Adam went aboard the ship and returned to shore minutes later with his brother, the captain of the *Diego*. "The whole of the population met them at the landing stage," the magistrate's report recounts, "uttering loud shouts, and demanding to see the invoice" listing the prices for articles sold at the shop. The crowd accompanied Adam and his brother to the manager's house "shouting and threatening, climbed up the balcony stairs, and even into his dining room." There Adam unsealed the invoice. Someone in the crowd looked over Adam's shoulder and read the prices aloud. "Having noticed a mention in the official letter about a case of tobacco (plug) and the rise in the price . . . the crowd demanded the return of the case to Mauritius."[49]

At the next morning's call for work, none of the men appeared. When the captain of the *Diego* asked them why they were not coming to work, they told him they would only work if his brother and Dagorne were sent back to Mauritius. A standoff ensued. The ship eventually left with its cargo aboard, but with Manager Adam and Dagorne still in Peros.

Three months and two days after the beginning of the insurgency, Mauritian magistrate W. J. Hanning arrived in the atoll along with an armed guard of ten police constables, two police inspectors, and two noncommissioned officers. Hanning and Police Inspector Fitzgibbon charged, convicted, and sentenced 36 Chagossian men and women for offenses including "larceny soap," "larceny rope measure," "extortion of document," "coalition to prevent unloading cargo," and "coalition to prevent work." Two were convicted of "wounds & blows." Punishment for the charges of larceny and extortion ranged from three to twelve months' hard labor. Labiche received a total of 30 months' hard labor; others got up to 36 months. Hanning sent three commandeurs back to Mauritius and mandated the reading of the names of the convicted and their punishments throughout the rest of Chagos and the other Mauritian dependencies.[50]

"I have the honour to state that quiet has been restored at Peros," Magistrate Hanning wrote. Although he thought the insurgents' grievances "imaginary" and found the islanders "economically many times better off than the Mauritian labourer," he concluded his report by calling on the plantation owners to "exercise some leniency" over markups on prices for "articles of necessity" sold at the company store.[51]

GROWING CONNECTIONS

In 1935, new owners in Chagos established the first regular steamship connection between Mauritius and Chagos after completing the consolidation

Figure 1.3 Schoolchildren in Chagos, 1964. Photographer unknown.

of ownership over the various plantations, which had begun in the 1880s. Previously the islands sent copra, oil, and other goods to Mauritius and received supplies on twice-a-year boats. The new four-times-a-year steamship system decreased travel times significantly and provided a regular connection between Diego Garcia and the northern islands of Peros Banhos and Salomon, over 100 nautical miles away. Peros to Salomon transportation was by sailing ship and later motorboat. Transportation within each group and around Diego Garcia's lagoon was generally by small, locally built sailboats, and later by motorboats. News from the outside world came primarily from illustrated magazines and other reading materials supplied by the transport vessels visiting Chagos.

At the beginning of the twentieth century, Chagos had been so isolated that at the start of World War I, management on Diego Garcia supplied the German battleship *Emden* with provisions before learning that Britain and its colonies were already at war with Germany. By contrast, thirty years later during World War II, Diego Garcia became a small landing strip for Royal Air Force reconnaissance aircraft and a base for a small contingent of Indian Army troops. At war's end, the troops went home, leaving behind a wrecked Catalina seaplane that became a favorite playground for children.

By the mid-twentieth century, Chagos had moved from relative isolation to increasing connections with Mauritius, other islands in the Indian Ocean, and the rest of the world. Copra and coconut oil exports were sold in Mauritius and the Seychelles, and through them in Europe, South Africa, India, and Israel. Wireless communications at local meteorological stations connected the main islands with Mauritius and the Seychelles. Shortwave radios allowed reception of broadcasts from at least as far as the Seychelles and Sri Lanka.[52]

The Mauritian colonial government started showing increasing interest in the welfare of Chagos's inhabitants and its economy. Specialists sent by the government investigated health and agricultural conditions. With the help of their reports, the government established nurseries in each island group, schools, and a regular garbage and refuse removal system reported to be better than that in rural Mauritius.[53] Water came from wells and from rain catchment tanks. Small dirt roads traversed the main islands, and there were a handful of motorbikes, trucks, jeeps, and tractors.

"NOTHING WE HAD TO BUY"

By the 1960s, everyone in Chagos was guaranteed work on the plantations and pensions upon retirement.[54] The vast majority of Chagossians still worked as coconut laborers. A few male laborers rose to become foremen and commandeurs, and a few women were also commandeurs. Other men became artisans working as blacksmiths, bakers, carpenters, masons, mechanics, and in other specialized positions.

Wages remained low and paternalistic: Men harvesting coconuts earned about £2 a month, while women shelling the nuts earned less than half that. Artisans, foremen, and commandeurs earned six times what female laborers earned, and those in privileged "staff" positions earned considerably more. No matter the position or the gender, workers' monthly rations included about £3 worth of rice or flour, coconut oil, salt, lentils, fish, wine, and occasionally vegetables and pork.[55] Work benefits also included construction materials, free firewood, regular vacations—*promne*—with free passage to Mauritius, burial services, and free health care and medicines. Workers continued to occupy and receive land near their homes. Many used the land for gardens, raising crops like tomatoes, squash, chili peppers, eggplant, citrus and other fruits, and for keeping cows, pigs, goats, sheep, chickens, and ducks.

After the day's work task was completed, generally around midday, Chagossians could work overtime, tend to their gardens and animals, fish, or hunt for other seafood, including red snapper, tuna, and other fish, crab, prawns, crayfish, lobster, octopus, sea cucumber, and turtles.

"Whatever time it was, you went to your house and your day marched on," Rita recounted. "A commandeur passed by, asked you if you were going to do overtime. So then you went to work for another day's work. . . . If you didn't go do it, no one made you.

"But," she continued, "our money, at the end of the month we got it, we just put it in our account. And what we earned from overtime, that we used for buying our weekly supplies, understand?"

On payday people went to the store and "the women would go to buy a little clothing. . . . That was the only thing we had to buy: our clothing, cloth to make clothing, sugar, milk.

"Apart from that, there was nothing we had to buy. Apart from cigarettes, which if you smoked, you needed to buy. There was beer at the shop to buy. There was rum to buy, but we made our own drink," Rita added, referring to Chagossians' own fermented drinks of dhal-based *baka* and palm toddy *kalu*.

"Then, you know Saturday *laba*," Rita explained, "Saturday what we did, with our coconut leaf brooms, we swept the court of the manager's house, everywhere around the chapel, the hospital, everywhere. When we finished that, then we'd go to the house. Around nine o'clock, we finished and left. Then we had Saturday, Sunday to ourselves. Monday, then we went back to hard work."

But on Saturday "the house, all the family, everyone was there. We had some fun. . . . We had an accordion, later we had a gramophone. . . . On Saturday, Saturday night, we had our *sega*."

Although the long-standing popular institution featuring singing, playing, and dancing to sega music is found on islands throughout the southwest Indian Ocean, Chagos and most other islands had their own distinctive sega traditions. In Chagos, segas were an occasion for entire island communities to gather. On Saturday nights everyone met around a bonfire in a clearing. Under the moon and stars, drummers on the goat hide–covered *ravanne* would start tapping out a slow, rhythmic beat. Others would begin singing, dancing, and joining in on accordions, triangles, and other percussion and string instruments.

The sega allowed islanders to sing old traditional songs or their own originals, which were often improvised. Most segas followed a call-and-response pattern, with soloists singing verses, supported by dancers, musicians, and onlookers who joined in a chorus, providing frequent shouts, whistles, and outbursts of encouragement. In Chagos, segas were filled with themes of love, jealousy, separation, and loss. Much as in the blues and other musical traditions, the sega was an important mode of expression and a way to share hardships and gain support from the community.

"The segas," Rita recounted, "at night, people opened their doors, everyone came out, beat the drum, sang, danced. And we carried on until early in the morning. Early in the morning, six o'clock. . . . six o'clock, until seven o'clock too, and then even the old ones went home."

I asked Rita if she danced to the sega. She said, "Yes."

I asked if she sang sega. She said, "Yes."

"What did you sing?" I asked.

"Everything. Those that I knew, I sang. I know how to sing sega very well. . . . I'm full of segas that I know," said Rita. And then she started to sing . . .

My father, you're yelling "Attention passengers! Embark passengers!"
This madame, her husband's going but she's staying.

Crying, madame, enough crying madame.
On the beach, you're crying so much,
The tears from your eyes are drowning the passengers list.

Crying, madame, even if you cry on the beach, even if you cry
Capitan L'Anglois isn't going to turn the boat around to come
get you.

O li la e, O la e, O li la la.
O li le le, O li le la la.

L'Anglois answer me, L'Anglois, my friend
Answer me, L'Anglois, this sega that you left down in Chagos.

"FRENCH COASTAL VILLAGES"

"The people of Île du Coin were exceptionally proud of their homes," Governor Scott wrote of Rita's Peros Banhos after World War II. "The gardens usually contained an arrangement of flower-beds and a vegetable patch, almost always planted with pumpkins and loofahs trained over rough trellis-work, with a few tomato plants and some greens."[56]

By that time Salomon had a large timber industry for export and was known as the home of Chagos's boat building industry, widely renowned in the southwest Indian Ocean. Three Brothers, Eagle Island, and Six Islands had been settled for most of the nineteenth and early twentieth centuries before the plantation company moved their inhabitants to Peros and Diego to consolidate production. Eagle's population rose to as many as 100 and was "regarded by its inhabitants," according to Scott, "as a real home," with a "carefully tended" children's cemetery and evocatively named places like Love Apple Crossing, Ceylon Square, and Frigates' Pool.[57]

Looking on "from the seaward end of the pier," Scott compared Diego Garcia's capital East Point to a French coastal village: "The architecture, the touches of old-fashioned ostentation in the *château* and its relation to the church; the disposition of trees and flowering shrubs across the ample green; the neighbourly way in which white-washed stores, factories and workshops, shingled and thatched cottages, cluster round the green; the lamp standards along the roads and the parked motor-lorries: all contribute towards giving the village this quality."

Clearly charmed by the islands, Scott continued, "The association of East Point with a synthesis of small French villages, visited or seen on canvas, was strengthened by the warm welcome of the islanders, since their clothes and merry bearing, and particularly the small, fluttering flags of the school-children, were wholly appropriate to a *fête* in a village so devised."[58]

"Funny little places! Indeed they are. But how lovely!" wrote Scott's predecessor as governor, Sir Hilary Blood. "Coconut palms against the bluest of skies, their foliage blown by the wind into a perfect circle; rainbow spray to the windward where the South-East Trades pile in the Indian Ocean up on the reefs; in the sheltered bays to the leeward the sun strikes through shallow water to the coral, and emerald-green, purple, orange, all the rich colours of the world, follow each other across the warm sea," glowed Sir Hilary. "Its beauty is infinite."[59]

A WARNING

In 1962, ownership of the islands changed hands, purchased by a Mauritian-Seychellois conglomerate calling itself Chagos-Agalega Ltd. Around the same time, Chagossians saw the introduction of a more flexible labor supply revolving around single male laborers from the Seychelles, as well as the "drift" of permanent inhabitants from Chagos to Mauritius, drawn by the allure of Mauritius's "pavements and shop-windows, the cinemas and football matches, the diversity of food and occupation." Scott compared the movement to the migration of people in Great Britain from villages to cities after World War I, but emphasized, "it is still only a drift."[60]

On the eve of the expulsion that no one in Chagos could have anticipated, Mauritian historian Auguste Toussaint wrote, "The insularity of this archipelago is total and, in this regard, Chagos differs from the Mascarenes and the Seychelles, which are linked with the rest of the world. The conditions of life there are quite specialized and even, believe me, unique."[61]

"The life that I had, compared to what I am experiencing now, David. All the time, I will think about my home because there I was well nourished and I didn't eat anything preserved or stored. We ate everything fresh," Rita told me.

"Doctors know that when we left the islands—they know—your health here isn't the same. Here, we eat frozen food all the time. . . . But *laba*, no. Even if something is only three or four days old, it isn't the same as fresh, David. . . . There we ate everything fresh."

"There, I tell you, you didn't have strokes, you didn't have diabetes. Only rarely did an old person die. A baby, maybe once a year, an infant might die at birth, that's it. Here, every day you hear about—I'm tired of hearing about death."

"Yes," I said softly.

"It's not the same, David. . . ." Rita continued, "I—how can I say this—I didn't leave there because the island closed. . . . I didn't realize" that the islands were being closed down. "And then I had a little girl named Noellie."

Writing in 1961, Governor Scott concluded his book with a sympathetic (if paternalistic and colonialist) description of the Chagossians. In it, one hears a chilling warning from one who as governor of Mauritius may well have known about developing plans aimed at realizing Lieutenant La Fontaine's original vision for harboring a "great number" of vessels in Diego Garcia's lagoon:

> It must also be recognized, however, that ignorance of the way of
> life of the islanders might open the way to attempts to jerk them
> too rapidly into more highly organized forms of society, before they
> are ready. They have never been hurried. Their environment has

probably inoculated them with an intolerance towards hurry. . . .
This is far from being a plea to make the Lesser Dependencies a
kind of nature reserve for the preservation of the anachronistic. It
is, however, very definitely a plea for full understanding of the islanders' unique condition, in order to ensure that all that is whole-
some and expansive in the island societies is preserved.[62]

CHAPTER 2

THE BASES OF EMPIRE

Around Washington, DC naval circles, Stu Barber was known as being "exceptionally far-sighted."[1] Two decades before President Carter announced his foreign policy doctrine—the consequences of which the world is feeling to this day—that the United States would intervene militarily in the Persian Gulf against threats to its interests, Stu proposed his own version. He called it the "South Atlantic and Indian Ocean Monroe Doctrine and Force." Developed during the 1960 presidential election campaign, Stu intended the idea "to be fed, somehow, to both Presidential candidates."[2]

During World War II, Stu served in naval intelligence on Ford Island, Hawai'i. Rising to the rank of lieutenant commander, he spent most of his time tracking and analyzing statistics from land-based air combat operations in the Pacific—combat flights launched primarily from island bases. After the war, Stu worked for the war housing authority before returning to the Navy as a civilian analyst.

Working at the Pentagon, he helped found a somewhat obscure new office, the Long-Range Objectives Group, in 1955. Called "Op-93" by the Navy bureaucracy, the Group was charged with planning the Navy's long-term technological, weapons, and strategic needs. The Group's first annual report declared it "mandatory" to have a "courageous approach" to its mission.[3] According to its highest-ranking staff members, "the brains of the outfit" belonged to Stu.[4]

Stu began work on his Strategic Island Concept idea around 1958. The premise of the plan was his recognition that in the age of decolonization, local peoples and the governments of newly independent nations were increasingly endangering the viability of many of the Navy's overseas bases. One of his first memoranda warned that in the event of hostilities in the Indian Ocean region, "access via Suez, and undisputed access via Singapore or through the Indies may be denied, as may air communications other

41

than via Australia or Central Africa. Access to anchorages and airfields may be denied or limited north of the equator, as the product of anti-colonialist feelings or Soviet pressures."[5]

Stu realized that finding base locations somehow lacking "local problems" was the best long-term solution to maintaining the Navy's positions overseas. The best place to find such locations, Stu saw, was on strategically located, lightly populated, isolated islands still controlled by friendly Western powers. In the words of former Navy official Vytautas Bandjunis, who later helped plan the base, Stu and soon others in the Navy realized that "remote colonial islands with small [colonial] populations would be the easiest to acquire, and would entail the least political headaches."[6]

Stu realized, however, that opportunities for acquiring such islands were rapidly disappearing as territories around the world were gaining their independence. If the United States was going to secure islands as potential base locations, it would have to move quickly to purchase them outright or win guarantees from the remaining colonial powers not to grant independence and to provide the United States with long-term basing access.

COMING TO TERMS WITH EMPIRE

From the Roman Empire to the British and French empires in the Indian Ocean and around the globe, bases have long been essential tools for securing empires and political, economic, and military control over vast lands. Prior to World War II, the United States had few bases outside its territory, although as we shall see, a series of U.S. Army forts played a critical role in enabling the westward conquest by the original thirteen states. By the end of World War II, the nation had more than 30,000 installations at more than 2,000 base sites globally.[7]

Today the United States has what is likely the largest collection of military bases in world history, totaling more than 5,300 globally and an estimated 1,000 bases outside its own territory of the 50 states and Washington, DC.[8] Slowly, awareness has been growing about this massive deployment of U.S. forces on the sovereign territory of other nations. Many have started referring to the United States as an "Empire of Bases."

People in the United States have long had trouble seeing their nation as an empire of any kind, given its powerful and important founding ideologies of democracy and freedom.[9] Many thought that if the country was ever an empire, it was only briefly and perhaps absent-mindedly so around the 1898 Spanish-American War and the acquisition of the Philippines, Puerto

Rico, and Guam. (Interestingly, many of the founders had little trouble reconciling imperial and democratic visions of the nation: George Washington referred to the United States as the "rising American Empire.")

Following the rapid invasion and conquest of Afghanistan and Iraq in 2001 and 2003, however, political scientists, historians, pundits, and others began acknowledging widely that the United States is indeed an empire.[10] The notion is no longer dismissed as an accusation or conspiracy theory; debate now revolves around what kind of empire the United States has become and the legitimacy of imperialism.

Some scholars and commentators like Niall Ferguson and Michael Ignatieff have embraced and even promoted the idea of the United States as a benign "liberal empire" or as a kind of humanitarian "empire lite."[11] Ferguson believes "many parts of the world would benefit from a period of American rule." People, he suggests, would benefit under an empire "that enhances its own security and prosperity precisely by providing the rest of the world with generally beneficial public goods: not only economic freedom but also the institutions necessary for markets to flourish."[12]

Ignatieff says the question "is not whether America is too powerful but whether it is powerful enough." Arguing in 2003 in support of invading Iraq, he asked, "Does it have what it takes to be grandmaster of what Colin Powell has called the chessboard of the world's most inflammable region? . . . The case for empire is that it has become, in a place like Iraq, the last hope for democracy and stability alike."[13]

Skeptical of such claims, others have long been critical of the U.S. Empire. They doubt that increasing U.S. power will do anything more than just that—increase the power and wealth of the United States and its economic elites. Focusing especially on the economic dynamics of U.S. Empire, revisionist historians and others have generally held that following the conquests of 1898, the United States primarily became an empire of economics, as exemplified by Open Door trade policies initiated in China after the Boxer Rebellion.[14] These scholars argue that the nation largely avoided the colonialism of the European powers based on territorial expansion and direct rule over subject peoples in favor of a more discreet, nonterritorial kind of economic imperialism. Economic control and exploitation, scholars say, have largely emanated from policies of the Open Door and later the International Monetary Fund (IMF) and the World Bank. "The best-preferred strategy," says geographer Neil Smith, "was to organize resource and commodity extraction through the market rather than through military or political occupation."[15] The market and the use of state power to open up capitalist opportunities became the basis

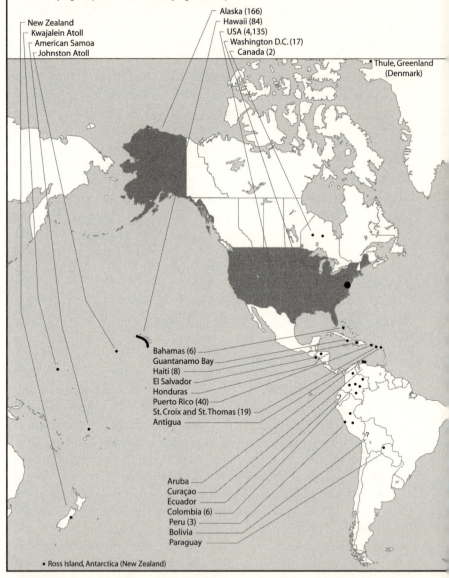

U.S. Military Bases

Because of the base network's size, complexity, and secrecy, base numbers cited are the most accurate available; locations are not always precise. "?" indicates a base under development or negotiation or where a base is suspected but cannot be confirmed.

Sources: Department of Defense, "Base Structure Report, Fiscal Year 2007 Baseline (A Summary of DoD's Real Property Invento 2007; Transnational Institute, "Military Bases Google Earth File," available at http://www.tni.org/detail_page.phtml?act_id=17; Chalmers Johnson, *The Sorrows of Empire: Militarism, Secrecy, and the End of the Republic*: (New York: Metropolitan Books, 2004); Chalmers Johnson, *Nemesis: The Last Days of the American Republic* (New York: Metropolitan Books, 2007); GlobalSecurity.org <http://www.GlobalSecurity.org>; news reports.

New Zealand
Kwajalein Atoll
American Samoa
Johnston Atoll

Alaska (166)
Hawaii (84)
USA (4,135)
Washington D.C. (17)
Canada (2)

Thule, Greenland (Denmark)

Bahamas (6)
Guantanamo Bay
Haiti (8)
El Salvador
Honduras
Puerto Rico (40)
St. Croix and St. Thomas (19)
Antigua

Aruba
Curaçao
Ecuador
Colombia (6)
Peru (3)
Bolivia
Paraguay

Ross Island, Antarctica (New Zealand)

Figure 2.1 The Global U.S. Military Base Network.

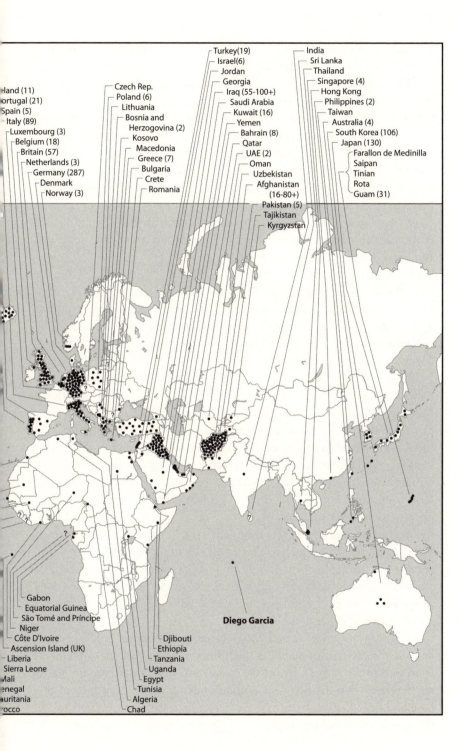

Turkey(19)
Israel(6)
Jordan
Georgia
Iraq (55-100+)
Saudi Arabia
Kuwait (16)
Yemen
Bahrain (8)
Qatar
UAE (2)
Oman
Uzbekistan
Afghanistan
(16-80+)
Pakistan (5)
Tajikistan
Kyrgyzstan

India
Sri Lanka
Thailand
Singapore (4)
Hong Kong
Philippines (2)
Taiwan
Australia (4)
South Korea (106)
Japan (130)
Farallon de Medinilla
Saipan
Tinian
Rota
Guam (31)

Czech Rep.
Poland (6)
Lithuania
Bosnia and
Herzogovina (2)
Kosovo
Macedonia
Greece (7)
Bulgaria
Crete
Romania

land (11)
ortugal (21)
Spain (5)
Italy (89)
Luxembourg (3)
Belgium (18)
Britain (57)
Netherlands (3)
Germany (287)
Denmark
Norway (3)

Gabon
Equatorial Guinea
São Tomé and Príncipe
Niger
Côte D'Ivoire
Ascension Island (UK)
Liberia
Sierra Leone
Mali
enegal
auritania
rocco

Djibouti
Ethiopia
Tanzania
Uganda
Egypt
Tunisia
Algeria
Chad

Diego Garcia

for exploitation and continued imperialism, with geopolitical and military tools of only secondary importance.[16]

Other scholars have pointed to the significance of military bases. Among them, Chalmers Johnson argues that unlike older European empires that relied on a series of colonies and direct rule over other peoples to exert their power, the United States has for the most part avoided colonial rule. Since World War II the United States has instead used its bases to exert control, influence, and economic domination over weaker nations. Bases, he and others say, have become a primary means by which the United States keeps other nations within a global political-economic order most favorable to the United States, thus maintaining its global political and economic supremacy.[17] Former Deputy Assistant Secretary of Defense and Air Force Undersecretary James Blaker describes the role of bases most bluntly when he says the United States came to use bases to "structure the character of other nations" and shape the future of the world.[18] Harnessing all its power, the nation has, like previous empires, exerted significant and substantive control over the affairs of other nations and peoples by combining a collection of bases in other people's lands with other forms of economic, political, and military power.

The economic power can be seen as the influence exercised over other nations through organizations like the World Bank, the International Monetary Fund, and the World Trade Organization. The political power can been seen in the system of Cold War alliances and client regimes nurtured since World War II and in the use and manipulation of the United Nations, NATO, and other multinational organizations for political and economic ends. The military power can be seen in frequent military interventions and wars abroad including more than 200 overseas military operations between the end of World War II and the invasion of Iraq, the maintenance of the world's most lethal nuclear and nonnuclear armed forces (with funding equaling that of all the other nations in the world combined), the deployment of military advisers and arms transfers to other nations, public displays of military force, and numerous CIA-orchestrated coups and other covert and paramilitary activities to intervene in the domestic affairs of other nations.

Exploring how the United States came to possess its 1,000 overseas bases is critical to understanding the history of Diego Garcia and requires us to turn to the earliest days of the nation and its westward expansion. As we shall see, from the first days of independence to the development of a base on Diego Garcia, bases have played an increasingly important role in the expansion of the United States and its development as an empire.[19]

BASES AND AN EXPANDING EMPIRE

When the thirteen North American colonies began moving toward independence from Britain in the middle of the eighteenth century, the colonies' leaders looked to the European empires as models for what the colonies might become. An "expansionist consensus" helped unify the revolutionaries around the "notion of preemptive right to the continent" and the vision of a united continental empire stretching across North America.[20] (The idea that the land might rightfully belong to native groups was hardly considered.)

Fueled by such expansionist desires, surging feelings of nationalism, a growing population, fears about the other imperial powers in North America, and a government desperate to pay off its war debts by selling western lands (inconveniently occupied by Native Americans), waves of settlers and speculators moved westward after independence, pushing Indians progressively away from the east coast. According to Horsman, "land and more land" is what settlers and many state governments wanted. To the settlers, native peoples were mere obstacles "to drive out or annihilate"; their land claims were simply "invalid."[21]

Assisting the process, the U.S. Army became what one scholar calls the "advance agent" and "pry bar" of Euro-American westward expansion. The Army was aided by a growing chain of forts marking the line of expansion.[22] By the mid-nineteenth century, there were more than 60 major forts west of the Mississippi River, from Fort Leavenworth in Kansas to the Presidio in San Francisco. Forts helped enable and protect what became a mass migration west, assisting the Army in forcing indigenous groups off their lands, into treaties, and onto "reservations."[23]

Over the course of the nineteenth century, most of the major native peoples in the east were forced into western reserves. Federal forts encircled the reserves to keep native peoples in and whites out, though the new reserves would soon face white encroachment. The Cherokee's 1832 "Trail of Tears" forced march westward, during which one in four may have died, was just one example of the systematic population displacements.[24] It's estimated that the government expropriated approximately 100 million acres of land from native groups in the east alone.[25] Across the continent, Indians faced starvation and the growing dissolution of their societies.[26]

By 1853, the United States had conquered most Native Americans, invaded and conquered large parts of Mexico, and seized or annexed Texas, the southwest, and Oregon. After the Civil War, interest in bases shifted primarily to the Pacific and increasingly, to island bases. The nation increased its commercial capabilities in the Pacific with the establishment of coaling stations—necessary for new steamship travel—in 1857, on Jarvis Island, Baker Island, and Howland's Island, southwest of Hawai'i.[27]

In 1867, the same year that the United States purchased Alaska from Russia, the government increased its possessions in the Pacific by acquiring Midway Island. Within a decade, the United States had signed an agreement to lease a naval station in Samoa; while the Senate failed to ratify it, the United States eventually gained possession of what became American Samoa in 1899, the same year it acquired Wake Island.

In this period, the most powerful proponent for increasing the nation's collection of island bases and building up a powerful navy to protect a growing commercial empire was naval historian Rear Admiral Alfred Thayer Mahan. Called the "prophet" of the Navy by World War II Secretary of War Henry L. Stimson, Mahan has proved the most influential U.S. naval thinker for over a century. Based largely on an analysis of the wars between Britain and France from 1660 to the fall of Napoleon in 1812, Mahan argued that "sea power," or the lack thereof, had determined the course of every major conflict as a result of each power's relative ability to control the enemy's commerce.[28] Applying these historical lessons to the United States, Mahan (and soon others) argued for the maintenance of a navy equal to or greater than Britain's, able to operate globally, and supported by new coaling stations and bases from China to Hawai'i to the Caribbean.[29]

Spurred by Mahan, the Navy grew interested, beginning in the 1890s, in creating additional bases in the Pacific to support U.S. commerce in Asia. In 1894, the United States gained access to a base in Hawai'i as part of a U.S.-supported overthrow of the local Hawai'ian monarchy by white sugar planters and settlers. The islands maintained limited sovereignty until the United States formally annexed Hawai'i in 1898; the annexation was realized in no small part because the growing empire needed a halfway base from which to deploy its power into Asia.[30]

The major movement of the United States into Asia came with the outbreak of the Spanish-American War and the largest seizure of territory by the United States since the completion of its continental expansion. In what was a rapid and ignominious defeat for a once mighty empire, the United States routed Spanish forces, claiming the Philippines, Puerto Rico, Guam, and (as a "protectorate") Cuba. The Philippines alone included more than 7,000 islands and a population of 7 million.[31] Although scholars will continue to debate the motivations of President William McKinley and the nation for acquiring the distant Spanish possessions, it is beyond debate that the United States expanded its territory, and with it the basing of military forces outside North America, in dramatic fashion. The Navy ultimately gained an indefinite lease for a base at Guantánamo Bay, Cuba (now the oldest U.S. base on foreign territory), control of a base in the Philippines' Subic Bay, and bases that came with Hawai'ian annexation. After warships again steamed eastward to stamp out the Boxer Rebellion in 1900, the Navy proposed to Congress the creation of additional bases in both the Far East and the Caribbean.

Following the conquests of 1898, the United States began to pursue a new kind of imperialism that generally avoided the bald-faced seizure of territory. Most scholars emphasize how this period was characterized by informal assertions of dominance exemplified by the Open Door policies in China.[32] While the Open Door became an important template for the extension of U.S. power abroad, the era between 1898 and World War II also featured frequent (and largely underestimated) military interventions in Latin America and the accompanying basing of forces abroad.[33]

In this period, the United States intervened militarily in (and in some cases occupied) Mexico (1914, 1916–19), Guatemala (1920), El Salvador (1932), Honduras (1903, 1907, 1911, 1912, 1919, 1920, 1924, 1925), Nicaragua (1898, 1899, 1909–10, occupied 1912–33), Costa Rica (naval presence 1921), the Dominican Republic (1903, 1904, 1914, occupied 1915–24), Haiti (1914, occupied 1915–34), and Cuba (occupied 1898–1902, 1906–9, 1912, 1917–22).[34] The military occupations in particular depended on the establishment of local military bases and garrisons to station U.S. troops. In Nicaragua, for example, between 1930 and 1932, the United States established at least eight military garrisons.[35] In Panama, where the United States intervened 24 times between 1856 and 1990, the nation built fourteen bases as part of gaining access to the Panama Canal Zone in perpetuity, as well as extensive powers of land expropriation and interference outside the Zone.[36] Like Cuba, Panama became an "American colony in all but name."[37]

Elsewhere in the hemisphere, during World War I, the Wilson administration grew worried that Germany would overrun Denmark and create a base in the Danish Virgin Islands. In a move that foreshadowed both the unprecedented expansion in the number of U.S. overseas bases and Stu Barber's Strategic Island Concept, the government purchased the soon renamed U.S. Virgin Islands from Denmark for $25 million.[38]

DESTROYERS FOR BASES

On September 3, 1940, President Franklin Delano Roosevelt informed Congress that as commander in chief, he was authorizing an agreement with the United Kingdom to provide nearly bankrupt wartime Britain with fifty World War I–era destroyers in exchange for U.S. control over a string of air and naval bases in Britain's colonies. Under a program known as "lend-lease" or "destroyers-for-bases," the United States acquired 99-year leases and near-sovereign powers on bases in the Bahamas, Jamaica, St. Lucia, St. Thomas, Antigua, Aruba-Curaçao, Trinidad, and British Guiana, and temporary access to bases in Bermuda and Newfoundland.[39]

Ostensibly the bases were for the defense of the western hemisphere against the Axis powers. Importantly, they were also used to preempt Germany and Italy from establishing their own bases in Latin America. Functionally, the military came to use the bases primarily to shuttle arms and aircraft to the battlefields of Europe and Africa, as well as for intelligence gathering, antisubmarine warfare, and hosting naval convoys. Ultimately, the bases created the foundation for a network of U.S. bases that would soon span the globe.

With the entrance of the United States into World War II after the attack on Pearl Harbor, the question for the U.S. military was not *if* it should expand its collection of bases but *how* to expand the number as quickly as possible.[40] The government followed lend-lease with deals to station U.S. forces in Iceland, Greenland (Denmark), Ascension (U.K.), Haiti, Cuba, Suriname (Netherlands), the Azores (Portugal), Acapulco (Mexico), the Galapagos Islands (Ecuador), Palmyia (south of Hawai'i), and Recife and Fortaleza (Brazil).[41] Major regional base networks emerged in the southwest Pacific, the central Pacific, North Africa, and from India through Burma and into China.

In addition to war-making interests, the multiplication of bases likely had other motivations, including a "strong element of imperial rivalry."[42] Roosevelt first became interested in obtaining island bases in the Caribbean in 1939, prior to lend-lease. Within a year of entering the war, the Joint Chiefs of Staff were already making plans for a network of postwar bases around the globe. In 1943, a paper for the Joint Chiefs declared that "adequate bases, owned or controlled by the United States, are essential and their acquisition and development must be considered as amongst our primary war aims." Domestic planners likewise saw the advantage of maintaining the base structure after the war for the nation's burgeoning airline industry, which needed access to airfields to service growing intercontinental air travel.[43]

During the war, base construction was particularly rapid in the Pacific, where the military built strings of small island bases to battle Japan. After the shock of the attack on Pearl Harbor and the subsequent loss of bases in the Philippines, Guam, and Wake Island, the U.S. military remembered the strategic doctrine of Admiral Mahan: Island bases were a way to win the war and ultimately to control the peace—to ensure that there would never again be a Pearl Harbor (part of the Japanese attack came from an island base on tiny Kwajalein in the Marshall Islands, west of Hawai'i). The military fought its way slowly through the ocean in a series of deadly and costly battles, retaking its lost islands and fighting from island chain to island chain toward mainland Japan. A construction "frenzy" followed the battles for each island group, building bases to launch assaults on other islands and Japan itself;[44] many of the affected islands and the local peoples living on them faced "devastation."[45]

The battle for the Marshall Islands, one of Japan's "mandates" (i.e., internationally legitimated colonies) from World War I, illustrates the deadly fighting that went on in the Pacific and the nature of the basing complexes that followed. In a span of eight days in 1944, the United States assaulted and captured all six square miles of Kwajalein Island with a force of 40,000 troops. The United States suffered 372 dead and 2,000 wounded in the fighting. Japan suffered 8,000 dead. No U.S. historians or military officials seem to have bothered to count the Marshallese dead.[46]

Within two months, the U.S. Army had turned Kwajalein into its main base in Micronesia, hosting 22,000 troops. (Later the island would become a major missile-testing base.) Within three months of taking what is now the Marshallese capital, Majuro, the Army and Navy had built a 5,800-foot airstrip and a naval anchorage. On Enewetak Atoll, another base hosted more than 11,000 troops.[47]

By the end of the war, the United States had built or occupied thousands of bases in the Pacific. Globally, the U.S. military was building base facilities at an average rate of 112 a month. In a matter of five years, the U.S. military developed a global network of bases that, according to some, became the world's largest collection ever held by a single power.[48]

THE POSTWAR BASING NETWORK

With the end of the World War II, the United States, like previous empires, was reluctant to give up territories and bases acquired in wartime. Even if the military had little interest in using a base or a territory, military principles of "redundancy"—the more bases, the safer the nation—and "strategic denial"—preventing enemies from using a territory by denying them access—held that the United States should almost never cede its acquisitions.

Especially in the Pacific, because of the high human and financial costs of acquiring "its" bases, the military felt justified in retaining control of captured islands as the "spoils of war."[49] "Having defeated or subordinated its former imperial rivals in the Pacific," several base experts explain, "the United States military was in no mood to hand back occupied real estate."[50] Congress agreed. It "shared the feeling that no one had the right to give away land which had been bought and paid for with American lives." Louisiana Representative F. Edward Hébert explained the logic prevalent after the war: "We fought for them, we've got them, we should keep them. They are necessary to our safety. I see no other course."[51]

The maintenance of such an extensive collection of military bases was driven by a widely held strategic belief that the security of the nation and the prevention of future wars depended on dominating the Pacific (and to a lesser extent the Atlantic) through a Mahanian combination of unparalleled naval forces and island bases. "Most importantly," Hal Friedman writes, "this imperial solution to American anxieties about strategic security in the postwar Pacific exhibited itself in a bureaucratic consensus about turning the Pacific Basin into an 'American lake.'"[52]

For General Douglas MacArthur, the Supreme Commander of Allied Forces in Japan, and other Navy leaders, securing the Pacific meant creating what they called an "offshore island perimeter." The perimeter was to be a line of island bases stretching from north to south across the western Pacific like a giant wall protecting the United States, yet with thousands of miles of moat before reaching U.S. shores. "Our line of defense," MacArthur explained, "runs through the chain of islands fringing the coast of Asia. It starts from the Philippines and continues through the Ryukyu Archipelago, which includes its main bastion, Okinawa. Then it bends back through Japan and the Aleutian Island chain, to Alaska."[53]

The island base plan found support from the architect of early Cold War strategic policy, George Kennan, who saw the island perimeter as equally beneficial for hosting air power to control East Asia without large ground forces. To carry out the plan, military leaders demanded complete sovereignty over Guam, the other islands in the Marianas and in Micronesia, and the retention of other captured Japanese islands. Some suggested full incorporation of Guam and other Pacific islands into the country as states or as part of a new Hawai'ian state. In the process of breaking up the British and French empires and sensitive to being attacked as colonialists, State Department and other Truman administration officials opposed outright U.S. sovereignty.

Eventually the administration struck a compromise to turn most of Micronesia and some of the other Pacific islands into a "strategic trust territory." Under the auspices of the United Nations, this Trust Territory of the Pacific Islands (TTPI) would be administered by the United States until the islands could assume self-government. Among other UN-granted powers, the United States had the right to establish military facilities in the TTPI and effectively governed the islands as part of the nation. (Until 1951, the Navy maintained direct administrative control of the islands.) As one observer put it, the trusteeship was "de facto annexation, papered over with the thinnest of disguises."[54]

THE BASE SYSTEM EVOLVES

The grandest plans for postwar bases were initially trumped by concerns about costs and (partial) demilitarization after the war. In the Pacific, the military abandoned its plans for an extensive offshore island perimeter (which would have resembled something like an offensive, oceanic Maginot Line), instead relying on key bases in Japan, Guam, and Hawai'i, and continued control over the TTPI.

To the disappointment of military leaders, the nation returned about half its foreign bases with the close of the war.[55] And yet, the United States still maintained what became a "permanent institution" of bases in peacetime.[56] In Germany, Italy, Japan, and France, U.S. forces retained rights of occupation as a victor nation. The United States signed deals to maintain three of its most important bases in Greenland, Iceland, and the Azores. The nation retained facilities in most of the British territories occupied under lend-lease, continued occupying French bases in Morocco, and gained further access to British facilities in Ascension, Bahrain, Guadalcanal, and Tarawa. When Britain wanted to grant complete independence to India and Burma, the U.S. State Department asked its ally to maintain control of three airfields in the former and one in the latter. U.S. bases in Great Britain proper turned the British Isles into what one journalist called an "emergency parking lot for the Strategic Air Command."[57] And the U.S. military had access to an even wider array of British and French bases still held in their remaining colonies.

Among its own colonial possessions, the United States retained important bases in Guam, Puerto Rico, Wake Island, and Cuba. When the Philippines gained its independence in 1946, the United States pressured its former colony into granting a 99-year rent-free lease on 23 bases and military installations.[58]

BEYOND COLONIALISM: THE POWER OF BASES

Alongside U.S. postwar economic and political power, the base network constituted a major mechanism of U.S. imperial control. While the total acreage of territory acquired may have been relatively slight (especially compared to prior European empires), in the ability to rapidly deploy the U.S. military nearly anywhere on the globe, the basing system represented a dramatic expansion of U.S. power and a significant way in which the United States came to maintain dominance over other nations.

In the nineteenth century, Britain and other European powers tied their expansionist success to the direct control of foreign lands. World War II made this no longer an option for the United States. The European powers had already divided most of the world among themselves, and the ideological mood of the time was clearly against colonialism and territorial expansion.[59] The allied powers had made World War II a war against the expansionist desires of Germany, Japan, and Italy, and the United States had framed the war as an anticolonial struggle, criticizing the colonial powers, and pledging to assist with the decolonization of colonial territories upon war's end. After the war, the creation of the United Nations enshrined the decolonization process and the right of nations and peoples to self-determination and self-government.

"In the 1950s era of decolonization," writes anthropologist Carole McGranahan, "empires did not go away, but went underground, surfacing in guises ranging from socialist empire in the Soviet Union to various forms of neo-imperialist aggressive democracy as in the case of the United States. Yet each of these polities," she explains, "fiercely guarded themselves against any accusations of empire or imperialism."[60]

Which meant the United States came to exert its power through increasingly subtle and discreet means: most importantly through economic markets, international agreements, and foreign bases. Without a collection of colonies, the United States used what is likely the greatest collection of bases ever as well as periodic displays of military might to keep wayward nations within the rules of an economic and political system favorable to the United States.[61] Indeed, it was the nation's unchallenged military superiority at the end of World War II that left it in a position to dictate much of the postwar international economic system upon which U.S. geo-economic power is based.[62]

U.S. forces abroad came to be "used to influence and limit the political, diplomatic, and economic initiatives of host nations," explains base expert Joseph Gerson.[63] In the Philippines, for example, the United States used military and economic aid and defense promises to extract not only decades' worth of base access but favorable terms of trade and political influence as well.[64] "Global economic access without colonies" was the postwar strategy, explains geographer Neil Smith, "matched by a strategic vision of necessary bases around the globe both to protect global economic interests and to restrain any future military belligerence."[65]

During the Korean War, shortly before Stu Barber began his work on Diego Garcia, the U.S. military increased its number of overseas bases by 40 percent, bringing the total to near the heights of World War II.[66] By the end of the 1950s, around one million U.S. troops and their families lived on or near bases abroad. By 1960, the United States had entered into eight mutual defense pacts with 42 nations and executive security agreements with more than 30 others, most of which provided various kinds of basing access. After some post-Korea reductions, there would be another 20 percent increase in base sites during the war in Vietnam.[67] One was Diego Garcia.

CHAPTER 3

THE STRATEGIC ISLAND CONCEPT AND A CHANGING OF THE IMPERIAL GUARD

Within three months of the United States' entrance into World War II, a U.S. Army Corps of Engineers "Capetown Clipper" seaplane was skidding to a halt across Diego Garcia's lagoon. Two officials stepped out of the plane and went to meet Diego's administrator. After signing his autograph book, they began surveying the northwest tip of the island for construction of a 4,000-foot runway.[1] The Army never built the runway; instead the ruling power in the ocean, Great Britain, developed a corner of the atoll into a small base for ships, reconnaissance seaplanes, and communications traffic.

Between the fall of Napoleon in 1814 and the end of World War II, Britain dominated the Indian Ocean without peer. During the war, the ocean was a relatively minor theater but saw periodic German attacks on allied shipping and Japan's seizure of the Andaman Islands and threats against India and Ceylon (Sri Lanka). Fearing the fall of Ceylon and its naval base there, Britain established an alternate base in the Addu Atoll, at the southern tip of the Maldives, 400 miles from Diego Garcia. The smaller base on Diego became a precautionary move against having to retreat even further south. British troops remained on the island through the end of the war, though the island saw no military action.[2]

After the war, Britain's power globally and in the Indian Ocean was clearly on the wane. Observing this and the growing importance of petroleum reserves in the Middle East, the United States established a small Middle East naval force, MIDEASTFOR, in 1949, in the Persian Gulf state of Bahrain. Composed of a handful of aging vessels, the force was mostly a symbolic gesture aimed at maintaining a political and military presence in the area. A larger presence and a base on Diego Garcia were, for the moment, deferred.

"FORWARD STRATEGY" AND MILITARIZATION'S CREEP

Following the end of World War II, the "containment" policy of George Kennan came to guide "national security" strategy (using the same kind of obscuring language that transformed the War Department into the Department of Defense). In the eyes of Kennan and other government officials, the aim of containment was to establish a worldwide balance of power favorable to the United States. For Kennan, this meant the use of not just military force but political, economic, and psychological power as well. Economic aid came to be a primary tool of Truman administration foreign policy in an attempt to rebuild Japan and the nations of Western Europe as strong allies opposed to the Soviet Union. NATO and other treaty organizations played an equally important political-military role as part of Kennan's vision for a selective approach of defending key strategic strongpoints with military force.[3]

After the Soviet Union successfully tested its first atomic weapon in 1949, a new iteration of the containment policy emerged with the drafting of National Security Council Report 68 of 1950 (NSC-68). The report was written in large part by Paul H. Nitze, a leading foreign policy official who would play a key role in the creation of the base on Diego Garcia and whose influence would extend into the Reagan administration. Unlike earlier Kennan-derived strategy, NSC-68 emphasized the military aspects of containment. Instead of defending key strategic strongpoints, NSC-68 saw danger everywhere and emphasized defending the United States and the West at every point on its "perimeter."[4]

Also known as the "forward strategy," this policy held that the United States should maintain its military forces as close as possible to the Soviet Union (and later China). These forces would create a line of defense against Soviet and Chinese expansion and allow rapid military deployment (nuclear and nonnuclear) to meet any perceived threat to the United States. A paper from a decade later outlined the "essential" role of the base network to the forward strategy: The base network

provides a basis of support and dispersal necessary for the retaliatory forces of the Air Force and the Navy and for other forces in

forward areas. It permits the forward deployment of ground, sea
and air forces in or close to potential spots in areas throughout
the world where the security interests of the United States require
military strength to deter or deal swiftly with any military action
against areas of the Free World.[5]

Both NSC-68 and Kennan's containment strategy shared a newly global
vision of U.S. foreign policy and an aim of encircling the Soviet Union
and, increasingly, China, with offensive nuclear and non-nuclear military
power as close to enemy borders as possible. Although there are precedents
for such a policy dating to the nineteenth-century acquisition of naval and
coaling stations in the Pacific, the postwar military policies of Kennan and
Nitze represented a shift in U.S. foreign policy. "The security of the United
States, in the minds of policymakers," one scholar explains, "lost much of
its former inseparability from the concept of the territory of the United
States."[6] For the Navy in particular, the forward strategy meant employing
an "offensive defense" to, in the tradition of Mahan, "project" U.S. naval
forces as close to the shores of the Soviet Union, keeping it hemmed in
and unable to project its own power outside Soviet territory.[7] At a broader
level, this "dominant mode of thought" crowded out all alternative visions
and to this day, as Catherine Lutz says, "necessitates an exhaustive sorting
of the world into friendly and unfriendly nations and the globe to be sliced
comprehensively into military zones patrolled twenty-four hours of each
day by American troops."[8]

A new vision had emerged of an "intrinsically threatening world," where
instability, no matter how far removed from the United States, was seen
as a threat to the nation. And in this world, the role of the military had
become that of a "permanently mobilized force" ready to confront threats
wherever they might appear.[9]

In a process that started before World War II and accelerated during the
war, military interests were entering into almost every corner of civilian
life.[10] Perhaps the most "pernicious feature" of this creeping militarization
is "not only the expansion of military influence into civilian areas from
which it should have been excluded, but the injection of the military élan
throughout our society—a constant pressure driving American life toward
the reactionary."[11] Thus when President Eisenhower left office, he warned
the nation that the military's influence was not just a problem of politics
and public policy but "an insidious penetration of our own minds."[12] The
United States and its people, writes Lutz, had become a "society made"—

socially, culturally, economically, politically, and psychologically—"by war and preparations for war."[13]

LOSING BASES AND THE "THIRD WORLD"*

As the Cold War proceeded into the 1950s, the relative supremacy of the United States gradually declined. The Soviet Union, as its nuclear weapons tests suggested, was emerging as another empire able to at least challenge the United States, and China soon emerged as a regional competitor.

With Britain, France, and other western European nations giving up their colonial possessions, their power and thus the power and influence of the United States and the West was eroding. Decolonization left the alignment of new nations up for grabs. With the United States allied with most of the former colonial rulers, a perception grew that many of the new nations and the balance of the Cold War were tilting toward the East. Amid the independence movements, opposition to foreign military facilities was growing throughout the decolonizing world. As nations gained their independence, countries like Trinidad and Tobago evicted the United States from bases in their territories.

In this context, Stu Barber and others grew concerned that the United States would be evicted from more bases. With these losses, officials worried that U.S. influence over the future of non-Western nations would decline as well. Many officials particularly feared losing control of the regions bounding the Indian Ocean, from southern Africa through the Middle East, south Asia, and southeast Asia.

The disastrous outcome, from Britain's standpoint, of the 1956 Suez Canal crisis called into question Britain's ability to assert long-term control over the Indian Ocean and the Middle East. U.S. military strategists began to foresee the development of a "power vacuum" in the region as British power declined. For the first time, some in the Navy and the wider national security establishment began to look seriously at establishing a larger presence in the ocean.[14]

Stu grew interested in the region, as he later explained, "not because of a visualized specific requirement but because of a realization that Western

* The term is one I prefer not to use because of the racial and other hierarchies it implies. I repeat it because it is the term that U.S. officials often used and thus conveys the way most thought about a broad area of colonized and formerly colonized lands inhabited primarily by non-Western peoples and featuring lower levels of industrialization than the United States and its Western allies.

power and influence in that part of the world had been dependent mainly on British forces and bases, and these were clearly on the way down." France's colonial presence was likewise on the wane.[15]

Part of this concern stemmed from a growing interest in ensuring the flow of Persian Gulf oil to the U.S. economy and, as much, to the increasingly Gulf-dependent economies of Europe and Japan. "More significant" in Stu's mind and the minds of other officials was the broader concern that "Western nations cannot afford to be without means of exerting power and influence in so large a sector of the world (which the USSR could potentially threaten at shorter range from the north). And looking ahead, the U.S. Navy seemed to be the service most likely to retain the potential of doing so."[16]

"We just can't bug out," Stu told Senator Ted Stevens in a letter.[17]

To this point, however, other than the token MIDEASTFOR ships, the Indian Ocean was largely unknown to the Navy, distant from the United States, and rarely visited by Navy vessels. (The CIA had started to work in the region, helping to overthrow the government of Iran in 1953 and installing the Shah.) For the Navy to operate in the ocean, it needed to be able to supply and repair its ships. In the Atlantic and Pacific, the United States had coastal ports and island bases like those at Pearl Harbor, Guam, and Puerto Rico. Other than the small outpost in Bahrain, the Navy had little capacity to operate in this new ocean.

Stu's Strategic Island Concept offered an answer, The Navy, for its part, was "buoyed by the fact that there were so many such islands in the Indian Ocean." Most of the islands were controlled by the British, and the Navy "did not see any real difficulty in persuading Great Britain to enter into . . . an agreement" to create island bases.[18] As with the Pacific Lake strategy after World War II, government officials ultimately hoped to ensure U.S. dominance in another ocean by controlling every available piece of territory, or at least by denying their use to the Soviet Union and China.

Stu's work on the Strategic Island Concept reflects the recognition by the late 1950s that the power of the United States had diminished relative to that of its Cold War opponents. The shift was probably less significant in real terms than it was in its perception, but this made little difference at the time to U.S. officials and others in the world. At the same time, domestic political concerns about appearing "weak" on "defense" or giving ground to the communists were probably as significant as perceptions of growing U.S. weakness in shaping foreign and military policy.

Indeed, most U.S. officials understood that the United States remained the most powerful nation on Earth. By the time President Kennedy took office, both the President and Secretary of Defense McNamara knew that fears about a "missile gap" with the Soviet Union were unfounded, that the Soviet Union and China no longer represented a unified threat, and that the United States enjoyed "overwhelming strategic dominance." In quantitative terms, Gareth Porter shows that although U.S. military strength narrowed from forty times greater than the Soviet Union in 1954 to nine times greater in 1965, the difference still represented the greatest disparity between a major power and its nearest rival since the seventeenth century.[19]

Aware of this power imbalance, that the United States possessed a dominance so great that in effect no other nation could constrain most of its contemplated activities, officials across successive presidential administrations exploited a "new freedom of action" to pursue "more aggressive and interventionist policies."[20]

SELECTING DIEGO GARCIA

Although Stu and the Long Range Objectives Group researched scores of islands (see table 3.1), they increasingly focused their attention on Diego Garcia. While looking for islands, the Navy considered not just an island's strategic location but certain political, economic, cultural, and social factors. As Stu explained, island selection was based on a weighing of "military and political factors": "Our military criteria were location, airfield potential, anchorage potential," he wrote. "Our political criteria were minimal population, isolation, present [administrative] status, historical and ethnic factors."[21]

After a survey of Diego Garcia, Stu and Op-93 determined that Diego Garcia was ideal: On "military" grounds, Diego Garcia was close to perfect, as Stu had recognized. Among the "political" criteria, the Navy found that Chagos had a small population and was "among the most neglected minor backwaters of the world."[22]

Importantly, Navy officials understood that the archipelago was not only of marginal interest globally but also of marginal interest to Mauritius: Given Chagos's limited economic output, Britain would have an easy time convincing Mauritian leaders to give up the islands. People of Indian descent dominated Mauritius, and officials understood that the Indo-Mauritian leadership would probably care little about uprooting an isolated, mostly African population whose ties to Mauritius were historically tenuous. Given the general isolation and obscurity of Chagos and its people, the Navy realized that few elsewhere would notice, let alone object.

TABLE 3.1
"Strategic Island Concept": Information on Potential Sites

Island and Controlling Power	Land Area Sq Mi	Approx. Population	Nearest Island
Indian Ocean			
Cocos Islands (Australia)	9	650	550
Diego Garcia (UK)	11	500	60
Aldabra (UK)	40	50	15
Desroches (UK)	2	75	20
Atlantic Ocean			
Sal, C.V.I. (Portugal)	87	2000	20
Ascension (UK)	34	400	700
Príncipe (Portugal)	54	5000	80
Annobon (Spain)	6	1700	100
Caribbean			
Little Cayman (UK)	9	60	4
Barbuda (UK)	62	1000	30
Grenadines (UK)	1–13	100–700	Varying
British Virgin Islands	67	7300	N/A
Pacific Ocean			
Saipan (TTPI/US)	47	7000	3
Tinian (TTPI/US)	39	500	3
Ulithi (TTPI/US)	2	500	3
Kwajalein (TTPI/US)	6	1300	30
Enewetak (TTPI/US)	2	0	170
Bikini (TTPI/US)	2	0	50
Tarama Jima (US-occupied Japan)	10	4500	20
Kerama Retto (US-occupied Japan)	18	4500	12
Iwo Jima (US)	8	0	35
Chichi Jima (US)	15	200	20
Marcus (US)	2	0	550
Ninigo (TTNG/Australia)	8	300	50
Hermit (TTNG/Australia)	3	50	50
Nukumanu (TTNG/Australia)	3	100	30
Christmas (UK)	223	300	160
Canton (US/UK)	4	300	40
Oneata (UK)	2	300	10
Ontong Java (UK)	2	800	30

SOURCE: Roy L. Johnson, memorandum for Deputy Chief of Naval Operations (Plans & Policy), July 21, 1958, NHC: 00 Files, 1958, Box 4, A4-2 Status of Shore Stations, 2–3. NOTE: U.S. Navy statistics not necessarily accurate.

THE BIKINIANS

The Navy's search for strategically located islands with small easy-to-re-move non-Western populations was not without precedent. After World War II, the U.S. Navy was given the responsibility for orchestrating post-war nuclear weapons tests and first needed to find an isolated island test site. "We just took out dozens of maps and started looking for remote sites," explained Horacio Rivero, one of two officers responsible for finding a location. "After checking the Atlantic, we moved to the West Coast and just kept looking."[23]

Rivero knew a lot about islands. He was born in Ponce, Puerto Rico in 1910. During World War II he served on the USS *San Juan* in battles for islands across the Pacific, including those at Kwajalein, Iwo Jima, Oki-nawa, Guadalcanal, the Gilbert Islands, the Santa Cruz Islands, the Solo-mon Islands, and Rabaul. After the war, Commander Rivero worked at the Los Alamos nuclear weapons lab under William S. Parsons; "Deak," as he was known, was a crew member on the Enola Gay, helping to arm the atomic bomb dropped on Hiroshima.[24]

In his next posting, Rivero and colleague Frederick L. Ashworth con-sidered more than a dozen nuclear test sites around the world's oceans. Of-ficials ruled out most because the waters surrounding the islands were too shallow, the populations too large, or the weather undependable. Rivero and Ashworth considered the Caroline Islands in Micronesia, Bikar and Taongi in the Marshall Islands, and even the Galapagos (the Interior De-partment had the foresight to strike Darwin's famed islands from the list be-cause of their rare species).[25] Initially the Navy was most interested in one of the Carolines, as one memorandum explained, "partly because evacuation of natives would not be a major problem." Eventually Rivero and Ashworth selected the Bikini Atoll in the Marshall Islands. The Navy was particularly pleased that Bikini had an indigenous population of only about 170.[26]

The Navy sent a commodore—"Battling Ben" Wyatt—to "ask" the Bi-kinians for use of their islands. However, the outcome was a foregone con-clusion: President Harry Truman had already approved the removal, and preparations for the test had begun on the islands.[27]

For their part, the Bikinians were "awed" by the U.S. defeat of Japan and grateful for the help the United States had provided since the war. They "believe[d] that they were powerless to resist the wishes of the United States."[28]

On March 7, 1946, less than one month after posing its "question," the Navy completed the removal of the Bikinians to the Rongerik Atoll, elsewhere in the Marshall Islands. Within months it became clear that the move to Rongerik had been "ill-conceived and poorly planned," leaving the Bikinians in dire conditions. The *New York Times* wrote in classically ethnocentric language that the Bikinians "will probably be repatriated if they insist on it, though the United States military authorities say they can't see why they should want to: Bikini and Rongerik look as alike as two Idaho potatoes."[29]

By 1948, the Bikinians were running out of food and suffering from malnutrition. After planning to move them to Ujelang, the Navy sent them to a temporary camp on Kwajalein Island, near a major U.S. base. Later that year, the Navy moved the islanders to a new permanent home on Kili Island. By 1952, the government was forced to make an emergency food drop on Kili as conditions again deteriorated for the people. In 1956, the United States paid the Bikinians $25,000 (in $1 bills) and created a $3 million trust fund making annual payments of about $15 per person. "The Bikinians were completely self-sufficient before 1946," explains attorney Jonathan Weisgall, "but after years of exile they virtually lost the will to provide for themselves."[30]

Between 1946 and 1958, the Navy conducted 68 atomic and hydrogen bomb tests in Bikini,[31] removing an additional 147 people from Enewetak Atoll and all the people of Lib Island. On March 1, 1954, the first U.S. hydrogen bomb test spread a cloud of radiation over 7,500 square miles of ocean, leaving Bikini Island "hopelessly contaminated" and covering the inhabitants of the Rongelap and Utirik atolls.[32] In addition to deaths and disease from this and other radiation, the removals and the disruption to Marshallese societies led to declining social, cultural, physical, and economic conditions, high rates of suicide, infant health deficits, and slum housing conditions, to name just a few of their debilitating effects.[33]

One of the two officers responsible for selecting Bikini, Horacio Rivero, was rewarded for his work by being made an admiral. Appropriately sharing a first name with both the figure from bootstraps mythology (Alger) and the naval hero from the Battle of Trafalgar (Nelson), Rivero became the first Latino admiral in U.S. Navy history. (That Rivero married Hazel Hooper, of Horacio, Kansas, seems beyond coincidence, underlining the significance of Rivero's name.) Rivero's next promotion was to become the third director of the Long Range Objectives Group, where he discovered another search for islands and Stu Barber's "brilliant idea" for Diego Garcia.[34]

BASE DISPLACEMENT

That Horacio Rivero would come to play a role in the displacement of both the Bikinians and the Chagossians is hardly a coincidence. Around the world, often in isolated locations, often on islands, and often affecting indigenous populations, the U.S. military has displaced local peoples as part of the creation of military facilities. Almost always, these removals have led to the impoverishment of those affected. And among the services, Rivero's Navy has frequently been involved. In total there are at least sixteen documented cases of base displacement outside the continental United States. Some of these took place prior to World War II. Other displacements initially began during World War II combat under the pretext of wartime necessity; most of the people removed in wartime, however, were prevented from returning at war's end, with the early displacements only paving the way for the displacement of even greater numbers in peacetime. The sixteen cases followed more than a century during which the United States engaged in the systematic displacement of native peoples in North America.[35]

In Hawai'i, the United States first took possession of Pearl Harbor in 1887 when officials coerced the indigenous monarchy into granting exclusive access to the protected bay.[36] Half a century later, after the Japanese attack on Pearl Harbor, the Navy seized Koho'olawe, the smallest of the eight major islands, and ordered its inhabitants to leave. The service turned the island, which is "home to some of the most sacred historical places in Hawai'ian culture," including 544 archaeological sites, into a weapons testing range.[37] In 2000, the Navy finally returned the environmentally devastated island to the state of Hawai'i.

In 1899, a year after the United States seized Guam from Spain, the U.S. Navy designated the entire island a U.S. naval station. The Navy administered the island until Japan captured it three days after the attack on Pearl Harbor. After the United States retook Guam in 1944, the military acquired more than 45 percent of its available land. Today, the military controls around one-third of the island and has plans for a major expansion of the base's capacity to host more than 20,000 troops shifted from bases in Japan, South Korea, and Europe.[38]

In Panama, the United States carried out nineteen distinct land expropriations around the Panama Canal Zone between 1908 and 1931. Some were for fourteen bases established in the country and some were for the canal.[39]

In the Philippines, Clark Air Base and other U.S. bases were built on land previously reserved for the indigenous Aetas people. According to McCaffrey, "they ended up combing military trash to survive."[40]

In Alaska, in 1942, the Navy displaced Aleutian islanders from their homelands to live in abandoned canneries and mines in southern Alaska for three years. The military also seized Attu Island for a Coast Guard station; it was eventually designated a wilderness area in 1980. In 1988, an act of Congress delivered some compensation to the surviving islanders.[41]

In the U.S. territory of Puerto Rico, the Navy carried out repeated removals on the small island of Vieques. Between 1941 and 1943, and again in 1947, the U.S. Navy displaced thousands of people from their lands, seizing three-quarters of Vieques for military use. In 1961, the Navy announced plans to seize the entire island and evict all 8,000 inhabitants before Governor Luis Muñoz Martin convinced President Kennedy to halt the expropriations in light of UN and Eastern bloc scrutiny of the relationship between Puerto Rico and the United States. Few benefits followed military occupation. Stagnation, poverty, unemployment, prostitution, violence, and the disruption of subsistence and other productive activities became the rule.[42]

On the neighboring island of Culebra, in 1948, the Navy seized 1,700 acres of land for a bombing range. By 1950, the population had shrunk to 580, from 4,000 at the turn of the century. The Navy controlled one-third of the island and its entire coastline, encircling civilians with the bombing range and a mined harbor. Beginning in the 1950s, the Navy started drafting plans to remove the rest of Culebra's inhabitants. In 1970, the Navy would attempt to remove the islanders again. When the issue became a "*cause célèbre* of the Puerto Rican independence movement," the Navy started looking for another island and ceased use of the bombing range. Ultimately this came at the expense of those in Vieques, where bombing increased until protesters won its cessation in 2003.[43]

In Okinawa, the military seized large tracts of land and bulldozed houses for bases during the 1945 Battle of Okinawa. Within a year, the United States had taken 40,000 acres, equal to 20 percent of the island's arable land. Displacement continued into the 1950s, affecting 250,000 people or nearly half of Okinawa's population. Initially the military forced Okinawans to relocate to refugee camps and prevented them from returning to their homes. With the island growing increasingly overcrowded, between 1954 and 1964, the United States found at least 3,218 "volunteers" to resettle off the island. They sent them about 11,000 miles across the Pacific Ocean to landlocked Bolivia. Promised new farmland and financial assistance, most found jungle-covered lands, incomplete housing and roads, disease, and none of the promised aid. By the late 1960s, "there was a steady exodus" to Brazil, Argentina, and back to Okinawa and Japan.[44]

In 1953 in Danish Greenland, the United States made plans to expand its air base in Thule and signed a secret agreement with the Danish Government to remove 150 indigenous Inughuit people standing in the way. Families were reportedly given four days to move or face U.S. bulldozers. The Danish Government gave the Inughuits some blankets and tents and left them in exile in Qaanaaq, a forbidding village 125 miles from their native lands.[45] The expulsion severed the people's connection to a homeland to which they were "intimately linked," causing them physical and psychological harm and the loss of ancient hunting, fishing, and gathering skills, and endangering their entire existence as a people. In recent years, Danish courts have ruled the Danish Government's actions illegal and a violation of the Inughuits' human rights. And yet the courts said they have no right to return.[46]

In the Marshall Islands' Kwajalein Atoll, the U.S. military displaced hundreds between the end of World War II and the 1960s to create a missile-testing base. Most were deported to the small island of Ebeye, where the population increased from 20 prior to 1944 to several thousand by the 1960s in an area less than 27 square miles. In 1967, with overcrowding a major problem, U.S. authorities would remove 1,500 "unnecessary" people from Ebeye. Following protests from the Marshallese Government, they were later allowed to return.[47] By 1969, Ebeye was called "the most congested, unhealthful, and socially demoralized community in Micronesia." A population of more than 4,500 was living in what was widely known as the "ghetto of the Pacific."[48] By 1978, there were more than 8,000 people on the island, giving it a population density that one would find if the entire population of the United States moved to Connecticut. By 2001, the population reached more than 12,000.[49]

The displacement of local peoples for bases may best be characterized as a kind of "strategic population cleansing," which empires across many centuries have carried out for military purposes: That is, the "planned, deliberate removal from a certain territory of an undesirable population distinguished by one or more characteristics such as ethnic, religious, race, class, or sexual preference."[50]

In her study of Vieques, Katherine McCaffrey explains how "bases are frequently established on the political margins of national territory, on lands occupied by ethnic or cultural minorities or otherwise disadvantaged populations."[51] While the military generally selects base sites at a regional level on strategic grounds, McCaffrey points to how the selection of specific locations is heavily influenced at a local level by the ease of land acquisition. The ease with which the military can acquire land is in turn strongly related to the relative powerlessness of a group, which is linked to a number of factors including a group's socially defined "race,"** ethnicity, nationality, numerical strength, and economic and political power.[52]

THE WAVE OF THE FUTURE

"One of the important things that was done," Rivero said of his time in the Long-Range Objectives Group, was that "Stu, with help from some of us, got involved in looking at all the little islands around the world that might have some potential value. This was Stu's idea, that we should stockpile base rights . . . before a lot of these countries became independent." Rivero continued, "So, looking around, we picked a number of islands, and one of them was Diego Garcia."[53]

Still, the man who selected Bikini for nuclear testing made his own contribution. According to Stu, Rivero approved the plan but insisted "emphatically" that the base be "austere" and have "no dependents."[54]

Rivero worked hard to win supporters for the Strategic Island Concept within the Office of the Chief of Naval Operations, and then from the powerful and longest-serving CNO in Navy history, Admiral Arleigh A. Burke.[55] In June 1960, Rivero suggested that Burke talk to the British Navy about Diego.

Burke thought it a "good idea"[56] and broached the subject at an October meeting with his British counterpart, First Sea Lord Admiral Sir Caspar

---

** In line with anthropological and other scientific understanding dating to the middle of the last century, I consider "race" to have no biological or scientific validity as a way to categorize human populations or understand human diversity. At the same time, even if race has no biological reality, the idea that race exists has over the past 500 years developed into a profound social reality shaping the treatment of human beings according to essentially arbitrary criteria and influencing how most human beings understand themselves and others. That is, even if race is not real in a biological sense, people experience it as real, making racism a pervasive and insidious part of our world. Throughout, then, I try to call attention to the socially constructed nature of race and the existence of alleged "races," while analyzing the significance of race and racism in shaping the lives of the people in this story.

John.[57] (Burke later claimed to have "foreseen" soon after World War II the eventual withdrawal of the British from the Indian Ocean and "advocated a U.S. Indian Ocean presence as early as 1949").[58]

Working from Stu's idea for acquiring Diego Garcia, Burke proposed that the British Government detach the atoll and the rest of Chagos from colonial Mauritius, as well as several other island groups from colonial Seychelles, to create a new territory that would ensure basing rights for future U.S. and U.K. military use.[59] The British Navy liked the idea, and Burke returned from the meeting to submit a proposal on the Strategic Island Concept and Diego Garcia to the Joint Chiefs of Staff (JCS).

Despite some initial Air Force opposition to a plan (perhaps any plan) coming from its rival service, the JCS took the Navy's proposal under consideration and expanded its scope to a worldwide search for bases.[60] The Navy started base development studies for some 50–60 strategic islands, including ones in the Pacific and Atlantic, and worked to build support for the proposal in the Department of Defense.[61] Despite the broadened search, the Navy maintained its focus on Diego: As Stu later put it, "Burke's prompt and strong advocacy" quickly made the acquisition of the atoll "an article of Navy faith."[62]

The response within the DOD was immediately warm. "This is long overdue," wrote one Deputy Secretary of Defense.[63] Another Pentagon official forwarded the Op-93 plan to high-ranking Kennedy administration officials McGeorge Bundy, Walter Rostow, and NSC-68 author Paul Nitze, explaining, "The study has considerable appeal as a possible solution to the dilemma posed by our continuing problem of maintaining an overseas base structure."[64]

Under the guidance of new Op-93 director Rear Admiral Thomas Moorer, Stu formally briefed Nitze, then Assistant Secretary of Defense for International Security Affairs, in April 1961. Nitze soon raised the topic with his counterpart in the State Department, Deputy Assistant Secretary of State for Politico-Military Affairs, Jeffery Kitchen.[65]

Lobbied directly by Stu as well, Kitchen warned against the "outright purchase" of islands proposed by DOD (military officials believed that only with complete U.S. sovereignty would they have unrestrained base access and freedom of military action). But, he reported, "The Department of State would have no objection to initiating confidential talks with the United Kingdom regarding the detachment of Diego Garcia from the Mauritius group before the granting of self-government." Kitchen predicted "no major difficulties" in the discussions.[66]

THE "SPECIAL RELATIONSHIP"

The British, for their part, were "trying desperately to figure ways to hang on in the Indian Ocean," as Kennedy and Johnson administration national security official Robert Komer later explained.[67] Diego Garcia offered a way to remain in the ocean while shifting the major economic and military costs to the United States. "Seeing Malaya going independent; having lost their position in India, Pakistan, and Burma and Ceylon . . . sensing that it would be desirable from the standpoint of their strategic interests to get the Americans involved in yet another area where they could no longer carry the can," Komer said, "the British were, I would say, quite interested in having us come in."[68]

U.S. officials knew that the British were considering the withdrawal of some military forces in East Asia and the Middle East. They saw the Strategic Island Concept as an opportunity to encourage the British to maintain this "commitment" through collaborating on island base rights. (Providing base rights was, and is, widely considered to be an affirmation of both a military commitment and a *de facto* alliance or, in the Anglo-American case, a "special relationship" between nations.)

In July 1961, U.K. Minister of Defence Peter Thorneycroft informally notified Secretary of Defense Robert McNamara that because of financial difficulties, Great Britain might withdraw all its forces east of Aden (in what is now Yemen). The Navy promptly narrowed the focus of the Strategic Island Concept to efforts to secure base rights in the Indian Ocean alone.[69]

Early in 1962, the Joint Chiefs formally signed on to the Navy's plan, recommending to McNamara that "steps be taken to assure long-term access rights for the US for use of strategically located islands in the Indian Ocean."[70] In September 1962, over three days of major U.S.-U.K. talks in Washington, Secretary McNamara and Minister Thorneycroft began formal diplomatic negotiations on a "possible joint Indian Ocean base."[71]

A "Top Secret" JCS discussion of the Strategic Island Concept in the Indian Ocean shows how the Joint Chiefs and eventually the Pentagon accepted Stu's plan in its entirety. The sparse, bulleted language of the JCS illustrates their adoption of the concept point by point:

- With the withdrawal of British forces from the area east of Aden, a military power vacuum will exist in the Indian Ocean area. . . .
- The United States requires bases to provide for the projection of its military strength around the world. There are important

gaps developing in the Free World base structure which are opening up as the Western powers withdraw. . . . This need is most acute at present in the Indian Ocean area. . . .

- Encroachment of the Sino-Soviet Bloc into the areas which are loosely termed colonial could be made vastly more difficult by conclusion of treaties and agreements now for permanent union with the United States. . . .

- US bases on foreign continents are inherently under pressure from a wide variety of sources [including]. . . . nationalism [and]. . . . Communist influences. . . .

- Acquisition of suitable islands by the United States would appear to be the most advantageous procedure [to counteract these forces]. . . .

- Islands having a limited population which are removed from continental mainlands and do not appear economically attractive seem to offer the most feasible avenues for United States development.[72]

As studies and planning continued within the Navy, and the departments of Defense and State, the State Department sent the following classified note to the British Embassy:

Washington, April 25, 1963. The Government of the United States proposes to the British Government the initiation of discussions by appropriate military and civil representatives of the two Governments looking toward the possible strategic use of certain small islands in the Indian Ocean area. The two Governments share a common concern for an adequate long-term allied presence in the area, and it is thus considered important that there be effective coordination of strategic planning on the matter.[73]

The British Embassy responded by presenting "its compliments" to the State Department and its "honour" of offering the following reply:

Washington, July 29, 1963. Her Majesty's Government in the United Kingdom agree that the two Governments share a common concern for the effective defence of the whole area against Communist encroachment. In principle, therefore, they welcome the American initiative for exploratory discussions.[74]

CHAPTER 4

"EXCLUSIVE CONTROL"

The members of the Kennedy administration saw themselves as living in "an Olympian age," and the people crafting foreign policy were its gods. They were men who were full of "virility" and power, combining traditional notions of American masculinity based on physical force with the supposed heights of intellectual prowess.[1] And of those in fabled Camelot, the men surrounding McGeorge Bundy epitomized "the best and the brightest" generation that descended on Washington. This was the elite group of White House staffers working for the Special Assistant to the President for National Security Affairs. They came to be known as the "Bundy State Department." When President Kennedy grew dissatisfied with the size and cautiousness of Dean Rusk's State Department, Bundy's men filled the void, eventually surpassing the Rusk State Department in influence.[2]

As unofficial biographer of the Kennedy and Johnson administrations David Halberstam described the Bundy team, they were a group of "bright young men summoned from all areas of government and academe," generally from privileged upper-class backgrounds. Almost all were part of the generation that fought in World War II and "were fond of pointing out that they were the generation which had fought the war," Halberstam observes. Full of confidence from having conquered the Axis, "there was a sense that these were brilliant men, men of force, not cruel, not harsh, but men who acted rather than waited."[3]

"BLOWTORCH BOB"

One of the best, brightest, and most ambitious of the bunch was Robert W. Komer. "With his owlish eyeglasses and a briar pipe and his 15 years in the Central Intelligence Agency," a *New York Times* obituary later wrote, Komer was the "model of what novelist John le Carre calls an intellocrat."[4]

Komer had graduated from Harvard College before going off to World War II to work as an intelligence officer and a historian. After he got his Harvard business degree at 25, friends from the war convinced him to join a new government branch called the Central Intelligence Group. "[I] went to the CIA before it was the CIA and found that it was a perfectly fascinating career," Komer explained. "These fellows said to me . . . 'You know the war with the Germans and the Japs may be over, but the war with the Communists seems to be beginning and public service is just critically important. So with your wartime background. . . .'"[5]

Komer served in the CIA for almost a decade, helping to create the first National Intelligence Estimates and focusing on Middle East policy. After a year at the National War College and working as a liaison with the National Security Council in the Eisenhower administration, Komer was asked by Bundy and Walt Rostow to join the national security team in the Kennedy White House.[6] Before long, Komer became the White House expert on India and Pakistan, the Middle East, and Africa, earning one of the palest members of the administration the title of "White House African."[7]

He earned his other nickname, "Blowtorch Bob," after President Johnson sent Komer to Vietnam in 1967: U.S. Ambassador Henry Cabot Lodge explained that arguing with Komer was "like having a flamethrower aimed at the seat of one's pants." In Vietnam, Komer would earn a "reputation as a man with a take-no-prisoners attitude, a deathless optimism that the war would be won, and a near religious faith in the power of facts and statistics to help win it."[8] Chief among Komer's tools for winning the war was his "pacification" program, CORDS, and its Operation Phoenix. Designed to win the hearts and minds of the South Vietnamese, Phoenix ultimately assassinated more than 20,000 suspected Viet Cong.

Years before entering that war, Komer was focused in the Kennedy White House on a large swath of the decolonizing world centered around the Indian Ocean. By 1963, Komer had seized on two ideas gaining momentum in the national security bureaucracy: Increasing the U.S. naval presence in the ocean and creating a chain of Indian Ocean bases with Diego Garcia as the centerpiece. "Look, this whole area from Suez to Singapore is heating up," Komer later recalled.

> We've had the Chinese making trouble in '62. We have the Paks starting to play footsie with the Chicoms* and then with the Russians. We have Bandaranaike in Ceylon. We have Sukarno over on

---

* Pakistanis and Chinese Communists from the Peoples Republic of China, respectively, in the bigoted bureaucratic lingo of the day.

the eastern end. We have . . . Nyerere in Tanzania sort of playing games with our friends the Chinese as well as the Russians. We have the Zanzibar business. I was saying, "Look this is an area of the world that is becoming more volatile at the very time when the former strategic balance-holders, the British essentially, are pulling back and that projecting the trend, it's a more important area."[9]

With the approval of his boss Bundy, Komer sent a memo to the President in June 1963 proposing the deployment of an aircraft carrier task force in the Indian Ocean supported by island bases.[10]

"Despite my parochial viewpoint," Komer started the memorandum, "I see an increasingly strong case for maintaining a small task force in the Indian Ocean." He continued, "It is a simple fact that our greatest lack of conventional deterrent power lies along the broad arc from Suez to Singapore. . . . We have traditionally left the defense of this region to the British, yet their strength is waning at a time when we face a potential show of force or actual combat needs ranging from Saudi Arabia to the Persian Gulf and Iran through India and Burma to Malaysia."[11]

Although he did not mention Diego Garcia** or the Strategic Island Concept by name, Komer clearly envisioned island bases supporting the task force in the face of what he saw as increased anti-Western sentiment and chaos in the region. "Mobile, sea-based, air power could be a real asset to us here," Komer wrote. "It would also minimize the need for expensive on-shore base rights, which would be politically difficult to obtain," and "especially if the Navy could settle for a protected anchorage or use of UK bases."[12] (Years later Komer would claim to have been "the one who proposed seeking from Britain a joint base in the Indian Ocean, which led to Diego Garcia."[13])

President Kennedy "jumped on it with enthusiasm," and told Komer, "Let's try it out for size. Take it up with McNamara."[14]

Komer cranked out a one-page memorandum in Kennedy's name asking McNamara to investigate the task force idea. The Indian Ocean area, he stressed, is one where "our military presence . . . is exceedingly light, and yet the pot is always boiling." Closing with an allusion to island bases, Komer emphasized that a naval task force should only be pursued on the grounds that it "would not require expensive base arrangements or involve significant flow of gold."[15]

McNamara was initially, as Komer put it, "very lukewarm" to the task force.[16] But "Blowtorch Bob" was not to be denied, keeping it on the agen-

---

** In a handwritten note on the same memorandum, Komer in fact seems to confuse the name Diego Garcia with Diego Suarez, the French port in Madagascar.

das of the departments of Defense and State. McNamara asked for the view of the JCS, which, as with the Strategic Island Concept, readily approved the plan. Secretary of State Rusk wrote to McNamara supporting the idea of a task force as "a significant stabilizing influence throughout th[e] area," adding that "we would view the establishment of the Indian Ocean base facilities at Diego Garcia which we are planning to negotiate with the British as an ideal protected anchorage to support an Indian Ocean Task Force. Indeed," he said, "it is our view that this negotiation should be pursued as a matter of some urgency."[17]

"CONSIDERATION NOW RPT NOW . . . LIMITED . . . "

As part of a separate project, McNamara had just approved a JCS recommendation to create a communications station in the Indian Ocean and passed the proposal on to the President. The station, codenamed "Project KATHY," was designed to fill a gap in military communications capabilities in the area south and east of the Suez Canal. Filling the gap would allow increased naval operations in the area, in part, JCS held, to "contain" any Chinese movements southward.

In the summer of 1963, Kennedy approved the proposal for a communications base and ordered McNamara to carry out the plan.[18] The State Department concluded that on political grounds Diego Garcia was the best available site. On August 23, State instructed its embassy in London to quietly approach the British about conducting an urgent and secret survey of the island.[19]

The response from the British Foreign Office was positive but mentioned in clipped official language, "HMG might feel it necessary to consider impact of large military installation on few inhabitants of this small island."[20]

An official at the U.S. Embassy in London replied "perhaps this aspect might better be considered during broader discussions," and asked that "consideration now rpt now be limited to survey question," using bureaucratic shorthand for the word *repeat*. The Foreign Office agreed, saying the "request would be given urgent attention."[21]

A TASK FORCE AND A TRANSFER OF POWER

Komer meanwhile continued to push McNamara on the "Indian Ocean Task Force." Komer went to see Navy officials to generate more support for his projects and reported back to Bundy that the "Navy of course is strong for it." Admiral Claude Ricketts, the Vice Chief of Naval Operations, told Komer that for a base, the "Navy could make do with no more than a communications facility ($15 million) which is needed anyway, plus an airstrip ($5 million). Of course," Komer added, "Navy would like more."[22]

By November, McNamara finally relented under Blowtorch Bob's pressure and directed the JCS to begin planning for deployment of the Indian Ocean Task Force. The flotilla steamed into the ocean four months after Kennedy's assassination, in April 1964. Officials renamed it the "Concord Squadron" to arouse fewer suspicions (among the Soviets, Chinese, and Indians especially) that the deployment signaled the major shift that it in fact represented: that is, the beginning of the first transfer of power in the Indian Ocean since Britain defeated France in 1814, and a major step toward the creation of a base on Diego Garcia and the expulsion of its people.

HIDDEN IN PARENTHESES

Jeffrey Coleman Kitchen started off closing bases. In 1944, at the age of 23, Kitchen began his State Department career in the Office of Foreign Liquidation, helping to close overseas military facilities acquired from Britain through lend-lease. After working for Secretary of State John Foster Dulles, serving as Deputy Director in the Office of Greek, Turkish, and Iranian Affairs, and spending five years at the RAND Corporation, Kitchen was back twenty years later leading discussions to open new bases on British territory.

For three days beginning February 25, 1964, now Deputy Assistant Secretary of State for Politico-Military Affairs Kitchen led a U.S. delegation in London for secret talks with their British counterparts on strategic island bases in the Indian Ocean. The meeting, which included officials from the DOD, Navy, Air Force, Army, and the U.K. Foreign and Colonial Offices and the Ministry of Defence, represented the major realization of the work of Stu Barber and the Navy, Nitze, and Komer to identify, promote, and push through the Diego Garcia idea within the national security apparatus

Entering the talks, two members of Kitchen's staff sketched out the joint State-Defense delegation's concerns and intentions: "On the one hand," they wrote, there are "threats to the stability and security of the area" from "massive communist military power" to the north and local disturbances that might offer the Soviets and Chinese opportunities to intervene in the region. "This, coupled with the fact that the Persian Gulf area is the largest source of petroleum available to the West on financially acceptable terms," they continued, "makes the [Arabian] Peninsula a key area."[23]

With rising costs in the war in Vietnam, they rejected continuous troop deployments or the construction of extensive military facilities, and proposed to the British the use of strategically located islands under U.K. control. Along with Diego Garcia and other islands in Chagos, the team identified some of the outlying islands of the Seychelles archipelago as prime possibilities. "They do not appear to us," they wrote, "to be capable of supporting serious independence movements and are probably too remote and culturally isolated to figure plausibly in the plans of any mainland government."[24]

On the first day of talks there was quick consensus on the basic plan to augment the U.S-U.K. military presence in the region and to gain permanent control over strategic islands to support new military activity.

"May be possible to transfer Diego Garcia from Mauritius to Seychelles which will be easier to deal with," the Navy's representative telegrammed back to the JCS about an initial idea for retaining control over Diego by separating it from Mauritius and making it part of the Seychelles, which unlike Mauritius was not expected to gain independence soon. "Only 200 people involved."[25]

U.S. officials and their British counterparts agreed on ensuring total control over Diego Garcia and Chagos without the possibility of outside interference. "It would be unacceptable to both the British and the American defence authorities," a UK Colonial Office document explained, "if facilities of the kind proposed were in any way to be subject to the political control of Ministers of a newly emergent independent state," referring to soon-to-be-independent Mauritius or the Seychelles.[26]

On the last day of the talks, Kitchen returned to the U.S. Embassy to report back on his progress. "Re Diego Garcia—UK willing to move rapidly as possible to separate Diego Garcia from Mauritius," Kitchen telegrammed the State Department. "Thereafter, joint US/UK survey will be conducted under UK auspices. If survey satisfactory, UK will move to acquire entire island for US communications site and later development other austere facilities."[27]

The U.K. representatives were surprised, however, with what Kitchen and the DOD's Frank Sloan had to say about the local populations on the islands. Some archived versions of the initial agreement produced at the talks remain censored on this point; but elsewhere uncensored documents show that the British (concerned about the future of their before-long ex-colonies) were "clearly disappointed" to hear that the United States was not interested in offering aid or base employment opportunities that might benefit the economies of Mauritius and the Seychelles. Instead, Kitchen and Sloan explained that the U.S. Government had something entirely different in mind. Tellingly, in the official record, they conveyed the demand in a parenthetical phrase: The United States wanted the islands under its "exclusive control (without local inhabitants)."[28]

"FREEDOM OF MANOEUVRE, DIVORCED FROM THE NORMAL CONSIDERATIONS"

The United States wanted the Chagossians gone. Or as other documents would later, more directly put it, they wanted the islands "swept" and "sanitized."[29] Despite their surprise, British representatives quickly agreed to the parenthetically presented expulsion order: "H.M.G. should be responsible for acquiring land, resettlement of population and compensation at H.M.G.'s expense," the representatives agreed. The United States would assume responsibility for all construction and maintenance costs.[30]

For U.S. officials, the aim was to avoid not just having to answer to a non-Western government like Mauritius or the Seychelles, but equally, having to deal with a (potentially antagonistic) local population. Worst of all was the possibility that a local population could press claims for self-determination at the United Nations and threaten the life of the base.

"The Americans made it clear during the initial [1963] talks," detailed a secret U.K. document, "that they regarded freedom from local pressures as essential."[31] Another Foreign Office brief, marked "secret and guard," was even more explicit:

> The primary objective in acquiring these islands from Mauritius and the Seychelles . . . was to ensure that Her Majesty's Government had full title to, and control over, these islands so that they could be used for the construction of defence facilities without hindrance or political agitation and so that when a particular island would be needed for the construction of British or United States defence facilities Britain or the United States should be able to clear it of its current population. The Americans in particular attached great importance to this freedom of manoeuvre, divorced from the normal considerations applying to a populated dependent territory.[32]

The document continued, "It was implied in this objective, and recognized at the time, that we could not accept the principles governing our otherwise universal behaviour in our dependent territories, e.g. we could not accept that the interests of the inhabitants were paramount and that we should develop self-government there." If the needs of the local population were treated as "paramount," the brief explained, the United States would likely cancel its participation.[33]

British officials felt that any apparent contradiction between their "principles" and the expulsion plan was "not an insurmountable problem": They would simply remove the people and tell the world "there were no permanent inhabitants in the archipelago." This step was crucial because, in classic Orwellian logic, "to recognise that there are permanent inhabitants will imply that there is a population whose democratic rights have to be safeguarded."[34]

For U.S. officials, the plan for Diego Garcia thus had all the advantages and almost none of the disadvantages of an overseas military base. It had all the advantages as a relatively surreptitious way to exercise U.S. power, and was controlled by "a longstanding ally (the United Kingdom) unlikely to toss [the United States] out for governmental changes or U.S. foreign policy initiatives."[35] In the British Government, the United States had a partner willing to ignore British law and international human rights guarantees. The British would do the dirty work of the expulsion. They would dispose of the population. All the while the United States would have the legal and political alibi that Great Britain was the sovereign, retaining ultimate responsibility for the islanders.

With the people scheduled for removal, the U.S. Government would have almost the perfect base: strategically located, free of any potentially troublesome population, under *de facto* U.S. control yet with its closest ally as sovereign to take any political heat, and almost no restrictions on use of the island, save the need to consult periodically with the British. Free reign over an idyllic and strategically located atoll in the Indian Ocean. No wonder the Navy would come to call it "Fantasy Island."

"SOME LOGICAL COVER"

Before the U.S. delegation left London, the two sides agreed to a series of recommendations and future steps involving the development of what officials were calling a "strategic triangle" of bases on the islands of Diego Garcia, Aldabra in the Seychelles on the western edge of the Indian Ocean, and Australia's Cocos/Keeling Islands to the east.[36] Notably, while U.S. officials demanded that the "local" (read: non-white) governments of Mauritius and the Seychelles cede their sovereignty claims, U.S. officials were willing to have the local Australian Government retain sovereignty in the Cocos/Keeling Islands (the ongoing Anglo-American-Australian coalition of the pale has of course been visible in Iraq).

The British Cabinet approved the recommendations in principle on the day the talks concluded. Six days later, Secretary Rusk approved the agreements; DOD and the JCS approved them the following month.[37]

When both the U.S. and U.K. delegations to the United Nations heard news of the plans, however, they expressed concern. Officials jointly suggested a slow implementation of the strategy "to minimize adverse reaction at the UN and throughout the world." Each step should have "some logical cover," they recommended. "Discreet timing and spacing" of the steps should be employed. "Any step which clearly reveals the true intentions should be taken after other preliminary steps" so as to reduce the amount of time opposition would have to build against the base. In particular, the delegations warned, "The transfer of population no matter how few . . . is a very sensitive issue at the UN. It should be undertaken on the basis that the populations must be induced to leave voluntarily rather than forcibly transferred."[38]

SURVEYS, SECRECY, AND A "CONSIDERABLE SERVICE" TO THE U.S. GOVERNMENT

Despite attempts to maintain the total secrecy of the discussions and planning, the *Washington Post* was ready to run a story about the London agreements by June 15, 1964. Fearing that the story might derail their plans, Kitchen and Assistant Secretary of State Jeff Greenfield went to meet with the managing editor of the *Post*, Alfred Friendly, to ask him to hold the story.

In an off-the-record conversation, Kitchen explained to Friendly the background of U.S. involvement in the Indian Ocean and the plans for island bases. Kitchen stressed how publication of the story would endanger British negotiations to remove the islands from Mauritius and the Seychelles, as well as a secret U.S-U.K. survey of the islands. Friendly promised not to publish his story until after a U.S. or U.K. announcement. Rusk later called it "a considerable service to the USG."[39]

A month later, White House and State officials feared that both the *Post* and the *Economist* might break the story within a matter of days.

In a heavily underlined memorandum hurriedly delivered by Komer to President Lyndon Johnson, Rusk alerted the President and provided him with background in case of press inquiries. Rusk described the islands as "*virtually uninhabited*," citing numbers of one to two hundred people.[40]

Under continued pressure from the State Department, the *Post* did not publish the story, and the secret island survey went off without interruption (the *Economist* also held the story). A team of Navy and Air Force engineers and construction experts left for the Indian Ocean at the end of July and completed its work within a month.

Upon the survey team's return, the Air Force expressed interest in Diego Garcia for the first time, as a base for B-52 bomber operations.[41] The Navy's evaluation was even more enthusiastic. A telegram back to Navy headquarters reported: "Anchorage excellent with minimum blasting coral heads. . . . Logistic airstrip feasible [at two sites]. . . . Island excellent for COMMSTA [communications station] regards interference and ground conductivity. . . . Sufficient land available other support as required."[42]

Briefed by the survey team at the Pentagon, Admiral Horacio Rivero, now Vice Chief of Naval Operations, exclaimed, "I want this island!"

Rivero "turned to one of his staff and told them to write a letter to the British using whatever words or justification that were necessary" to get it.[43] There is no record of any discussions about another of the survey team's findings: that a distinct native population was living on Diego. The team reported, "The problem of the Ileois*** and the extent to which they form a distinct community is one of some subtlety and is not within the grasp of the present manager of Diego Garcia."[44]

The *Washington Post* finally ran its story on August 29, more than two months after it had been written, buried in the media void of end-of-August vacations. The last column of the article described the population of Diego Garcia as consisting "largely of transient laborers" most of whom were "understood to have left."[45]

A day prior to publication, the article's author, Robert Estabrook, met with U.S. Embassy officials in London. They convinced him to remove references to the detachment of islands from Mauritius and the Seychelles and to make the story less definitive about which islands were the focus of attention. An embassy cable reported that Estabrook initially refused to delete a paragraph explaining that the *Post* had held the story at the

*** They appear not to have bothered asking how to spell the name.

request of the State Department; the published article included no such reference.[46] The story gained little attention and was soon forgotten.

PLATINUM HANDSHAKES

On the British side, the U.K. Government began pressuring Mauritian representatives during its independence negotiations in 1965 to give up Chagos in exchange for Mauritian independence. During meetings with Secretary Rusk in Washington in April, new Labour Party Prime Minister Harold Wilson brought up the detachment and said that Britain would "pay a price" at the UN for its actions.[47] In 1960, the UN General Assembly had passed Declaration 1514 (XV) "on the Granting of Independence to Colonial Countries and Peoples." The declaration called for the complete independence of non-self-governing territories, like Mauritius and the Seychelles, without alteration of their borders, thrice demanding that states respect their "territorial integrity" during decolonization, and condemning "any attempt aimed at the partial or total disruption of the national unity and the territorial integrity of a country."[48]

The British understood that they would thus have to pay Mauritius and the Seychelles to silence any protests over the detachment and trump any Soviet voices likely to encourage protest: "If we do not settle quickly (which must mean generously) agitation in the colonies against 'dismemberment' and 'foreign bases' (fomented from outside) would have time to build up to serious proportions, particularly in Mauritius."[49]

A British official was even blunter during face-to-face meetings. He told U.S. representatives that British officials could not proceed in detaching the islands (by this point agreed to be Chagos, and the Aldabra, Desroches, and Farquhar groups) from Mauritius and the Seychelles until they knew what "bribe" they could offer the local governments.[50]

A few days later, Foreign Office official E. H. Peck told Kitchen he was "red-faced" over the matter but stressed the need to give Mauritius a "platinum handshake."[51] British Foreign Secretary Michael Stewart officially inquired in an aide-mémoire if the United States was willing to make a financial contribution. Stewart estimated the total cost at £10 million, or $28 million, and explained that the money would "include compensation for the inhabitants and commercial interests displaced."[52]

The Joint Chiefs took the matter under consideration and decided "perpetual access" to the islands was worth $15 million. Although McNamara initially disagreed (he believed payment would be a signal to the British that the United States was ready to assume Britain's position in the Indian Ocean), the Secretary of Defense changed his mind. On June 14, 1965, McNamara authorized a contribution of up to half—or $14 million—of Britain's BIOT expenses.[53]

With the financial arrangement secured, Kitchen led another State-Defense team to London to finalize the foundations of the deal. The meetings were held on September 23–24, at the same time British ministers were concluding independence negotiations with Mauritian representatives. The leading Mauritian official, Seewoosagur Ramgoolam, who would become the first prime minister of Mauritius, was given little choice: Accept the detachment of Chagos from Mauritius and £3 million, or no independence. Ramgoolam chose independence and the money.[54]

The Seychelles, which was further from independence, had even less choice in the matter but won construction of an international airport, now essential to its tourism-based economy. The Seychelles eventually negotiated the return of its three groups when it gained independence in 1976.

As the Mauritian independence negotiations concluded, the British Cabinet informed Kitchen's delegation that it would detach the Mauritian islands and the three Seychellois groups and maintain them under British sovereignty. "After two years of, at times, intensive negotiation," reported a memorandum for Paul Nitze in his new job as Secretary of the Navy, "the use of the islands on acceptable terms for US defense requirements has been secured. The principal task remaining is to work out the details on making the islands available, particularly the status of the local population."[55]

The decision to retain the islands was not announced publicly. On November 8, 1965, the British Government invoked an archaic royal prerogative of the monarch to pass laws without parliamentary approval. (Prime ministers did the same to take the nation into wars in Egypt in 1956 and Iraq in 2003.)[56] The government, in the name of the Queen, used what is called an Order in Council to quietly declare that Chagos and the three groups of islands from the Seychelles "shall together form a separate colony which shall be known as the British Indian Ocean Territory (BIOT)."[57]

Investigative journalist John Pilger describes how they did it: "The British Indian Ocean Territory was brought into being by an order-in-council, a decision approved not by Parliament but by the monarch, acting on the advice—in effect, the instructions—of a secretive, unaccountable group known as the Privy Council. The members of this body, the Privy Councillors, include present and former government ministers. They appear before the Queen in Buckingham Palace, standing in a semi-circle around her, heads slightly bowed, like Druids; they never sit down." The Orders in Council are read out by title, and the Queen simply says, "Agreed." Pilger explains, "This is government by fiat: the use of a royal decree by politicians who want to get away with something undemocratically. Most British people have never heard of it."[58] (As we shall see, this would not be the last time the British Government would employ the Order in Council in this story.)

More than a month later, the UN General Assembly passed Resolution 2066 noting its "deep concern" over actions taken by Great Britain "to detach certain islands from the Territory of Mauritius for the purpose of establishing a military base." Citing the UN prohibition on disturbing the territorial integrity of non-self-governing territories, the General Assembly asked Britain "to take no action which would dismember the Territory of Mauritius and violate its territorial integrity," and instead to implement fully 1960's Declaration 1514 on decolonization.[59]

Blowtorch Bob moved more quickly than the UN. Two days after the BIOT was created, Komer sent the following nine-word memo to "Jeff" Kitchen: "Congratulations on the islands. Now how about some forces."[60]

"OBE"

In the at times exotic bureaucratic language of Washington, "OBE" stands for "overtaken by events," meaning that an issue is no longer relevant because of changed circumstances. Not long after the creation of the BIOT, the Joint Chiefs of Staff reviewed the communications station proposal for Diego Garcia and found that it had been "overtaken by events" and "that the high cost of construction did not warrant" the project.[61] The relevant "events" were the development of satellite technology that made the need for a communications station on Diego Garcia essentially obsolete. The U.S. Embassy in London informed the Foreign Office of the change. The embassy said that for the time being, no population removal would be necessary.

Undeterred, Navy planners began drafting a new base proposal. One rear admiral suggested to Secretary of the Navy Nitze that creating a fuel station for ships transiting the Indian Ocean might offer a "suitable justification" for a facility.[62] Under the name of Vice CNO Rivero, a four-page draft proposal emerged for a $45 million "fleet support activity," comprising an anchorage, a runway, austere communications equipment, berthing and recreation facilities for 250 men, and 655,000 barrels of petroleum, oil, and lubricants (POL) storage. Nitze received the Rivero proposal and revised it personally before sending it to Secretary McNamara.[63]

One of Nitze's staff members, Robert Murray, explained that the staff considered the base a "contingency facility" for the future. From his office as President and CEO of the consulting firm the Center for Naval Analyses, Murray recalled in 2004 that he and his colleagues said at the time, "None of this makes a lot of sense in today's world. It's only if you believe that you don't know what the world's going to look like, or what our interests are going to be in it, that you would want to do this. And if the cost is low . . . then, why not?" Murray clarified, "I mean, it was speculation against the future. Or a hedge against the future."[64]

Because hedges and speculations do not frequently earn funding from Congress and thus priority within DOD, Nitze offered McNamara three justifications for the base: the loss of naval ports in littoral nations as a result of anti-Western sentiment; "tenuous" naval communications capacity in the Indian Ocean; and the need for the United States to augment its military presence in the ocean as Britain appeared on the verge of reducing its forces "East of Suez."[65]

Nitze closed his memo to McNamara by saying the facility was the "minimum" necessary to meet the Navy's existing requirements but could serve as a "nucleus around which to build an altogether adequate defense base." Known for his aggressively persuasive writing style, Nitze argued, "We should plan now for the orderly development of a fleet support facility before the need for it reaches emergency proportions with attendant higher costs."[66]

The reply from the Pentagon came from Nitze's former deputy at ISA, John McNaughton. McNaughton politely informed Nitze that it was "prudent and necessary" for the Navy to continue in-house studies of the project.[67]

The Navy dutifully complied and later the same year offered a little-changed but repackaged facility at the same cost as Nitze's proposal. Just before the end of 1966, however, the Pentagon rejected a proposed congressional notification package that would have asked for funding for the base. McNamara's people were concerned about expected opposition on Capitol Hill, a pending military budget review in the midst of the Vietnam buildup, and the lack of British financial commitment to the project.[68] The base and the Chagossians' fate were again deferred.

"A-L-D-A-B-R-A"

With Nitze and the Navy temporarily stymied, the Air Force and JCS were simultaneously moving ahead with a proposal to build a joint U.S.-U.K. air base on Aldabra, one of the Seychelles island groups now part of the BIOT. In July, McNamara discussed the issue in a mid-morning telephone call with President Johnson, who was preparing for a visit by Prime Minister Wilson later that day.[69]

"What about this—his wanting to help you, uh, uh," Johnson began. "Wanting you, to build, uh, uh—wanting us to participate in building an airport, when he moves out of Aden?"

"Uh—that, that. Alebra, in the Indian Ocean," McNamara replied, misremembering the island's name. "We can go in on a 50/50 basis, and I think it will cost us on the order of, of, uh, uh [pause] 10 million, I think.**** The island's name is A – L – D –A – B – R – A. Aldabra."

"Alright. And have you agreed to that?" Johnson queried.

"Uh, not in detail. No. And if you want to, it's, it's fine with us. [Pause] 50/50."

"Alright. Anything else?" Johnson asked, moving the conversation to other issues.[70]

Six days later McNamara approved a proposal to accept cost sharing for the Aldabra base and to alert the British to new planning for Diego Garcia.[71]

"UNDER THE COVER OF DARKNESS"

While the Navy continued its studies and planning to win funding for Diego Garcia, Jeffrey Kitchen continued hammering out an official government-to-government agreement for use of the BIOT islands.[72] In mid-November, Kitchen returned to London for more secret talks, accompanied by a team of six, including officials from the Pentagon, the Navy, and the Air Force. Over two days, Kitchen initialed the agreements with his counterparts in the Foreign Office. Kitchen noted that although financing was not yet secured for Diego Garcia, the Secretary of Defense had approved the Navy's plan for a facility that could be expanded quickly in the future.[73]

A little more than a month later, the U.S. Ambassador to Britain, Honorable David K. E. Bruce, and a representative for the British Secretary of State for Foreign Affairs, George Brown, M.P., met to sign the final agreements. As others were preparing for year's end parties, they gathered, as one of Kitchen's negotiators who witnessed the signing later said, "under the cover of darkness," the day before New Year's Eve, 1966.

The agreement signed that night was to be completed by an "exchange of notes." It was innocuously titled, "Availability of Certain Indian Ocean

**** The correct estimated cost for half of the project was $25 million.

Islands for Defense Purposes." A treaty would have had to survive time-consuming legislative approval before Congress and Parliament; an exchange of notes accomplished the same thing without the legislative approval and public notification.

Published without notice months later in the United States by the Government Printing Office, the agreement made all the islands of the British Indian Ocean Territory "available to meet the needs of both Governments for defense." As agreed, the United Kingdom would remain sovereign in the territory. The United States would have access to the islands for fifty years with an option to extend the agreement for an additional twenty years. Each government would pay for constructing its own facilities, though in general access would be shared. According to the published notes, the islands would be available to the United States "without charge."[74]

In a set of confidential accords accompanying the notes, however, the U.S. Government agreed to make secret payments to the British of up to $14 million, or half the cost of creating the BIOT, as McNamara had agreed months earlier. These payments helped reimburse the British for "all costs pertaining to the administrative detachment of the Indian Ocean islands in question and to the acquisition of the lands thereon"—diplomatic legalese for the costs of deporting the Chagossians, buying out the plantation owners, and paying off Mauritius and the Seychelles.

A secret British document explained the arrangement:

> Besides the published Agreement there is also a *secret* agreement under which . . . the US effectively, but indirectly, contributed half the estimated cost of establishing the territory (£10m). This was done by means of a reduction of £5m in the research and development surcharge due from Britain for the Polaris missile. Special measures were taken by both the US and UK Governments to maintain the secrecy of this arrangement.[75]

Seeking to avoid congressional oversight and required congressional approval for a budget appropriation, the DOD credited the British for payments owed on research and development costs on the purchase of Polaris missiles. Another British document described the evasion of Congress:

> The second point, and of even more importance to us, is the American insistence that the *Financial Arrangements must remain secret.* . . . The Americans attach great importance to secrecy because the Unites States Government has, for cogent political reasons of

its own, chosen to conceal from Congress the substantial financial assistance which we are to get in the form of a remission of Polaris Research and Development dues.[76]

No money was exchanged directly, but in effect, a $14 million debt was wiped off the books for Great Britain.

Yet this was not the only secret agreement. Another confidential "agreed minute" referred to a paragraph in the public notes where the United States agreed to notify the United Kingdom in advance of using any island so that Britain might take those "administrative measures" necessary to make the islands available for use. Those administrative measures, the secret notes show, were any actions necessary for closing down the plantations and "resettling the inhabitants."[77]

CHAPTER 5

"MAINTAINING THE FICTION"

So far we have seen how officials were worried that despite the advantages of overseas bases for controlling large territories, bases also carry with them significant risks. The most serious, as Stu Barber realized, is the possibility that a host nation will evict its guest from a base. There is also the danger that for political or other reasons a host will make a base temporarily unavailable during a crisis. During the lead-up to the most recent invasion of Iraq, for example, Turkey's Islamist ruling party refused to allow the United States use of its territory for a large troop deployment, though it permitted the basing of warplanes and the use of its airspace. In most cases, guest nations are forced to negotiate continually for a variety of base rights with their hosts.

The other main risk facing bases on foreign soil is that posed by the people outside a base's gates. As recent U.S. experience in Saudi Arabia, South Korea, and Okinawa has shown, foreign bases can become targets of attacks and lightning rods for local protest and criticism about foreign intrusion and imperialism.[1] Worst of all, the military fears outright revolt against a base, or that locals could press claims to self-determination before the United Nations and thus threaten the life of the base. This was of special concern for U.S. officials during an era of rising nationalism and anti-imperialism in Africa and Asia.[2] U.S. military officials also worry that local populations pose risks of espionage, security breaches, and uncontrollable sexual and romantic liaisons between troops and their neighbors.

In short, soldiers and diplomats view local peoples as the source of troubles, headaches, and work that distracts the military from its primary missions. If civilian workers are needed as service personnel, importing outsiders without local ties or rights, who can be controlled and sent home at will, is typically preferred.

For these reasons, in the eyes of soldiers and diplomats, a base free of any nonmilitary population is the best kind of base. For these reasons, after World War II, U.S. officials increasingly looked for bases located in relatively unpopulated areas.[3] The Strategic Island Concept was premised on the threat to bases posed by rising anti-Western sentiment and the search for *people-less* bases. With the islanders scheduled for removal from Diego Garcia, military planners were thrilled at the idea of a base with no civilian population within almost 500 miles. U.S. officials and their British counterparts wanted total control over the island and the entire archipelago without the slightest possibility of outside interference—be it from foreign politicians or local inhabitants.

Diego Garcia was attractive once it became British sovereign territory precisely because it was not subject to, as one Navy official explains, "political restrictions of the type that had shackled or even terminated flexibility at foreign bases elsewhere."[4] The "special relationship" between the United States and the United Kingdom ensured the U.S. military near *carte blanche* (pun intended) use of the island.

The priorities of the U.S. and U.K. governments were clear: maintaining complete political and military control over the islands; retaining the unfettered ability to remove any island populations by force; and assuming an intentional disregard for the rights of inhabitants. The U.S. Government wanted unencumbered freedom to do what it wished with a group of "sparsely populated" islands irrespective of the treatment owed to the people of dependent territories. In simplest terms, the U.S. Government wanted the Chagossians removed because officials wanted to ensure complete political and military control over Diego Garcia and the entire archipelago.

PLANNING THE REMOVALS

Four days after the government of the United Kingdom created the British Indian Ocean Territory in November 1965, the British Colonial Office sent the following instructions to the newly established BIOT administration, headquartered in the Seychelles: "Essential that contingency planning for evacuation of existing population from Diego Garcia . . . should begin at once."[5]

While planning between the British and U.S. governments had been underway since at least 1964, officials began to plan the removals in earnest after the creation of the BIOT. British officials again faced the untidy problem of how to get rid of the Chagossians, given UN rules on decolonization and the treatment due permanent inhabitants of colonial territories. In a 1966 memorandum, Secretary of State for the Colonies Francis Pakenham proposed simply rejecting "the basic principle set out in Article 73" of the UN Charter "that the interests of the inhabitants of the territory are paramount." "The legal position of the inhabitants would be greatly simplified from our point of view—though not necessarily from theirs," another official suggested, "if we decided to treat them as a floating population." They would claim that the BIOT had no permanent inhabitants and "refer to the people in the islands as Mauritians and Seychellois."[6]

Another official, Alan Brooke-Turner, feared that members of the UN Committee of Twenty-Four on Decolonization might demand the right to visit the BIOT, jeopardizing the "whole aim of the BIOT." Brooke-Turner suggested issuing documents showing that the Chagossians and other workers were "belongers" of Mauritius or the Seychelles and only temporary residents in the BIOT. "This device, though rather transparent," he wrote, "would at least give us a defensible position to take up in the Committee of Twentyfour."[7]

"This is all fairly unsatisfactory," a colleague responded in a handwritten note a few days later. "We detach these islands—in itself a matter which is criticised. We then find, apart from the transients, up to 240 'ilois'* whom we propose either to resettle (with how much vigour of persuasion?) or to certify, more or less fraudulently, as belonging somewhere else. This all seems difficult to reconcile with the 'sacred trust' of Art. 73, however convenient we or the US might find it from the viewpoint of defence. It is one thing to use 'empty real estate'; another to find squatters in it and to make it empty."[8]

A response came from Sir Paul Gore-Booth, Permanent Under-Secretary in the Foreign Office: "We must surely be very tough about this. The object of the exercise was to get some rocks which will remain *ours*; there will be no indigenous population except seagulls who have not yet got a Committee (the Status of Women Committee does *not* cover the rights of Birds)."[9]

Below Gore-Booth's note, one of his colleagues, D. A. Greenhill (later Baron of Harrow), penned back, "Unfortunately along with the Birds go some few Tarzans or Men Fridays whose origins are obscure, and who are being hopefully wished on to Mauritius etc. When this has been done, I agree we must be very tough."[10]

---

* U.K. and U.S. documents offer widely varying, and mostly inaccurate, estimates of the numbers of Chagossians. In fact, there were probably 1,000–1,500 in Chagos and at least 250–500 living in Mauritius at this time.

British officials eventually settled on a policy, as Foreign Office legal adviser Anthony Aust proposed, to "maintain the fiction that the inhabitants of Chagos are not a permanent or semi-permanent population."

"We are able to make up the rules as we go along," Aust wrote. They would simply represent the Chagossians as "a floating population" of "transient contract workers" with no connection to the islands.[11]

GRADUAL DEPOPULATION

Following the signing of the 1966 agreement, British officials moved to purchase the islands in the BIOT that were privately owned. After conveniently appointing themselves as the legislature for the new colony, British ministers passed "BIOT Ordinance No. 1 of 1967," allowing for the compulsory acquisition of land within the territory. In March 1967, the United Kingdom bought Chagos from Chagos-Agalega Ltd. for £660,000.[12]

The next month the British Government leased the islands back to Chagos-Agalega to continue running the islands on its behalf. Until this point, Chagossians could, as they had been accustomed since emancipation, leave Chagos for regular vacations or medical treatment in Mauritius and return to Chagos as they wished. After May 1967,[13] the BIOT administration ordered Chagos-Agalega to prevent Chagossians, like Rita Bancoult's family, from returning to Chagos. When, at the end of 1967, one of Chagos-Agalega's parent companies, Moulinie & Co., took over management, it also agreed to serve as the United Kingdom's agent in Chagos and prevent the entry of anyone without BIOT consent.[14] Like Rita, Chagossian after Chagossian appearing at the steamship company in Mauritius for return passage was turned away and told, "Your island has been sold."[15]

By February 1968, Chagossians in Mauritius had begun to protest their banning to the Mauritian Government. Mauritian officials asked Moulinie & Co. to allow their return on the next ship to the islands. When Paul Moulinie, Moulinie & Co.'s director, asked BIOT officials if they would allow some Chagossians to return, they refused. The company's steamer, the M.V. *Mauritius,* left on its next voyage for Chagos with no Chagossians aboard.

Later in 1968, with labor running low on the plantations, Moulinie & Co. requested permission from BIOT authorities to bring some Chagossians back from Mauritius. Amid ongoing consultations with U.S. officials, BIOT authorities denied the request. British officials understood, as one wrote, "if we accept any returning Ilois, we must also accept responsibility for their ultimate resettlement."[16] To keep the plantations running at a "basic maintenance level," the BIOT administration allowed Moulinie & Co. to replace the stranded Chagossians with imported Seychellois workers.[17]

DETERIORATING CONDITIONS

Back in Chagos, BIOT administrator John Todd found that "the islands have been neglected for the past eighteen months, due to uncertainty as to their future."[18] With military talks ongoing and the start of base construction uncertain, the BIOT and its agents gradually reduced services on the islands, making only basic maintenance repairs to keep the plantations running.

Beginning in 1965 with the creation of the BIOT, Chagos-Agalega began importing three-month stocks of food rather than the six-month stocks ordered previously. This left staple supplies of rice, flour, lentils, milk, and other goods lower than normal, making Chagossians increasingly reliant on fish and their own produce to meet food needs.[19]

After 1967 (and perhaps as early as late 1965) medical and school staff began leaving the islands. The midwife at the hospital in Peros Banhos left Chagos sometime before August 1968. She was not replaced, leaving only a single nurse at the hospital.[20] Around the same time, in 1967, the school in Peros Banhos closed due to the lack of a teacher.[21] In the Salomon Islands, the midwife departed during the first half of 1969, leaving a single nurse employed there as well. Salomon's teacher left sometime before July 1970, and the school there closed.[22]

At first Chagos-Agalega neglected the islands to avoid making capital investments on plantations it knew the BIOT might soon shut down. After the company sold the islands and gave up its lease, the BIOT institutionalized the neglect in the contract Moulinie & Co. signed to manage the islands: No improvements of more than Rs2,000 (around $420 at the time) could be made without BIOT permission.[23]

STRANDED IN MAURITIUS

With conditions worsening, some Chagossians left for Mauritius, with hopes that life in Chagos would improve and allow their return. Others left as usual for vacations or medical treatment. Some Chagossians report being tricked or coerced into leaving Chagos with the award of an un-scheduled vacation in Mauritius.[24] When the new arrivees and other Chagossians in Mauritius attempted to book their return passage, they, like their predecessors, were again refused. Because there was no telephone service in Chagos and because mail service between Mauritius and Chagos had been suspended, news of Chagossians being stranded in Mauritius did not reach those in the archipelago. By 1969, there were at least 356 Chagossians already in exile.[25]

This growing number found themselves having lost their jobs, separated from their homes and their land, with almost all of their possessions and property still in Chagos. Most were separated from family members left behind. All were confused about their future, about whether they would be allowed to return to their homes, and about their legal status in Mauritius.

The islanders also found themselves in a country that was highly unstable after gaining its independence in March 1968. Just after independence, riots between Afro-Mauritians and Indo-Mauritian Muslims broke out in many of the poor neighborhoods where Chagossians were living and continued through most of 1968.

Meanwhile, unemployment in Mauritius was over 20 percent.[26] British experts warned that the island was a Malthusian disaster in the making and would soon lack the resources to feed and support its rapidly growing population. A secret British telegram acknowledged "the near impossibility of [Chagossians] finding suitable employment. There is no Copra industry into which they could be absorbed."[27] The result was that most were left, as another British official put it, languishing "on the beach."[28]

As one Chagossian explained to me in 2004, life was turned completely upside down. Suddenly, "Chagossien dan dife, nu de lipie briye"—Chagossians were in the fire, with both our feet burning.

"LIKE QUESTIONING APPLE PIE"

As Paul Nitze's staff member Robert Murray recalled, the British "relieved us of a lot of problems. I mean, we didn't have to think through" the question of the removals anymore. "We didn't have to decide how we were going to manage our force relative to the local population, because there wasn't a local population."

I asked Murray if there were discussions about the fate of the Chagossians.

There were, he said, but "it was something the British thought they could manage. We didn't, we didn't try to get ourselves involved in it. Unless Kitchen and State did. We had the practical interest in having the base. And the British said that they could manage the transition. And they went about it and some of it was legal and some of it was otherwise. They were doing whatever they were doing. To the best of my knowledge they weren't consulting with us on the—now maybe that's not true, but I don't remember it anyway."

"And your sense was that you wanted to leave that to them and it was something you didn't particularly look into, or—" I asked before Murray interrupted.

"Yeah, we wanted to leave it to the British, I think, to manage that transition of the people and the sovereignty. We saw that as their responsibility. It was their island. . . . We personally saw, in Defense, no need or opportunity for us to inject ourselves—at least that's how I saw it at the time."

Murray's memory of the Chagossians reflects a striking consistency in former officials' responses when I asked what they remembered thinking about the Chagossians. Almost all remembered spending little time thinking about the islanders. The people were, as State Department official James Noyes put it, a "nitty gritty" detail that they never examined. Or as another said, they were something to which officials turned a "blind eye." The removal was a "*fait accompli* . . . a given" never requiring any thought.

I asked former State Department official George Vest if he disagreed in any ways with the Diego policy.

"I didn't have that deep a sense, [that] deep a feeling about it," he explained. "There was never any conflict. My attitude, which I expressed, was what I call an inner internal marginal attitude. I accepted the premises which led us to do what we were doing there without any real questioning."

That he and the United States were doing good in the world, Vest and others took for granted. Noyes said, "It was taken as a given good."

Indeed, Noyes explained that by the time he arrived at the State Department in 1970, there was no policy analysis about Diego Garcia because the base was treated as already being in place. There was no questioning of the British about "'What are you guys doing with the natives?'" he said. "It was an accepted part of the scenery."

"It was—the question, the ethical question of the workers and so on," Noyes said hesitatingly, "simply wasn't, wasn't in the spectrum. It wasn't discussed. No one realized, I don't think . . . the human aspects of it. Nobody was there or had been there, or was close enough to it, so. It was like questioning apple pie or something."

THE WHIZ KIDS

With the population already gone in the minds of most U.S. and U.K. officials, the Pentagon simultaneously pursued the Air Force's interest in Aldabra and the Navy's proposal for Diego Garcia. The Air Force budgeted $25 million in fiscal year 1968 for the 50/50 base on Aldabra. For the Diego Garcia proposal, Secretary of the Navy Nitze asked McNamara to "reconsider" McNamara's 1966 decision to withhold the Navy's request from Congress. This time Nitze had a new justification for the base, pitching it around the war in Vietnam as an "austere" refueling port for ships traveling to and from southeast Asia. The plan had a revised $26 million budget, divided into two funding increments beginning in fiscal year 1969. The austere facility, Nitze noted, would still offer a "nucleus" for expansion into a larger base, "if need arose."[29]

For this new incarnation, Nitze and the Navy had allies at DOD in Nitze's former office and its new Assistant Secretary of Defense for International Security Affairs, John McNaughton. Together, Nitze and McNaughton now pushed McNamara to approve the new Diego-as-fueling-depot plan.

Still hesitant, McNamara referred the proposal to the office in the Pentagon that, bureaucratically speaking, defined his tenure as Secretary of Defense: Systems Analysis. When McNamara joined the Kennedy administration, he brought with him, from his tenure at Ford Motor Company, a mode of statistically based economic analysis that had started to grow in popularity in the 1950s. McNamara saw it as a way to seize control of the Pentagon from the military services by imposing rationality on Defense decision-making and hired a group that became known as the "Whiz Kids" to implement the changes.

"Young, book-smart, Ivy League," these "think-tank civilian assistants," many coming from the RAND Corporation, championed rational calculation and statistical analysis as the basis for all policy decisions. "Everything was scrutinized with the cost-benefit and cost-effectiveness analysis" of RAND, Fred Kaplan writes in *Wizards of Armageddon* (1991[1983]). The questions of the day were ones like, "'What weapon system will destroy the most targets for a given cost?' or 'What weapon system will destroy a given set of targets for the lowest cost?'"[30]

McNamara charged Systems Analysis, and its head Alain Enthoven, with providing this analysis. In Systems Analysis, statistically based cost-effectiveness and cost-benefit calculations helped shape, justify, and evaluate military policymaking. Nearly every weapons purchase, every troop deployment, and every base decision had to pass through Systems Analysis for approval.

"McNamara would not act on a proposal without letting Alain's department have a chop at it," explained Earl Ravenal, a Systems Analysis staffer who worked on the Diego Garcia proposal. "Systems analysis became accepted as the buzz word, the way that decisions were rationalized, the currency of overt transactions, the *lingua franca* inside the Pentagon," Kaplan writes.[31] Often, this language and the use of statistical data alone were enough to create the veneer of rationality and justify policy decisions. This is exactly the type of language one sees in the Strategic Island Concept, in the talk of "stockpiling" islands like "commodities" and "investing" in bases as "insurance" to obtain future "benefits." As anthropologist Carole Cohn has shown among "defense intellectuals," and as the recollections of officials suggest, this language played an important role in shaping a particular version of reality and in shielding officials from the emotional and human impacts of their decisions.[32]

But at this time Ravenal's team in Systems Analysis received the proposal for Diego Garcia with instructions to "look into the quantitative rationale" for the base and "see if it makes sense." They took the Navy at its word and evaluated its most recent justification for the project—to create a new fueling depot for ships traveling to and from Vietnam. Ravenal's team found the base was not cost-effective: Given the distances involved and the costs of transporting fuel, it was simply cheaper to refuel ships at existing ports.

McNamara wrote to the new Secretary of the Navy, Paul R. Ignatius (by the end of June 1967, Nitze was back at the Pentagon as Deputy Secretary of Defense), to inform him that he would again defer "investment."[33]

Ravenal explained that the Navy and ISA were "extremely annoyed." They were "hopping up and down" mad, he said. Even people within Systems Analysis were concerned that Ravenal's team had taken on and defied the Navy over what they saw as such a relatively small project (thinking only in dollar terms). Rear Admiral Elmo Zumwalt, Senior Aide to the Secretary of the Navy, who had worked on Diego Garcia since serving under Nitze at ISA, immediately knew that the Navy had picked the wrong rationale to get the base.

"We knew it would be a billion before long," Ravenal said of the base's cost. "They said, 'Why are you opposing an austere communications facility?' I said, 'That's not what's going on here. You're going to have a tremendous base here. It's gonna be a billion'—of course it's over that now."

I asked Ravenal if any discussion of the Chagossians had surfaced in the work of Systems Analysis. Ravenal said he "heard about birds" on the island—some flightless rails, he thought—but "very little" about any people. "It was sort of out in the middle of, we thought, nowhere," he explained. "We thought nowhere because even though someone may have mentioned that there were some coconut farmers there, it didn't register. I never heard a single thing. Just birds. That's all."

"Why do you think it didn't register?" I asked.

"Well," Ravenal paused. "The mindset of almost anyone on the political-military side of government, they simply were not sensitized to those kinds of issues," Ravenal replied. "And I think it would have been my assumption, if you had twelve hundred people there, if you're going to have a military base there . . . everyone's better off getting them off there. But I would have made the assumption in my mind—but probably not bothered to check it out, I have to admit—that we were going to give them a lot of money and relocate them somewhere. Now if we didn't, I think that's a terrible shame."

"THE ALDABRA AFFAIR"

While the Navy was facing continued resistance at the Pentagon, the British Government was still pursuing a base on Aldabra. At the time, however, the United Kingdom was undergoing a severe financial crisis and looking for ways to cut its overseas expenditures. In April and May 1967, British officials informed their U.S. counterparts that they remained interested in a Diego facility but the U.K. financial participation would be no more than a nominal one.[34] In July, a U.K. white paper announced the withdrawal of all British troops from Singapore and Malaysia by mid-1970.

As the British continued plans for construction on Aldabra, U.K. and U.S. scientists who had been sent by the governments to survey the islands of the BIOT began to rally public opposition against the base. In what soon became known as the Aldabra Affair, scientists from the Royal Geographic Society and the Smithsonian Institution argued against a base on Aldabra. They said the military would endanger local populations of giant tortoises and rare birds, like the red-footed booby, which made Aldabra the "Galapagos of the Indian Ocean."[35]

By contrast, according to David Stoddart, one of the scientists who surveyed the islands, Diego Garcia "was simply a coconut plantation. The plants were common and the birds and land animals few."[36]

CHAPTER 6

"ABSOLUTELY MUST GO"

"When it came to writing official, top-secret reports that combined so-phisticated analysis with a flair for scaring the daylights out of anyone reading them," writes Fred Kaplan, "Paul H. Nitze had no match."[1] For five decades, Nitze was at the center of U.S. national security policy, begin-ning and perhaps most centrally with his authorship of the 1950 NSC-68 memo, which became one of the guiding forces in U.S. Cold War policy.

In NSC-68, and throughout his career, Nitze became an ardent pro-ponent of building up "conventional, non-nuclear forces to meet Soviet aggression on the peripheries" (i.e., in the so-called Third World). But NSC-68's language was "deliberately hyped," admitted another of its au-thors, Nitze's boss, Secretary of State Dean Acheson. They used it as a "bludgeon," for "pushing their own, more militaristic views into official parlance."[2] In NSC-68 and again in 1957 when Nitze helped spawn un-founded fears about a "missile gap" with the Soviets, as well as in his later work, the Democrat and former Wall Street financier continually inflated the Soviet threat. He offered a "highly pessimistic vision of Soviet military might, and the idea that the only real answer to the Soviet challenge lay in the construction of a gigantic, world-wide U.S. military machine."[3]

In June 1967, with Diego Garcia detached from Mauritius as part of the BIOT and an agreement for a base signed but still facing stiff opposi-tion on financial grounds from Robert McNamara, Nitze left his job as Secretary of the Navy to become Deputy Secretary of Defense, the second highest-ranking official in the Defense Department. Half a year later, with Britain having devalued the pound and still facing deep military spending cuts and scientific opposition to a base on Aldabra, Prime Minister Wil-son announced the cancellation of the Aldabra base. McNamara, Nitze, and other U.S. officials were little interested in going it alone on Aldabra (which they had always viewed primarily as another way to keep a British military presence "East of Suez"). Nitze and other Pentagon leaders returned their focus to Diego Garcia.[4]

Before long, however, changes came closer to home. By March 1968, McNamara had left the Defense Department for the World Bank, and Clark Clifford became Johnson's new Secretary of Defense. With Clifford focused almost entirely on Vietnam, Nitze was left to run most of the rest of the Pentagon. Having worked on Diego Garcia since 1961 during his tenure at ISA, Nitze soon began meeting with Navy officials to discuss plans for the base.

Barely a month after McNamara's departure, the Joint Chiefs offered a "reappraisal" of the Diego Garcia proposal in light of the 1967 Arab-Israeli war and the January 1968 British decision to withdraw their forces east of Suez by the end of 1971. Once again predicting the development of a "power vacuum" in the region and ensuing Soviet and Chinese "domination," the JCS recommended "the immediate establishment" of a base on Diego. They proposed a $46 million joint service facility capable of supporting limited forces in "contingency situations" (the euphemism for combat), Army and Air Force infrastructure, and a 12,000-foot runway capable of landing B-52 nuclear bombers and C-5A transport aircraft.[5] So much for "austere."

Internally the JCS crafted a strategy to dissuade new Secretary of Defense Clifford from being "unduly influenced" by Systems Analysis: "The project is analogous to an insurance policy," their rationale explained. "Low premiums now could lead to large returns later if military requirement does develop." The Chiefs continued, "We are trying to buy preparedness which is never cost-effective."[6]

Systems Analysis was again unconvinced. It urged the Secretary to "reject the JCS proposal" because it was not cost-effective and risked starting an arms race in the Indian Ocean.[7]

Surprisingly, Deputy Secretary of Defense Nitze agreed. He found there was "no justification" for a major base. However, he decided that "adequate justification exists" for what he called a "modest facility" on Diego Garcia, at a cost of $26 million, which, it just so happened, was exactly the price he had previously suggested as Secretary of the Navy.[8]

In this case, Nitze let the JCS provide the "bludgeon" with its warnings of Soviet "domination" and Chinese "expansion." In the face of these articulated threats and with the major JCS proposal on the table, Nitze's plan looked like a cheap, rational option, challenging the heart of Systems Analysis's opposition.

The Navy submitted a plan for the base along Nitze's suggested lines. It sent Nitze's former staffer Elmo Zumwalt back to Ravenal at Systems Analysis to make the case. "What is so striking about the succession of proposals," Ravenal later said, was "the kaleidoscopic change of rationales to support the same proposals."[9]

But this time, "they knew they were going to win," Ravenal recalled of Zumwalt's visit. "They were going to do it right this time. . . . They weren't going to make some sort of a [weak] case."

Still Systems Analysis continued its opposition, questioning the urgency of the Diego project and asking for it to be deferred until fiscal year 1971. But this time, Ravenal explained, "We lost."

ISA approved the plan as expected and in November 1968, Nitze signed off on the Navy's request to include $9,556,000 in the fiscal year 1970 military construction budget.[10] Within days, the Navy had notified the armed services committees of both houses of Congress. Under Nitze's leadership, an interdepartmental group of top officials from the Pentagon, State Department, CIA, and Treasury Department began arguing for the base on Capitol Hill.[11] In January 1969, a classified line item for Diego Garcia appeared in the fiscal year 1970 Military Construction budget. The funding process for the base was finally underway.

"It is the persistence of the military services," Ravenal would tell Congress years later, "that eventually wears down opposition within the Pentagon, within the executive branch, and ultimately within Congress and succeeds in attaining what they were after in the first place."[12]

In the case of Nitze, Ravenal told me, one has to see, "He threw the football as Secretary of the Navy, and he caught it as Deputy Secretary of Defense."

PLANNING THE "EVACUATION"

While DOD was quarreling over funding, the State Department's Bureau of Politico-Military Affairs and the embassy in London were coordinating the removals with the British.

"U.S. would desire removal of migrant laborers from Diego Garcia after due notice in accord with Minutes to BIOT Agreement," read an August 1968 telegram to the embassy in the name of Secretary of State Rusk. The joint State-Defense message instructed the embassy to inform British officials of the State and Defense departments' concern that the removals might arouse the attention of the United Nations' Committee of Twenty-Four. The message asked that the removals be carried out in a manner minimizing such negative publicity, preferably with resettlement taking place outside the BIOT (and thus technically removing it from the purview of the Committee of Twenty-Four).[13]

The telegram further noted that some British officials had still been using the term "inhabitants" to describe the people of Diego Garcia. Following the Foreign Office's plan to deny there was a settled population, the message asserted that the islanders were in fact "migrant laborers."

"We suggest, therefore, that the term 'migrant laborers' be used in any conversations with HMG as withdrawal of 'inhabitants' obviously would be more difficult to justify to littoral countries and Committee of Twenty-four."[14]

The embassy spoke with the Foreign Office the next day. Ambassador David Bruce telegrammed back to the State Department that the Foreign Office's representative "took the point on 'migrant laborers'" but noted that although "it was a good term for cosmetic purposes . . . it might be difficult to make completely credible as some of the 'migrants' are second generation Diego residents."[15]

MORE "FICTIONS"

"Negligible. . . . For all practical purposes . . . uninhabited." Or so the U.S. Navy said when characterizing Chagos's population in briefing papers delivered to members of Congress to secure Diego's funding in the 1970 military construction budget. When pushed by Senate Appropriations Committee member Senator Henry Jackson about the local population, one Navy official "told him that it consisted entirely of rotating contract copra workers, and that the British intended to relocate them as soon as possible after Congressional action was complete." Recounting Jackson's reaction, the official explained, "He came back to this question twice more. He was obviously concerned about local political problems. I assured him that there should be none."[16]

On Capitol Hill however, the political problems mounted for the Navy. First the Senate Armed Services Committee rejected the project, only to have it restored in a House-Senate conference. Then, after the House Appropriations Committee authorized funding, Jackson's Senate committee disapproved it, despite an intensive Navy lobbying campaign led by new Chief of Naval Operations Admiral Thomas Moorer.

In appropriations committee conference, senators led by Democrat Mike Mansfield refused to yield to Diego backers in the House through four meetings on the military appropriations. Democrats argued the project was a new military commitment overseas at a time when the Nixon administration had already indicated its desire to withdraw from Vietnam. Others wanted to "hold the Brits feet to the fire," and keep the U.S. from assuming their role in the Indian Ocean. The conferees ultimately left the project unfunded but offered the Navy an oral agreement: It should return in the following year's budget cycle with a pared-down request for a communications station without the other proposed facilities.[17]

Following the congressional defeat, newly elected President Richard Nixon's Secretary of Defense Melvin Laird gave the Navy equally simple instructions: "Make it a communications facility." Within two weeks, John H. Chafee, the new Secretary of the Navy, submitted to Laird a proposal for a $17.78 million "communications facility," with an initial funding increment of $5.4 million for fiscal year 1971.[18]

This of course was the same proposal that in 1965 had been "overtaken by events." Navy documents indicate that while the station was supposed to address gaps in the naval communications network in the Indian Ocean, the only such gaps were in the ocean's southernmost waters, closest to Antarctica and far from any potential conflict zones. A closer examination of the Navy's budget shows too that half the cost of the revised "communications station" project was for dredging Diego Garcia's lagoon and building an 8,000-foot airstrip; both were said to allow the resupply of a facility that featured a mere $800,000 worth of communications equipment. The "austere" project featured the construction of a 17-mile road network, a small nightclub, a movie theater, and a gym.[19]

Under the guise of a communications station, the Navy was asking for the nucleus of a base whose design allowed for ready expansion and the restoration of previously envisioned elements of the base.[20] As the CNO's Office of Communications and Cryptology put it, "The communications requirements cited as justification are fiction."[21]

FUNDING SECURED

By the spring of 1970, with congressional funding looking likely for the following year, British officials wanted to begin making arrangements for the deportations. The British were eager to begin negotiations to convince the Mauritian Government to receive the Chagossians and arrange for their resettlement. State and Defense officials on the other hand were concerned that Mauritian officials would leak news of the negotiations and endanger congressional funding by drawing international attention to the removals. State and Defense moved quickly and secured agreement from British officials not to begin negotiations until funding had been secured.[22] With members of Congress concerned at the time about increasing problems between U.S. overseas bases and local populations, presentations to Congress were careful to maintain that there would "be no indigenous population and no native labor utilized in the construction."[23]

At the same time, Defense and State emphasized in internal discussions that they needed "to retain enough distance" from the details of the deportations to ensure that British officials would not look to the United States for assistance and to avoid anyone making the connection between the impending base construction and the removals. Accordingly, the departments rejected a suggestion from the embassy in London to send an engineer to assist simultaneously with the base planning and the resettlement program.[24]

As expected under the previous year's oral agreement, in November 1970, Congress appropriated funds for an "austere communications facility." The funds were again listed as a classified item in the military construction budget. In a closed-to-the-public "executive" session of the House Appropriations Committee, Navy representatives told members of Congress for the first time that the BIOT agreement included the "resettlement of local inhabitants" and $14 million in Polaris missile payments.[25] Neither issue ever found its way out of the closed-door session.

With the money secured, Navy officials worked "to pursue the early removal" of those they were now simply calling "copra workers."[26] On December 7, 1970, a joint State-Defense message, telegrammed in the name of Secretary of State William P. Rogers, delivered instructions to the U.S. Embassy in London. Rogers asked the embassy to inform British officials that it was time "for the UK to accomplish relocation of the present residents of Diego Garcia to some other location":

> All local personnel should be moved from the western half of the island before the arrival of the construction force in March 1971. We hope that complete relocation can be accomplished by the end of July 1971 when aircraft begin using the air strip and the tempo of construction activities reaches its full scale.[27]

In turn, the embassy reported that the British were facing serious difficulties in arranging the deportations, given the bar on discussing resettlement with the Mauritians until after base funding was secured.[28]

"We recognize the British problem," State and Defense replied, but deporting the population "was clearly envisioned as United Kingdom's responsibility in 1966 agreements," and one for which the United States had paid "up to $14,000,000 in Polaris Research and Development charges."[29]

At 10:00 a.m. Washington time, on Tuesday, December 15, the Nixon White House for the first time publicly announced the United States' intention to build a joint U.S.-U.K. military facility on Diego Garcia. The State and Defense departments provided embassies with a list of anticipated questions and suggested answers to handle press inquiries, including the following:

Q: *What is the purpose of the facility?*
A: To close a gap in our worldwide communications system and to
   provide communications support to U.S. and U.K. ships and
   aircraft in the Indian Ocean.

Q: *Is this part of a U.S. build-up in the Indian Ocean?*
A: No.

Q: *Will other facilities be built in this area?*
A: No others are contemplated.

Q: *What will happen to the population of Diego Garcia?*
A: The population consists of a small number of contract laborers from the Seychelles and Mauritius engaged to work on the
   copra plantations. Arrangements will be made for the contracts
   to be terminated at the appropriate time and for their return to
   Mauritius and Seychelles.[30]

AN ORDER

If, as Earl Ravenal indicated with one of today's ubiquitous sports metaphors, Paul Nitze helped get the plan for Diego Garcia moving as Secretary of the Navy (in fact he started even earlier at ISA) and got the base funded as Deputy Secretary of Defense, the man who saw the project to its completion was Admiral Elmo Zumwalt.

Born in San Francisco in 1920 to two doctors, Elmo Russell Zumwalt, Jr., a prep school valedictorian and Naval Academy graduate, enjoyed an unprecedented rise to the top of the Navy hierarchy. At 44, Zumwalt was the youngest naval officer to be promoted to Rear Admiral. At 49, Zumwalt became the Navy's youngest-ever four-star Admiral and the youngest-ever CNO. His record of awards, decorations, and honorary degrees runs a single-spaced page, including medals from France, West Germany, Holland, Argentina, Brazil, Greece, Italy, Japan, Venezuela, Bolivia, Indonesia, Sweden, Colombia, Chile, South Korea, and South Vietnam.[31]

As CNO from 1970 to 1974, Zumwalt gained attention for integrating the Navy, for upgrading women's roles, and for relaxing naval standards of dress in keeping with the times. In an order to the Navy entitled "Equal Opportunity in the Navy," Zumwalt acknowledged the service's discriminatory practices against African Americans and ordered corrective actions. "Ours must be a Navy family that recognizes no artificial barriers of race, color or religion, " Zumwalt wrote in what was a pathbreaking statement for the U.S. armed forces. "There is no black Navy, no white Navy—just one Navy—the United State Navy."[32]

Nitze originally recruited Zumwalt in 1962 to work under him when Nitze was Assistant Secretary of Defense at ISA. In his memoirs, Zumwalt describes working closely with his "mentor and close friend." Zumwalt eventually following Nitze to his position as Secretary of the Navy, as Nitze's Executive Assistant and Senior Aide. Zumwalt was "at Paul's side" during the Cuban Missile Crisis and negotiations leading to the Nuclear Test Ban Treaty. Under Nitze's "tutelage," Zumwalt writes, he earned a "Ph.D. in political-military affairs."[33]

Nitze, for his part, rewarded Zumwalt by recommending him to receive the rear admiral's second star two years before others in his Naval Academy class were eligible and without having commanded a destroyer squadron or cruiser, as was the Navy's tradition.[34] Upon becoming the Navy's youngest-ever rear admiral, Zumwalt commanded a cruiser-destroyer flotilla and later became Commander of U.S. Naval Forces in Vietnam before his promotion by President Nixon to CNO.

Zumwalt worked on Diego Garcia from his time with Nitze at ISA and maintained the same interest in the base once he left Nitze's staff.[35] One of Zumwalt's staffers, Admiral Worth H. Bagley, remembered in 1989 how Zumwalt wanted to boost the U.S. naval presence in the Indian Ocean, in part out of concern for the "growing reliance on high oil imports at a time when things were looking unstable." Helped by the 1971 war between India and Pakistan, Zumwalt increased the pace of deployments in the ocean.

"He went out himself and visited the . . . African countries," Bagley explained. "Looking into the question of bases and things of that sort. . . . To see if he could find some economical way to increase base and crisis support possibilities there."[36]

"In dealing with Diego Garcia also?" Bagley's interviewer suggested.

"Moorer did that. Zumwalt finished it up for him," Bagley replied.[37]

And so Zumwalt did. Once Nitze and Admiral Moorer had secured funding from Congress, Zumwalt focused on removing Diego Garcia's population to prevent any construction delays. At a December 10, 1970 meeting, CNO Zumwalt told his deputies that he wanted to "push the British to get the copra workers off Diego Garcia prior to the commencement of construction," scheduled to begin in March 1971.[38]

A secret letter confirmed British receipt of the order to remove the Chagossians: "The United States Government have recently confirmed that their security arrangements at Diego Garcia will require the removal of the entire population of the atoll. . . . This is no surprise. We have known since 1965 that if a defence facility were established we should have to resettle elsewhere the contract copra workers who live there."[39]

As both governments prepared for the deportations and the start of construction, the U.S. embassies in London and Port Louis began recommending that the Navy use some Chagossians as manual laborers for the construction. Zumwalt refused. Two days after his December 17 order redressing racial discrimination in the Navy, Zumwalt stressed that by the end of construction all inhabitants should be moved to their "permanent other home."

In a small note handwritten on the face of Zumwalt's memo, a deputy commented, "Probably have no permanent other home."[40]

As planning proceeded into January 1971, Zumwalt received a memorandum from the State Department's Legal Adviser, John R. Stevenson, bearing on the deportations and the speed with which they would be accomplished. In the memo, Stevenson discussed "several legal considerations affecting US-UK responsibilities toward the 400 inhabitants of Diego Garcia." He pointed out that the 1966 U.S.-U.K. agreement "provides certain safeguards for the inhabitants," noting as well the commitment of both nations under the UN Charter to make the interests of inhabitants living in non–self-governing territories "paramount":

Although the responsibility for carrying out measures to ensure the welfare of the inhabitants lies with the UK, the US is charged under the [1966] Agreement with facilitating these arrangements. London 10391 [embassy memo] states that the US constrained the UK from discussing the matter with the GOM pending the outcome of our Congressional appropriations legislation. In light of this, we are under a particular responsibility not to pressure the UK into meeting a time schedule which may not provide sufficient time in which to satisfactorily arrange for the welfare of the inhabitants. Beyond this, their removal is to accommodate US needs, and the USG will, of course, be considered to share the responsibility with the UK by the inhabitants and other nations if satisfactory arrangements are not made.[41]

A day after Zumwalt received Stevenson's warning, two Navy officials were in the Seychelles to meet with the commissioner and administrator of the BIOT, Sir Bruce Greatbatch and John Todd. Together, they made plans for emptying the western half of Diego Garcia before the arrival of Navy "Seabee" construction teams, the "segregation" of Chagossians from the Seabees, and the "complete evacuation" of Diego Garcia by July.[42] Greatbatch and Todd explained that this was the fastest they could get rid of the population other than to "drop Ilois on pier at Mauritius and sail away quickly."[43]

Two weeks later a nine-member Navy reconnaissance party arrived on Diego Garcia with Todd and Moulinie & Co. director Paul Moulinie. On January 24, Todd and Moulinie ordered everyone on the island to the manager's office at East Point. Dressed in white and perched on the veranda of the office overlooking the assembled crowd, Todd announced that the BIOT was closing Diego Garcia and the plantations. The BIOT, he added, would move as many people as possible to Peros Banhos and Salomon.

A black-and-white photograph of the scene shows the islanders staring in disbelief (see figure 6.1). Some "of the Ilois asked whether they could return to Mauritius instead and receive some compensation for leaving their 'own country.'"[44] Not unlike the Bikinians before them, most were simply stunned.[45]

When given the "choice" between deportation to Mauritius or to Peros Banhos or Salomon, most elected to remain in Chagos. Many Seychellois workers and their Chagos-born children were deported to the Seychelles. Some Chagossians resigned themselves to deportation directly to Mauritius.

Many Chagossians say that they were promised land, housing, and money upon reaching Mauritius.[46] Moulinie's nephew and company employee Marcel Moulinie swore in a 1977 court statement that he "told the

Figure 6.1 Closing Diego Garcia, January 24, 1971. The BIOT announces the deportations, John Todd at center, hand on forehead; Paul Moulinie at right, in white hat. Courtesy Chagos Refugees Group, photographer unknown.

labourers that it was quite probable that they would be compensated." He continued, "I do not recall saying anything more than that. I was instructed to tell them that they had to leave and that is what I did."[47]

Within days, a Navy status report detailed the progress of the deportations:

> Relocation of the copra workers is proceeding in a satisfactory manner. The Administrator of the BIOT has given his assurance that the three small settlements on the western half of the atoll will be moved immediately to the eastern half. All copra producing activities on the western half will also cease immediately. The BIOT ship NORDVAER is relocating people from Diego Garcia to Peros Banhos, Salomon Islands, and the Seychelles on a regular basis.[48]

On February 4, a State-Defense message directed all government personnel to "Avoid all direct participation in resettlement of Ilois on Mauritius." The cable explained that "basic responsibility [is] clearly British," and that the United States was under "no obligation [to] assist with" the resettlement. On the other hand, the departments conceded, the government had some obligation to give the British "sufficient time" to adequately ensure

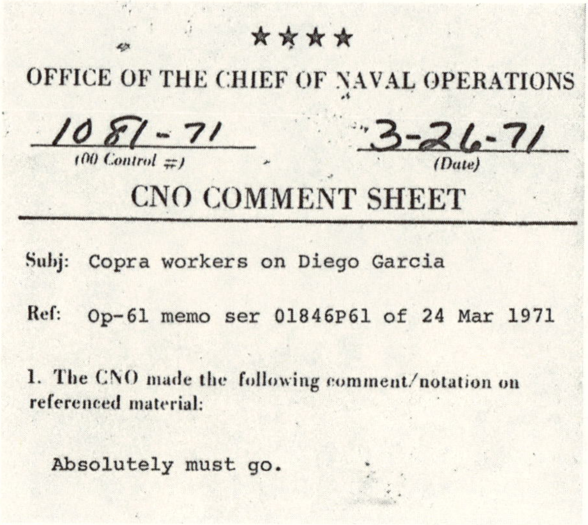

★★★★

OFFICE OF THE CHIEF OF NAVAL OPERATIONS

_1081-71_   _3-26-71_
(OO Control #)   (Date)

CNO COMMENT SHEET

Subj: Copra workers on Diego Garcia

Ref: Op-61 memo ser 01846P61 of 24 Mar 1971

1. The CNO made the following comment/notation on referenced material:

Absolutely must go.

Figure 6.2 CNO Comment Sheet, Admiral Elmo Russell Zumwalt, Jr., Navy Yard, Washington, DC, 1971. Naval Historical Center.

the welfare of the islanders. "USG also realizes," the telegram stated, "it will share in any criticism levied at the British for failing to meet their responsibilities re inhabitants' welfare."[49]

ECHOES OF CONRAD

The pace of deportations continued unabated, and within a few months, Marcel Moulinie and other company agents had forced all Chagossians on the western side of Diego Garcia, including the villages of Norwa and Pointe Marianne, to leave their homes and land to resettle on the eastern side of the atoll.[50]

On March 9, a landing party arrived on Diego to prepare for the arrival of a Seabee construction battalion later that month. Within days, unexpected reports came back to Navy headquarters from the advance team.

The commander "warns of possible bad publicity re the so-called 'copra workers,'" a Deputy CNO wrote. "He cites . . . fine old man who's been there 50 years. There's a feeling the UK haven't been completely above board on this. We don't want another Culebra," he said, referring to the opposition and negative publicity faced by the Navy during major protests in Puerto Rico against 1970 plans to deport Culebra's people and use their island as a bombing range.[51]

"Relocation of persons," Captain E. L. Cochrane, Jr. admitted to the Deputy CNO four days after the Seabees began construction, "is indeed a potential trouble area and could be exploited by opponents to our activities in the Indian Ocean." He added, "A newsman so disposed could pose questions that would result in a very damaging report that long time inhabitants of Diego Garcia are being torn away from their family homes because of the construction of a sinister U.S. 'base.'"[52]

The Navy, Pentagon, and State concluded, however, "that the advantages of having a station on an island which has no other inhabitants makes it worth the risk to ask the British to carry out the relocation." In fact, Cochrane wrote, the advantages of having the British relocate the inhabitants were "so great that the United States should adopt a strict 'let the British do it' policy while at the same time keeping as well informed as possible on the actual relocation activities."[53]

Weighing the concerns of the advance party and Cochrane's recommendation, Zumwalt had the final say. On a comment sheet with the subject line "Copra workers on Diego Garcia," Zumwalt had three words:

"Absolutely must go."[54]

CHAPTER 7

"ON THE RACK"

With the money finally secured from Congress and the British taking charge of the final deportations, the Navy set to work building its base. "Resembling an amphibious landing during World War II," writes a former Navy officer who worked on the project, "Seabees landed on Diego Garcia in March 1971 to begin construction."[1] A tank landing ship, an attack cargo ship, two military sealift command charter ships, and two dock landing ships descended on Diego with at least 820 soldiers and equipment to construct a communications station and an 8,000-foot airstrip. The Seabees brought in heavy equipment, setting up a rock crusher and a concrete block factory. They used Caterpillar bulldozers and chains to rip coconut trees from the ground. They blasted Diego's reef with explosives to excavate coral rock for the runway. Diesel fuel sludge began fouling the water.[2]

According to many Chagossians, there were threats that they would be bombed or shot if they did not leave the island. Children hid in fear as military aircraft began flying overhead.[3] The *Washington Post*'s David Ottaway later reported that "one old man . . . recalled being told by an unidentified American official: 'If you don't leave you won't be fed any longer.'"[4]

Navy officials continued to pressure their British counterparts to complete the deportations as quickly as possible. On April 16, the United Kingdom issued BIOT Immigration Ordinance #1 making it a criminal offense for anyone except authorized military personnel to be on the islands without a permit. A State Department official in the Office of the Assistant Secretary for Africa later acknowledged, "In order to meet our self-imposed timetable, their evacuation was undertaken with a haste which the British could claim has prevented careful examination of resettlement needs."[5] Construction continued unabated, with the runway operational by July 1971.

Figure 7.1 M.V. *Nordvær*, 1968. The BIOT cargo
ship used to deport Chagossians, at times with more
than 100 aboard. Photo courtesy of Kirby Crawford.

The BIOT administration and its Moulinie & Co. agents continued
to remove families to Peros Banhos and Salomon. Some Chagossians refused but were told they had no choice but to leave. Marcel Moulinie and
other Moulinie & Co. agents reiterated that there would be no more work.
There would be no more transportation to and from the island, food stores
had run out, and the boats were taking away the salvageable plantation
infrastructure.

For the voyage, passengers were generally allowed to take a small box of
their belongings and a straw bed mat. Most of their possessions and all their
animals were left behind. In August 1971, the BIOT dispatched its 500-
ton cargo ship, the M.V. *Nordvær*, to Diego to remove the last families from
the island. When the *Nordvær* experienced engine troubles before reaching
Diego, the BIOT administration sent another ship, the *Isle of Farquhar*, to
continue the removals.[6] By then food supplies were running dangerously
low, and BIOT officials started considering asking for emergency assistance.
The Navy's Seabee contingent eventually shipped food and medical supplies
across the lagoon to sustain the remaining islanders.[7]

In the days before the last inhabitants of Diego Garcia were removed,
BIOT commissioner Sir Bruce Greatbatch sent the order to Moulinie &
Co. to kill the Chagossians' pet dogs and any other remaining dogs on the
island. Marcel Moulinie, who had been left to manage Diego Garcia, was
responsible for carrying out the extermination.

According to Moulinie, he first tried to shoot the dogs with the help
of Seabees armed with M16 rifles. When this failed as an expeditious

extermination method, he attempted to poison the dogs with strychnine. This too failed. Sitting in his home overlooking a secluded beach in the Seychelles 33 years later, Moulinie explained to me how he finally used raw meat to lure the dogs into a sealed copra-drying shed, the *kalorifer*. Locking them in the shed, he gassed the howling dogs with exhaust piped in from U.S. military vehicles. Setting coconut husks ablaze, he burnt the dogs' carcasses in the shed.[8] The Chagossians were left to watch and ponder their fate.

THE FINAL DEPORTATIONS

After the *Isle of Farquhar* took a load of Chagossians and Seychellois from Diego, a repaired *Nordvær* returned to remove the final inhabitants. "There was a crowd of people there and a lot of them were crying," Marcel Moulinie remembered. "People were upset about" the killing of their dogs, "as well as being upset about having to leave the islands. I persuaded Marcel [Ono, a Diego Garcia *commandeur*] that he had to go as there were no more rations on the island and the boat had not brought in any food. The stores had been removed and there was no way of feeding anyone. . . . I last saw him as he walked on to the boat." With U.S. military personnel looking on shortly before the end of October 1971, the last boatload steamed away from Diego Garcia.[9]

Chagossians and others report that the boats were terribly overcrowded and that the open seas were often rough on the initial 1,200-mile, four-day journey to the Seychelles. The *Nordvær* had cabin passenger space for twelve and deck space for sixty (accommodating a total of 72 passengers). On the last voyage, 146 were packed on the vessel. At the orders of Sir Bruce Greatbatch, Diego's horses were given the best places on deck. All but a few Chagossians made the trip exposed to the elements elsewhere on deck or in the hold, sitting and sleeping on a cargo of copra, coconuts, company equipment, and guano—bird feces. Many became ill during the passage, vomiting on deck and in the hold. Two women are reported to have miscarried.[10]

Moulinie recalled:

The boat was very overcrowded. The boat deck was covered with stores, the belongings of the labourers, and a lot of labourers were traveling on deck. Greatbatch had insisted that the horses be carried back to Mahé and these were on deck with the labourers. The labourers also traveled in the holds. This was not unusual but there were more people than usual in them. The holds also held a lot of copra being taken out of Diego. When the boat finally arrived the conditions were filthy. They had taken four days to travel and many of the women and children were sick. The boat deck was covered in manure, urine and vomit and so was the hold.[11]

When the *Nordvær* arrived in the Seychelles, offloading the islanders before the second leg of the journey, another 1,200 miles to Mauritius, Moulinie & Co. arranged to have their management housed in hotels. The Chagossians were housed in a prison.[12]

A VOICE IN THE BUREAUCRACY

With the arrival in Mauritius of the last islanders from Diego Garcia, the U.S. Embassy in Port Louis grew increasingly concerned about the condition of what officials described as "1300 miserable and uneducated refugees."[13]

"The USG has a moral responsibility for the well-being of these people who were involuntarily moved at our request," the embassy argued to the State Department in Washington. U.S. moral responsibility was especially heavy given that the government had "resisted GOM and HMG efforts to permit Ilois to remain as employees of the facility." Even if legally speaking "primary responsibility" lay with the British, the Port Louis mission believed, the U.S. Government was responsible for ordering the removal and was vulnerable to criticism in public and at the UN.[14]

The embassy was equally unhappy about the lack of resettlement planning: "To our knowledge," the mission cabled, "there exists no operative plan and no firm allocation of funds to compensate them for the hardship of the transfer from their former home and their loss of livelihood." While the British were still in the midst of convincing the Mauritian Government to create a resettlement plan, such a scheme was "foredoomed," first, because of the "political impossibility" of giving special resources to the Chagossians while unemployed Hindus, Muslims, and Afro-Mauritians received nothing, and second, because of the Mauritian Government's own inability to make use of current British aid money, let alone new funds for a special Chagossian project.[15]

"The plight of the Ilois," the embassy wrote, "is a classic example of perpetuation of hardship through bureaucratic neglect." "The Embassy believes we have regrettably neglected our obligation toward them. We recommend that early and specific exchanges with HMG be undertaken in order to assure the welfare of the Ilois and that authority for this essentially political matter be appropriately centralized within the Department."[16]

The primary author of these remarkable cables was Henry Precht, the deputy to the ambassador in an embassy of just seven (Precht later worked on Iran at the State Department, playing a key role in the Carter administration's handling of the hostage crisis). Now living in the Washington area, Precht remembered that the Navy "didn't want to be bothered. They wanted an all-American facility," free of any labor problems, health issues, or anything that would have "complicated life there." It was "much neater" without the islanders, he said.

For three months, Precht and Ambassador William Brewer cabled strongly worded reports about the Chagossians, demanding, "Justice should be done." Lambasting the "inadequate and cavalier treatment so far accorded the Ilois," they traded charged dispatches with an undersecretary of the Air Force and others in the bureaucracy over the U.S. Government's responsibility.[17] It was "absurd" to say, as some in the bureaucracy continued to maintain, that Diego Garcia had "no fixed population," given its history of habitation dating to the eighteenth century. Moreover, "DOD acknowledged its responsibility for the removal of the Ilois by payment of $14 million to HMG." Precht and Brewer wrote that the Government didn't fulfill its obligation to the Chagossians by its $14 million payment, pointing out correctly that most of the money seemed to have gone toward building an international airport in the Seychelles.

"The point of our exercise," they said, is that "the USG should make sure that the British do an adequate job of compensation."[18] (Around the same time Brewer was also helping to "burnish the Diego public relations image" in Mauritius by delivering 3,000 bags of Christmas candy prepared by Navy personnel on Diego to underprivileged and children's groups.[19])

I asked Precht why he thought no one else spoke out on behalf of the Chagossians. "There weren't very many of them," he replied. "They didn't add up to much of a problem. They were easily pushed aside." And it would have taken someone in Washington, he said, to have enough interest "to pursue it. And pursuing something in Washington" takes a lot of political energy. It can be quite a "profitless enterprise."

Adam Hochschild's exploration of violence perpetrated by the Belgian Empire in the Congo helps explain Precht's observation: Because Belgian authorities sanctioned violence against the Congolese, "for a white man to rebel meant challenging the entire system that provided your livelihood.

Everyone around you was participating. By going along with the system, you were paid, promoted, awarded medals."[20]

As the embassy's failed protests show, challenges to the expulsion would likely have been fruitless save for those originating at the highest levels of the bureaucracy, from people like Nitze, Komer, Zumwalt, Moorer, Mc-Namara, and Rusk. "The individual bureaucrat cannot squirm out of the apparatus in which he is harnessed," Max Weber wrote half a century earlier. "The professional bureaucrat is chained to his activity by his entire material and ideal existence. In the great majority of cases, he is only a single cog in an ever-moving mechanism which prescribes to him an essentially fixed route of march. The official is entrusted with specialized tasks and normally the mechanism cannot be put into motion or arrested by him, but only from the very top."[21]

Back in the State Department bureaucracy in Washington, James Bishop was the desk officer who received Precht and Brewer's cables. "Vaguely" recalling the dispatches when I spoke to him in early 2008, Bishop said they came a "considerable time" before human rights "became a major part of our diplomacy." This "was the Kissinger era," when the Secretary of State and National Security Adviser was "chastising" the African bureau "as a bunch of missionaries." Plus, the Chagossians were not a very high issue on State's agenda when it came to relations with Bishop's "parish" Mauritius. On the other hand, he said, "there wasn't any question about their being recent arrivals. It was their homeland." Bishop added, "I do recall feeling that they were going to get screwed."

Jonathan "Jock" Stoddart had responsibility at the State Department for much of the implementation of the removals. I asked Stoddart if anyone investigated the embassy's reports.

"My answer would be, I don't think so," Stoddart replied from his apartment at The Jefferson, a retirement facility in the Washington, D.C. suburbs. "I doubt if the Navy sent somebody that was interested in human rights out to Diego to look into this. I think the Navy's attitude was, accept what the British say, and turn a blind eye to whatever was going on."

State and Defense officials seemed to choose the same tack. "It was, I would say, an issue that was lurking in the background but generally ignored," Stoddart said. "We were all leaving the whole problem up to the British—to justify, rationalize, whatever. We were quite aware that our original—the original information that we had received from the British was wrong: that this was an uninhabited archipelago. I think we fully accepted that fact."

Still, "this is one of the best deals the United States has ever negotiated," Stoddart added, from his apartment complex named for the president known for one of the nation's earliest land acquisitions.

"For a change," he said, it came "at a minimal cost."

The official response to Precht and Brewer from higher-ups in the State and Defense bureaucracies was a February cable from the State Department. "Basic responsibility" for the Chagossians lay with the British, the telegram said; but it directed the embassy in London to inform the Foreign and Commonwealth Office of the U.S. Government's "concern" over their treatment. The State Department conceded internally (in its clipped bureaucratic language), "USG also realizes it may well share in any criticism levied at British for failing meet their responsibilities re inhabitants' welfare." Concerned about the removal's Cold War implications, State added: "Continued failure resolve these issues exposes both HMG and USG to local criticism which could be picked up and amplified elsewhere."[22]

Former national security officials Anthony Lake and Roger Morris, who resigned from the Nixon administration to protest the invasion of Cambodia, describe memoranda from Washington like these and the effect of the geographical and, as they say, spiritual distance between decision makers and those affected by their decisions:

> We remember, more clearly than we care to, the well carpeted
> stillness and isolation of those government offices where some of
> the Pentagon Papers were first written. The efficient staccato of
> the typewriter, the antiseptic whiteness of nicely margined memo-
> randa, the affable, authoritative and always urbane men who wrote
> them—all of it is a spiritual as well as geographic world apart from
> piles of decomposing bodies in a ditch outside Hue or a village
> bombed in Laos, the burn ward of a children's hospital in Saigon,
> or even a cemetery or veteran's hospital here. It was possible in that
> isolated atmosphere, and perhaps psychologically necessary, to dull
> one's awareness of the direct link between those memoranda and
> the human sufferings with which they were concerned.[23]

In the summer of 1972, the State Department sent Precht to Tehran and Brewer to fill the place of the assassinated ambassador to Sudan.

DETERIORATING CONDITIONS

At about the time that Brewer was on his way to Khartoum, the British secured the agreement of the Mauritian Government to receive the Chagossians. Despite the fact that a majority of the Chagossians said they wanted to receive compensation in cash, a planned Anglo-Mauritian re-habilitation scheme called for the provision of housing, pig breeding jobs (never a significant economic activity in Chagos), and some cash payments. On September 4, 1972, Mauritian Prime Minister Ramgoolam accepted £650,000 to resettle the Chagossians, including the remaining few hundreds who were still to be removed from Peros Banhos and Salomon.

British officials realized that the project was "under-costed" for an adequate resettlement, but were happy to have struck such a cheap deal. Precht had earlier weighed in on the likelihood of the resettlement plan's working: "We doubt it."[24] The resettlement was never implemented, and Chagossians saw almost none of the £650,000 for more than five years.

After the emptying of Diego Garcia, around 370 Chagossians remained in Peros Banhos and Salomon. Like those who went to Mauritius and the Seychelles, those who went from Diego Garcia to Peros and Salomon had been required to leave most of their possessions, furniture, and animals in Diego. They received Rs500 (about $90) as a "disturbance allowance" to compensate them for the costs of reestablishing their lives. Those going to Mauritius and the Seychelles received nothing.

The neglect of Peros Banhos and Salomon by the BIOT and Mouli-nie & Co. continued as it had on Diego Garcia, and conditions worsened dramatically in 1972 and 1973. Food supplies declined and Chagossians remember how their diet became increasingly dependent on fish and coconuts. When milk supplies ran out, women fed their children a thin, watery mixture of coconut milk and sugar. Medicines and medical supplies ran out. With even ripe coconuts in short supply, people ate the spongy, over-ripe flesh of germinated nuts. The remaining staff in each island's hospital left, and the last school, in Peros Banhos, closed.

In June 1972, the *Nordvær* continued emptying Peros and Salomon. At least 53 left on this one voyage, telling BIOT agents they wished to "return later to the islands," hopeful that conditions would improve.[25] Again Chagossians say conditions on the ship were terrible. Marie Therese Mein, a Chagossian woman married to the departing manager of Peros Banhos, described the voyage:

> Our conditions were somewhat better than the other suffering passengers since we were given a small cabin [because her husband was the manager], but we had to share this between my husband, myself and our 8 children. We could not open the portholes since the ship was heavily laden, and the sea would splash in if we did. It was therefore extremely hot and uncomfortable. Many people were

in much worse conditions than us, having to share a cargo compartment with a cargo of coconuts, horses and tortoises. Some had to sleep on top of the deck of the ship. No meals were provided, and the captain, a Mr. Tregarden, told the families to prepare their own meals. By contrast the horses were fed grass. The passage was rough and many of the passengers were seasick. There was urine and manure from the horses on the lower deck. The captain decided to jettison a large part of the cargo of coconuts in order to lessen the risk of being sunk. The whole complement of passengers suffered both from an extremely rough passage and from bad smells of animals and were sick and weary after the 6 day crossing.[26]

Mein was three months pregnant at the time. She miscarried a day after arriving in the Seychelles.

A subsequent voyage of the *Nordvær* had 120 Chagossians on board, nearly twice its maximum capacity.[27] In December 1972, BIOT administrator Todd reported that Salomon had closed, with all its inhabitants moved to Peros Banhos or deported to Mauritius or the Seychelles. A small number of Chagossians remained in Peros, with only enough food to last until late March or April.

Early in 1973, Moulinie & Co. agents informed the remaining Chagossians that they would have to leave. At the end of April, with food supplies exhausted, the *Nordvær* left Peros Banhos with 133 Chagossians aboard. The *Nordvær* arrived in Mauritius on April 29.

By this time, however, the Chagossians on the *Nordvær* had heard about the fate of others arriving in Mauritius. They refused to disembark. They demanded that they be returned to Chagos or receive houses in Mauritius. After nearly a week of protest and negotiations, 30 families received a small amount of money and dilapidated houses in two of the poorest neighborhoods of Port Louis.

A month later, on May 26, 1973, the *Nordvær* made its final voyage, removing 8 men, 9 women, and 29 children from Peros Banhos. The expulsion from Chagos was complete.

EXPANSION

As early as Christmas Day, 1972, Bob Hope and Red Foxx were cracking jokes for the troops on Diego Garcia as part of a USO special.[28] Shortly before the final deportations from Peros Banhos in 1973, the Seabees completed their 8,000-foot runway and made the communications station operational. By October, the Navy was using the base to fly P-3 surveillance planes to support Israel during the 1973 Arab-Israeli war—quite a feat for a mere communications station.[29]

As Nitze and others in the U.S. Government had hoped, the original "austere communications facility" on Diego Garcia served as a nucleus for what became a rapidly expanding base. Before the base was operational, Zumwalt was already asking others in the Navy in 1972, "What do we do in 74, 75, and 76 for Diego Garcia?" referring to expansion ideas for the upcoming fiscal years.[30]

Restricted to the use of the Azores as its only base from which to resupply Israel during the October war, the Navy soon submitted an "emergency" request for $4.6 million in additional construction funds. The Pentagon turned them down. Within weeks, the Navy submitted a request to the Pentagon for an almost $32 million expansion of the base over three years, to include ship support facilities and a regular air surveillance capacity. Days later, Chairman of the Joint Chiefs of Staff Admiral Moorer sent a recommendation to Secretary of Defense James Schlesinger to expand the base beyond the new request, including a runway extension to accommodate B-52 bombers. In January 1974, the Air Force asked for a $4.5 million construction budget of its own.[31]

After an initial supplemental appropriation for fiscal year 1974 was deferred to the 1975 budget, additional appropriations for Diego Garcia soon became a minor political battle between the Ford administration and Democratic senators concerned about U.S. military expansion and a growing arms race with the Soviet Union in the Indian Ocean. Hearings were held in both houses of Congress. Amendments to defeat the expansion and to force arms negotiations in the Indian Ocean were introduced but defeated. Congress made new funding contingent on the President affirming that the expansion was "essential to the national interest of the United States," which Ford quickly did. "In particular," his justification said, "the oil shipped from the Persian Gulf area is essential to the economic well-being of modern industrial societies. It is essential that the United States maintain and periodically demonstrate a capability to operate military forces in the Indian Ocean."[32]

During House committee hearings, State Department representative George Vest was asked, was there "any question about Diego Garcia being in the open sea lanes?"

"No, it is open sea," he replied, before volunteering, "and uninhabited."

"There are no inhabitants in Diego Garcia?" queried Representative Larry Winn of Kansas.

"No inhabitants," Vest answered.

"None at all?"

"No."

Within weeks the Pentagon won appropriations for fiscal years 1975 and 1976 totaling more than $30 million.[33]

CONGRESSIONAL HEARINGS

On September 11, 1975, a page-one *Washington Post* headline read, "Islanders Were Evicted for U.S. Base." Reporter David Ottaway had become the first in the Western press to break the story. Democratic Senators Edward Kennedy of Massachusetts and John Culver of Iowa, who had opposed the expansion of the base, took to the floor of the Senate to propose an amendment demanding the Ford administration explain the circumstances surrounding the expulsion and the role of the U.S. Government in the removals. The amendment passed. A month later the administration submitted to Congress a nine-page response drafted by State and Defense.

The "Report on the Resettlement of Inhabitants of the Chagos Archipelago" described how Chagos had been inhabited since the late eighteenth century, and that "despite the basically transitory nature of the population of these islands, there were some often referred to as 'Ilois'. . . . In the absence of more complete data," the report said, "it is impossible to establish the status of these persons and to what extent, if any, they formed a distinct community."[34]

The report explained the removals by saying that the 1966 U.S.-U.K. agreement envisioned the total evacuation of the islands for military purposes, citing three reasons for wanting the islands uninhabited: security, British concerns about the costs of maintaining civil administration, and Navy concerns about "social problems . . . expected when placing a military detachment on an isolated tropical island alongside a population with an informal social structure and a prevalent cash wage of less than $4.00 per month."[35]—this was a polite way of referring to trumped up, racist fears about prostitution and other unwanted sexual and romantic relations between military personnel and the islanders.

As to the deportations, the report said, "All went willingly." It continued, "No coercion was used and no British or U.S. servicemen were involved." Although acknowledging that the "resettlement doubtless entailed discomfort and economic dislocation," the report concluded, "United States and United Kingdom officials acted in good faith on the

7.2 U.S. Government officials. Top from left: Adm. Arleigh Burke, Adm. Horacio Rivero, Paul Nitze. Bottom from left: Robert McNamara, Adm. Thomas Moorer, Adm. Elmo Zumwalt. Photos credits: Admirals courtesy Naval Historical Center; Nitze courtesy Harry S. Truman Library and Museum; McNamara courtesy Lyndon Baines Johnson Library and Museum.

basis of the information available to them." The last sentence of the report offered the Ford administration's final position: "There is no outstanding US obligation to underwrite the cost of additional assistance for the persons affected by the resettlement from the Chagos Islands."[36]

When the House Special Subcommittee on Investigations called for a day of hearings, administration representatives held firm. On November 4, 1975, Democrat subcommittee chair Lee H. Hamilton* asked State Department representative George T. Churchill if he considered the characterization "'all went willingly' to be a fair disclosure of the facts."

"In the sense that no coercion at all was used," Churchill replied.

"No coercion was used when you cut off their jobs? What other coercion do you need? Are you talking about putting them on the rack?"[37]

* Hamilton co-chaired the Iraq Study Group following the 2003 invasion.

Figure 7.3 "Aunt Rita," wearing her best for a Chagos Refugees Group festival and fundraising event, 2004. Photo by author.

At another point in the hearings Hamilton probed further with Churchill: "Is it the position of our Government now, that we have no responsibility toward these islanders? Is that our position?"

"We have no legal responsibility," Churchill replied. "We are concerned. We recently discussed the matter with the British. The British have discussed it with the Mauritian Government. We have expressed our concern."

"It is our basic position that it is up to the British. Is that it?" Hamilton pressed.

"It is our basic position that these people originally were a British responsibility and are now a Mauritian responsibility," Churchill explained.

"We have no responsibility, legal or moral?"

"We have no legal responsibility. Moral responsibility is a term, sir, that I find difficult to assess."[38]

Before testimony's end, Churchill said that it was the position of the Government not to allow the Chagossians to return to their homeland. Congress has never again taken up the issue.

CHAPTER 8

DERASINE: THE IMPOVERISHMENT
OF EXPULSION

Paradise Found: Twenty degrees south of the Equator, Mauritius lies at the crossroads of Europe, Africa, and Asia. Celebrated as the pearl of the Indian Ocean, it is truly a land of splendour and human warmth.

—*Anahita World Class Sanctuary Mauritius*[1]

If heaven is that painless place where pleasures never pall then Mauritian hideaways provide a close approximation.

—*Condé Nast Traveler*[2]

When you arrive in Cassis, you find a maze of rusting corrugated iron fences lining small passageways, dirt paths, and a few paved roads, surrounded by houses and shacks cobbled together in metal, concrete block, and wood. Four major cemeteries dominate the landscape of the slum neighborhood closest to the center of Port Louis. Trash often sits smoldering in empty garbage-strewn lots. Bent, rusted, and torn sheets of metal lie in piles that to an outsider seem like just more detritus but upon closer inspection reveal themselves to be emergency supplies for future home repairs. From the balconies of the few two or three story homes (in a neighborhood where the only upward mobility is usually literal), you see a tightly packed clutter of corrugated rooftops, many weighted down against Indian Ocean winds by bedsprings, broken-down bicycle parts, bricks. The rare palm tree juts up from below. An open drainage sewer runs through the middle of the neighborhood, past one of the cemeteries and toward the ocean.

Although Mauritius is known internationally for its beautiful beaches, and although most of Cassis is surrounded by the Indian Ocean, there is little water and beach access in the neighborhood: Between a power station on one side and a sand plant on the other, a small stretch of beach remains. A landing area for fisherfolk lies nearby, small wooden boats dotting the water at anchor just off the shore. Up from the water are about ten yards of beach, across which are scattered pieces of coral, broken shells, and decaying fly-ridden seaweed, along with a collection of shattered bottles, rusted-out cans, abandoned tires, lone shoes, shards of wood, plastic bags, car parts, and shards of splintering white styrofoam. At the end of the beach is a mountain of sand out of which emanate a sulfurous stench and nine large black industrial pipes stretching out over the ocean. A large red and white government sign stands nearby, the bottom half of its message all that hasn't been stripped away: "*BAIGNADE NON RECOMMANDEE*." SWIMMING NOT RECOMMENDED.

Cassis is the neighborhood where Rita and Julien Bancoult found themselves and their family following Noellie's death. After briefly sharing a home with Rita's mother and a group totaling seventeen, Rita and Julien found a little shack for the family. When the owner demanded Rs1,500 for the property—a price they couldn't come close to paying—they found themselves evicted.

For fifteen days they lived in another shack next to Cassis's St. George's cemetery. Then the owner told them that his son was getting married and needed the home. Out on the streets again, the family found a small plot of land, across the street from the cemetery, along with some sheets of metal and some wood. Paying the land's owner a yearly rent, they built a small three-room shack. "Inside there, I—we lived." That's where "we went through all our *mizer*," Rita said, using the Mauritian and Chagos Kreol word for not just poverty, but abject, miserable poverty.

Julien eventually found some on-again, off-again work as a casual laborer loading and unloading trucks late into the night around Port Louis. When the trucks needed laborers, Julien brought home some cash. When the trucks had plenty of men, Rita explained, he came home empty-handed. She went to work doing washing and ironing in a wealthy woman's house. But she had to be careful. "If a person went and said that I'm Ilois, the next day I go" to work "the madame pays me and tells me, 'Go! Don't come back to work.' Like we're inferior, you understand?"

Sometimes though, the woman she worked for was nice and would give her some curry and some bread. "I didn't eat it," she said. "I put it in my bag. I brought it home for my children. How will I eat it, David, when my children have nothing to eat? I didn't eat. I put it in my bag."

In those days, feeding the children was a daily struggle. "Then, David, I tell you, I had a difficult life, I did. At times the children didn't eat, didn't eat. I was worried. I didn't know what I would do."

At times, Rita waited for people to throw bags of stale bread in the trash. "I'm not afraid to say it. I only looked out to see if people were watching me. I just took the bag," got the bread, and went back home. With some wood for kindling, she would light a fire, warm the bread on top of a small shard of metal, and make a tea-like infusion with wild leaves and some sugar. "My children ate that and the bread," she said.

Other days she would make a thin watery broth with *bred murum*—another wild edible leaf known as the "food of the poor."

"I took the bred murum. I picked the leaves. I didn't have oil. I only had salt with a little bit of ginger. I grated the ginger. I put it in the boiling water. I put the leaves in. I added salt. The children wetted the bread that I had warmed, and they ate it.

"But on my island, I was never like that, David. How will I forget? My children went two days without eating."

Rita's story is typical of islanders who were barred from returning to Chagos beginning in 1968. They found themselves homeless and jobless in a foreign land, separated from their islands, their communities (both those living and those buried on the islands), and their entire way of life.

After the deportations began in 1971, Chagossians were literally left on the docks of Port Louis. "The Ilois walked bewildered off their ships and tramped through the slums of the capital," investigative journalist John Madeley recounts, "to try to find a relative or friend who would offer accommodation."[3]

Another reporter saw how many had "to go begging to survive, and live in shacks which are little more than chicken coops."[4] More than half lived in single-room houses with as many as nine people in a room. In one case in Cassis, seven Chagossian families moved into a single courtyard that already housed ten other families. They shared one water tap, one toilet, and one shower among them.[5]

Already scattered over 1,200 miles between Mauritius and the Seychelles, Chagossians dispersed further around Port Louis and the main island in the Seychelles, Mahé. Although many in Mauritius settled around other Chagossians, most of the social networks and village ties that had previously

Figure 8.1 Rita David in her home with box used to take personal belongings from Peros Banhos during deportation to Mauritius, 1972. Photo by author.

connected people were severely ruptured. Chagossians deported to the Seychelles were even more isolated, crowding into the homes of relatives or squatting on the land of others. Some families lived "*anba lakaz,*" or underneath another family's stilt-elevated house. One family lived in a vacant cowshed, slowly transforming it into a formal house over many years.

In Mauritius, Chagossians found themselves on an overcrowded island that population experts were warning might soon become a "catastrophe" given one of the fastest growing populations in the world.[6] Novelist V.S.

Naipaul called the island the "overcrowded barracoon."[7] Conditions in Port Louis were particularly bad, according to British experts:

> The housing conditions in parts of Port Louis are worse than anything we saw in the villages [in rural Mauritius]. Hundreds of people are crowded into tin shacks hardly fit for animals. Not surprisingly, Tuberculosis and other diseases are very common in these slums, and a large proportion of the families depend on the help, regular and irregular, of the Public Assistance Department. Urban rents are relatively high and there is a serious shortage of housing in the towns; a situation made worse by the cyclone damage in 1960.[8]

Although by most accounts health in Chagos was "if anything somewhat better than in Mauritius,"[9] soon after their arrival, many Chagossians began to fall ill and die. A survey conducted by a support group documented "an impressive number of cases where Ilois have found death after having landed in Mauritius, i.e. from one to 12 months' stay." The dead totalled at least 44 by 1975 "because of unhappiness, poverty and lack of medical care."[10] Among them were:

Bertin Cassambeu: Dead through illness, distress.

Eliezer Louis: Had gone to Rogers [shipping company] so as to return to Diego. When he failed, had much grief and died.

Ito Mandarin: Died after landing of grief and poverty.

Victorrien, Michel, Vivil, and Sabine Rabrune: Had no property. Were abandoned by everybody. Died in disgrace.

Willy Thomas: Died in poverty and of grief.

Daisy Volfrin: No food for three days, obtained Rs3 and no more as Public assistance. Died through poverty.[11]

At least eleven others were reported to have died by suicide. "According to an enquiry made with their parents and friends," the support group found, "the reasons behind these suicides are disgust of the life they have been living in Mauritius and of poverty: no roof, no job and uncared.

They were demoralized, and instead of living a depraved life, they found in death a remedy."

Among the suicides were Joseph France Veerapen Kistnasamy, born on Six Islands, who "burnt himself" two days before Christmas, 1972; Syde Laurique, who had "no job, no roof, drowned herself"; Elaine and Michele Mouza, who as "mother and child committed suicide"; and Leone Rangasamy, born in Peros Banhos, who "drowned herself because she was prevented from going back."[12]

Other deaths seem to have been the result of Chagossians' vulnerability to illnesses that were rare or unknown in Chagos.[13] By 1975, 28 children had died of influenza: "Adults and children died of the diphtheria against which Mauritians are automatically vaccinated," the *Manchester Guardian* wrote. "And the cultural shock of arriving in the teeming, humid, poorer quarters of Port Louis still takes its toll."[14]

At least fifteen more, in addition to Rita, were admitted for psychiatric treatment. They included one islander who "on the death of his child due to lack of food . . . burnt his wife and wanted to commit suicide." Another "was mentally affected" after having to admit his children to a convent when he was unable to support them. Another "lost his head" on the ship and "was admitted as soon as he landed."[15]

Amid their other problems, Chagossians faced a society beset by systemic unemployment and inter-ethnic tensions following gang violence and riots between Indo-Mauritian Muslims and Afro-Mauritians.[16] British officials had long acknowledged and anticipated the difficulty of finding employment, especially given the absence of a "copra industry into which they could be absorbed."[17] Following independence in 1968, Mauritius experienced sporadic outbreaks of communal violence. By the time of the last deportations from Diego Garcia in 1971, British officials were predicting a worsening of conditions, with unemployment leading to "outbreaks of disorder, perhaps comparable to those which in September 1970 led to appeals for British military assistance."[18]

With such high rates of unemployment, almost half of the islanders depended after their arrival, in whole or in part, on non-work income, including public welfare, the help of family and friends, charity, loans from moneylenders, and other sources.[19] By 1975, only around one-quarter of family heads in Mauritius had full-time work. Most of those who were employed at all were working in the lowest-paid jobs as dockers and stevedores, domestic workers, fisherfolk, and truck loaders.[20]

According to Madeley, by mid-1975, "at least 1 in 40 [Chagossians in Mauritius] had died of starvation and disease."[21] The support group's report describes how "The causes mostly are: unhappiness, non-adaptation of Ilois within the social framework of Mauritius, extreme poverty, particularly lack of food, house, job. Another cause of this mortality was family dispersion." The report concludes that "The main cause of the sufferings of the Ilois was the lack of proper plan to welcome them in Mauritius. There was also no rehabilitation programme for them."[22]

This conclusion is in fact exactly what forced displacement experts would predict for a population displaced against its will and finding no resettlement program upon arrival. Research aggregating findings from hundreds of forcibly displaced groups around the globe—pushed off their lands by dam construction, warfare, environmental disasters, and other causes—has come to an unambiguous conclusion: Absent proper resettlement programs and other preventative measures, involuntary displacement generally causes "the impoverishment of considerable numbers of people."[23]

"HE DIDN'T RESPOND"

It was 1973 and the middle of the night when Julien nudged Rita as they slept. "He nudged me. He told me the baby woke up," Rita remembered. Four years earlier, on July 4, 1969, she had given birth to a son Ivo, their only child born in Mauritius.

After rousing herself from an exhausted sleep and checking on Ivo, she returned and told Julien that he had a bottle and was fine. But "he didn't respond. I didn't realize that he was sick. I said to him, 'I'm speaking and you, you aren't responding.'"

When Julien still didn't answer, Rita yelled for her uncle, who, with his wife, was living in the other room. When he came and looked at Julien, he knew right away that he was sick. "His arm, his hand, his foot, it was all dead," paralyzed. They rushed him to the hospital. "He stayed a month, a month and fifteen days in the hospital. . . . It went on, and on, and on, until he died. He had *sagren*, David. *Sagren* is what he had.

"You know, he saw his children, every day they went without food. He didn't have a job that he could work to be able to give them food. That's what made him sick. He wasn't used to life like that, you understand? Oh la la."

Pointing to the gendered impact of forced displacement, Rita added, "What happened to me—how can I say it—I wasn't able to bear it. But my husband, he was able to bear it even less than I was, because a man—the load is supposed to be on him. He had six children to feed. How was he going to do it? He suffered a stroke."

FROM UNIVERSAL EMPLOYMENT TO STRUCTURAL DISADVANTAGE

The Mauritian economy that the Bancoults and other Chagossians encountered during the late 1960s and early 1970s was undergoing massive transformations. Since the island's permanent settlement in the eighteenth century, the economy and life of Mauritius had been dominated by sugar. By the twentieth century, Mauritius was the epitome of a colonial monocrop economy, dependent on the fluctuations of the sugar market and powerbrokers in England. When Chagossians began arriving, Mauritius's population growth, which ranked among the highest in the world, meant that increasing numbers of working-age Mauritians were entering a labor market dominated by a sugar cane sector unable to absorb additional workers.[24]

In 1970, following examples in Hong Kong, Puerto Rico, Taiwan, and Jamaica, the Mauritian Government began attempts to diversify its economy with the establishment of an export processing zone (EPZ) designed to lure foreign investment and create jobs in the production of cheap exports. Spurred by tax breaks, investment from Hong Kong and elsewhere, and loopholes in U.S. and European garment quotas, EPZ factories and employment boomed over the second half of the 1970s and the 1980s, in what some have described as one of the world's few examples of an EPZ success strategy; we shall see how limited this success was for some in Mauritius, contrary to this popular narrative.

Beginning in the 1970s, Mauritius further diversified its economy with a major expansion of its tourist industry. While sugar cane remained a dominant part of the economy, the two new sectors grew, largely on the basis of Mauritius's supply of cheap, relatively well-educated female labor. (In recent years, the government has attempted to diversify the economy again, encouraging "offshore" foreign financial investment, higher-end export development, and information-based technology industries, following the Indian model.)[25]

Over the same period, the economy of the Seychelles underwent a similar transformation. Prior to the 1970s, the Seychelles had an even more stagnant colonial economy dependent on a handful of globally insignificant agricultural exports like cinnamon. Unemployment was "even worse than that in Mauritius," reaching as high as 27.5 percent.[26] In 1971, the

Seychelles opened its first international airport, built, as we have seen, by the United Kingdom as compensation for taking three island groups for the BIOT. Weekly tourist arrivals jumped from numbers in the tens to numbers in the thousands; the airport's opening allowed the explosion of a tourism industry that continues to drive the Seychelles economy to this day. (More recently, the Seychelles has tried to develop its substantial fishing resources and to become, like Mauritius, a center for offshore finance and high-tech services, while continuing to expand its tourism industry.)[27]

Although the economic booms in Mauritius and the Seychelles have made both nations more economically prosperous on a per capita basis than almost any other nations in all of Africa, Chagossians for the most part have not shared in this prosperity. The experience of expulsion has left the Bancoults and others structurally disadvantaged in Mauritius and the Seychelles in a variety of ways that has largely prevented their benefiting from wider economic prosperity.

Perhaps most importantly, Chagossians arrived in Mauritius and the Seychelles before the major economic changes were underway or before they had taken hold. They arrived in one country, Mauritius, that had a sugar cane monocrop economy unable to absorb additional workers and in another, the Seychelles, described by anthropologists Burton and Marion Benedict as a "rundown plantation," with even higher unemployment than Mauritius.[28] And they arrived, for the most part, with few employable skills. Mauritius had no copra industry (except for a small one in its dependency Agalega, where a few Chagossians relocated). Though copra had been the main export in the Seychelles since the 1840s, the industry was diminishing rapidly in the period when the islanders arrived (overall agricultural employment declined 10 percent from 1971 to 1977, by which point just 2.8 percent of households were earning their primary income from farming).[29]

Some of the other skills the islanders brought with them were also rendered economically useless. The talents of Chagossian marine carpenters and boat builders were of little commercial use in countries where wood-based boat construction was nearly obsolete. Chagossians' fishing skills were relatively—but only relatively—more useful after the expulsion, and fishing has remained a source of employment for some to this day. A 1975 article illustrated some of the difficulty in trying to make a living from fishing in Mauritius: "Michel tried to become a fisherman when exiled, but the local [small-scale] fishermen, themselves unable to compete with the new fishing fleets with refrigerated holds, do not welcome further competition."[30]

With such competition, earning a profitable living in the fishing in-dustry in Mauritius (and to a lesser extent in the Seychelles) increasingly meant working for the long-distance fleets that cruise away from Mauri-tius for several months at a time. Employment on these ships thus resulted in further (temporary) displacement and the separation of families for sig-nificant parts of each year. One man, for example, left his family every year for six months at a time to work on a fishing boat, returning to work in temporary jobs for the rest of the year, mostly in construction.

Two of the most economically successful Chagossians who now are among the rare few to have secure, unionized jobs at the port of the Mau-ritian capital gained their starts at relative prosperity by finding jobs in the merchant marine. This came at the cost of separation from their fami-lies for far longer periods, lasting years at a time. One said he "sacrificed" eleven or twelve years of his life away from his parents, sending a portion of every paycheck back to them in Mauritius. As displacement expert Ranjit Nayak explains of many displaced peoples, "Certain occupations . . . may involve further expulsion. These occupations are taken . . . not by choice, but because of compulsion to earn their livelihood."[31]

The conventional, and idealized, view of the economic boom in Mauri-tius is that the nation achieved full employment by the late 1980s. Though unemployment decreased significantly as a result of the growth in EPZ and tourist industry employment, unemployment and underemployment have remained problems. For many poor Mauritians, and especially for Chagossians, moving from unstable, insecure jobs to stable employment has proved impossible.[32] Even near the height of Mauritian employment growth, in 1986, more than 30 percent of the labor force was working in the informal sector.[33] In short, most Chagossians joined other Afro-Mauri-tians making up a largely invisible army of low-wage, easily hired and fired workers upon which the Mauritian economy continues to depend. "While Mauritius made remarkable economic progress in the 1980s and a major-ity of Mauritians benefited from the island's development," anthropologist Rosabelle Boswell explains, "a significant heterogeneous [Afro-Mauritian] minority of Mauritians, known locally as Creoles, have not profited from Mauriti[an] economic success."[34]

A 1980 survey found 85.8 percent of male Chagossians underemployed and 46.3 percent of women completely unemployed. "The economic situ-ation of the Ilois community," observed a social worker, was (and we shall see, is) characterized "by low wages, unemployment, [and] underemploy-ment" for people with skills still ill suited for the Mauritian labor market.[35] Another 1981 survey showed a male unemployment rate of 41 percent and female unemployment at 58 percent. Most of the few families who had "satisfactorily remunerated jobs" were among a relatively small cohort who arrived in Mauritius prior to 1960 and married Mauritians.[36]

Not surprisingly, some turned to theft, prostitution, and illegal drug sales.[37] When the Chagos Refugees Group surveyed nearly the entire Chagossian population in Mauritius in 2001, 38 were in prison, yielding an adult incarceration rate easily surpassing the U.S. rate of 1 in 100, which ranks highest in the world.[38]

Given their employment difficulties and having little to no savings from Chagos, many quickly became indebted to local loan sharks to pay rent and other basic living expenses. Others ran up debts to the owners of small neighborhood grocery stores charging often equally exorbitant interest rates.[39] Relatively unfamiliar with interest and the Mauritian economy when they first arrived, the Chagossians were particularly vulnerable to exploitation. As social worker Francoise Botte writes, "even the shopkeeper cheated them."[40] Since the economic boom of the 1980s, buying furniture, electronics, and other household items from department stores with similarly high-interest credit has become a widespread phenomenon among the poor of Mauritius.[41] Many Chagossians are active participants in this kind of indebtedness, reflecting the multiplication of generally unfulfilled materialistic desires in nations enjoying widespread but unequal economic growth.[42]

As forced displacement expert Michael Cernea and others have shown among other displaced populations,[43] downward mobility was pronounced for the islanders: They were displaced from a society where they enjoyed lives of structural security, where they and their ancestors had worked and lived for generations with universal, nearly guaranteed employment, food, income, housing, health care, education, and other necessities of life, to societies where they were in positions of structural insecurity and marginalization in increasingly competitive economies, where the skills they possessed were generally not in demand, where formal education (which most did not have) was increasingly important to securing employment, and where, as we shall see, most found themselves lumped into dark-skinned "Creole" groups facing employment discrimination in rigid social hierarchies allowing little socioeconomic mobility.

CHAPTER 9

DEATH AND DOUBLE DISCRIMINATION

"I'm telling you, Mauritians, when they, how can I say it. They found out that you were Ilois, they laughed at you. They said things like, 'You walk barefoot!' if you didn't have flip-flops. What can you do, David? You can't steal from someone when you family is living in *mizer*," said Rita.

"At my children's school, everyone said, 'He's a little Ilois! A little Ilois!' My children came and told me this," she continued. "I said, 'Leave them be, leave them be. Let them talk. You don't need to say anything.' Do you understand? My children went to school, they didn't even have a little tea" to drink. "They didn't have anything."

THE BOTTOM OF THE BOTTOM

Arriving in Mauritius and the Seychelles, islanders like Rita found themselves in positions vulnerable to ethnic and racial discrimination, as Chagossians and as Afro-Mauritians. Their arrival at times of heightened social tensions was noted with considerable anxiety by many of their hosts sensitive to new economic competition. During the first years in Mauritius, the word "Ilois" shifted from a term of self-identification to a term of insult, pronounced derisively by some Mauritians *ZZZEEL-wah*.[1] As anthropologist Iain Walker noted, many Mauritians began to use the term to describe any person "behaving in an antisocial or immoral fashion."[2] In the Seychelles, Chagossians heard curses of "*Anara!*" a word suggesting they had no identity, that they were soulless, uncivilized pagans, and that as a people, they were the lowest of the low. Others in both nations were called *sovaz*—savage—and *bet*—stupid. Many heard people shout, "Go back to the islands!"[3]

Francine Volfrin, who was removed from Diego Garcia and then Peros Banhos as a teenager in the 1970s, remembered walking to school from their home in the Seychelles, a shack on a relative's land, with neighbors throwing apricots fallen from the trees at her and her siblings. Some spit on them. The neighbors were very mean and cruel, she said. Some would say she and her family had not been vaccinated and would make them sick. (This was a common insult aimed at the islanders. If they had not previously been vaccinated, they were vaccinated upon arrival in the Seychelles. And indeed, evidence points to the opposite of the insult's accusation: Living in the Seychelles and Mauritius has actually made many Chagossians sick.)

Discrimination extended beyond verbal abuse. Employment discrimination was common by Mauritian "employers who favor local Mauritians."[4] In the Seychelles, discriminatory treatment began with the housing of the islanders in a local prison, while Moulinie & Co. "staff" stayed in hotels.[5] This discrimination compounded difficulties Chagossians had in finding jobs because they lacked the social connections important to finding work in these small island societies.

Desperate to find work and earn money after their arrival, many used "intermediaries" to connect them with employers and jobs. When they were to be paid, the intermediaries took most of their salaries. Many intermediaries and employers also appear to have preyed upon Chagossians' innumeracy and relative inexperience with cash. Botte explains how the exploitation worked, particularly against women: "These 'intermediaries' explained to the employers that these Ilois women are not used to money and some money could be given to the intermediaries from the salary of that poor maid-servant or washerwoman. These Mauritian employers preferred to engage the Ilois women because [they] did not know about labour law and the employers had only to exchange a Rs10 note into many coins to make the employees believe that it was much money." Over time, women realized that they were being cheated and became more assertive with Mauritian employers.[6]

In Mauritius, and to a lesser extent in the Seychelles, Chagossians entered an environment of long-standing racism and discrimination against people of mostly or entirely African descent, known locally as Creoles. In Mauritius, bigotry and prejudice against Afro-Mauritians has been unabated since Franco-Mauritians began importing enslaved African peoples to the island. Bigotry increased with the post-emancipation introduction of indentured laborers from India, soon to make up the majority of Mauritius's population and against whom Afro-Mauritians were pitted by the "white" ruling class. Since the nineteenth century, people of French and

British descent have remained at the top of the social, political, and economic hierarchies; people of mixed and Indian ancestry have occupied a middle stratum; Afro-Mauritian Creoles have remained primarily working class, generally at the bottom of the hierarchies.[7]

In the Seychelles, where the population is a more homogeneous collection of people of mostly mixed African and European descent, there is somewhat less discrimination against people of recognizable African ancestry (in part because almost all Seychellois have at least some [recent*] African ancestry). Still, high social and economic status in the Seychelles remains closely linked to lightly pigmented skin and European ancestry. Discrimination is prevalent against those with the darkest skin.[8]

Being primarily of African or mixed African and Indian descent, almost all Chagossians in Mauritius have been perceived socially as part of the Afro-Mauritian Creole community, the community that has benefited least from Mauritian economic success. Increasingly in Mauritius, scholars and others recognize that Afro-Mauritians, marked as they are by their socially defined race, class, and segregated residential geography, have been excluded from the economic prosperity of the nation as a whole.[9] Arriving in a setting where they were lumped with this minority group, the islanders have faced additional barriers to economic success and social acceptance.

Even worse, Chagossians are thought to occupy a subset of Afro-Mauritian Creoles known as *ti-kreol* (literally, "little Creole"), who by definition are found in the most marginal and lowest-paying occupations. This group resides at the opposite end of the socioeconomic spectrum from the *grand blanc* or rich white ruling class. Anthropologist Thomas H. Eriksen describes in stark and commonly held racist terms the place in the national hierarchy of the ti-kreol: They are, "perhaps [the] most stigmatized category of people in Mauritius; that is, the segments of Creoles . . . comprising fishermen, dockers, unskilled workers and artisans." Eriksen adds, "As an ethnic category, the 'ti-kreol' are known by outsiders as lazy, backward and stupid people, as being too close to nature and resembling Africans in a not particularly flattering fashion."[10] With the ti-kreol at the bottom of Mauritian society, Chagossians are widely considered to reside, along with people from the small Mauritian dependency of Rodrigues, at the bottom of the ti-kreol—the bottom of the bottom.[11]

And these hierarchies are not just a matter of perception. They reproduce themselves in ways that have maintained Mauritius and the Seychelles

---

* I note the qualification in passing to point out that the ancestors of all humans come from Africa.

as relatively rigid hierarchical societies organized around class and ethno-racial stratification.[12]

Chagossians' inability to benefit from national macroeconomic growth thus stems in part from structural and individual discrimination and exclusion faced by Chagossians, both as Afro-Mauritians and specifically as Chagossians. Because they belong to two stigmatized groups, the discrimination they have faced often involves a complex array of overlapping prejudice, bigotry, and systemic marginalization. The expulsion thus put the islanders in a position of structural disadvantage in part by making them vulnerable to a kind of double discrimination in ethnically hierarchical societies.

For many, however, the most painful and symbolic form of discrimination and exclusion has been that of being barred from jobs on the Diego Garcia base. Since the 1980s, the base has employed nonmilitary service workers who are neither U.S. nor U.K. citizens, mostly from the Philippines, Sri Lanka, and Mauritius. When Chagossians (men for the most part) have applied for these jobs at recruitment offices in Mauritius, they have been repeatedly rejected. Since the expulsion, no one born in Chagos or the child of someone born in Chagos has ever worked on Diego Garcia. "It has been stipulated that no Ilois," two Indian Ocean scholars explain, "are to be allowed to go." When asked about employing Chagossians, a Mauritian recruiter told *60 Minutes* in a June 2003 broadcast, "Definitely no. . . . I was given instructions to be careful. They don't want any kind of claim or demonstration."[13] (Since 2006, a few Chagossian men have been allowed to work on the base.)

Jacques Victor, who was born on Diego Garcia, described going three times to apply for jobs and being rejected each time. As soon as they saw that he was born on Diego, he said, they turned him away. "They judge us" before even knowing us, Mr. Victor said, shifting to address the whole of his experience in exile. *It's as if life is a prison for us here in Mauritius—there's a lot of discrimination.*[14]

"Beaucoup, beaucoup discrimination. Beaucoup," he said, switching into French. Lots, lots of discrimination. Lots.

In Peros Banhos, Alex Bancoult and his siblings went to the small one-room schoolhouse on Corner Island. In Mauritius, he started school but didn't stay long. He left to earn money for the family, taking a job in a cologne factory making Rs9 a week. "He didn't go" to school for long, "but he was very clever," Rita recalled sadly.

Rita's only surviving daughter, Mimose, went to work at fourteen to earn money for the family. Mimose worked for a Mauritian family miles away as a domestic servant and cook. For years, she worked for the family, going stretches of three to four months without seeing her mother and siblings. It was very painful to leave her family, she said. But she had no choice because the family was poor and needed her income. "Plore," Mimose said. I cried. "Plore, plore, plore. . . ." I cried, I cried, I cried.

Never given a bed to sleep on, Mimose had to sleep on a mat under a flight of stairs. Frequently, the husband in the family abused her. One day she finally walked out of the house and returned to her mother. She told her she was ill and never told her family what had happened with the Mauritians.

"It's terrible what we experienced, do you understand?" Rita told me. "My children went to school without having flip-flops. My children went to school without having a book. Only Olivier persisted in always going" to school.

The youngest of Rita's sons born in Chagos, Louis Olivier stayed in school longer than his siblings. But when it came time to take exams at the end of high school, Rita didn't have the money for his exam fees. Some charitable Mauritians had been helping to pay for Olivier's after-school tutoring (essentially mandatory for educational success and a *de facto* part of the country's unequal educational system usually available only to the middle and upper classes). "I wasn't able to go and ask them again for the money to pay for his fees," Rita said.

Nor were Alex's Rs9 a week and Rita's jobs as a maid enough to pay the fees. So, Rita recounted, Olivier "went to take the exam. He went to take it—he passed. He didn't get a certificate because he didn't deposit the money."

BARRIERS AT SCHOOL

The structural disadvantage the islanders faced was compounded by the low levels of education they brought from Chagos and systematic educational disadvantage in exile (particularly in Mauritius). In Chagos, low levels of formal education and illiteracy were irrelevant to performing the vast majority of jobs. In Mauritius and the Seychelles, having little formal education and being illiterate, or nearly so, have been significant and increasing impediments to securing jobs and to achieving upward job mobility. Most of the new employment created in the two nations since the

1970s (i.e., in the EPZ and tourist sectors) has demanded at least some educational background. At the height of the EPZ boom in Mauritius, remember, it was "the availability of cheap, *literate and skilled* labour," in addition to financial incentives and infrastructure, that encouraged "a massive flow of foreign direct investment."[15] By contrast to relatively high levels of education in Mauritius, almost all Chagossians who were adults at the time of the expulsion left Chagos illiterate: Schools only opened in the archipelago in the 1950s, so by 1975, just 2 percent of adults could read "a little."[16]

Similarly, most of those who left Chagos as children arrived with a low-quality formal education that had worsened in the last years in Chagos. With their school interrupted, at least briefly, by the expulsion, children were in some cases barred access to Mauritian schools or had significant difficulty enrolling. Many school-age adolescents, like Rita's children Alex, Mimose, and Eddy, often had to curtail schooling to find jobs and help their families financially. By 1975, 27 percent of school-age children were not in school.[17] On the job market, even outside the EPZ and tourist sectors, Chagossians thus competed for jobs with Mauritians and Seychellois who almost always had more formal education than they had.

Among those who entered school, many experienced discrimination and verbal abuse from teachers and classmates. If children managed to finish primary school without having dropped out for work, family, or academic reasons, most could not afford secondary school, which only became "free" in Mauritius in 1976 (compulsory book, uniform, exam, transportation, and other fees make it far from free). Universal free secondary school in the Seychelles only became available in 1981.

Those children who have attended school in Mauritius have found themselves structurally disadvantaged in another important way: Living for the most part in the poorest areas of Mauritius, they have attended the worst schools with the worst teachers in a school system that has been shown to discriminate systematically against poor students.[18] Growing up with illiterate parents, moreover, meant they had little help with their studies.

I AM ALONE ON THE EARTH

I am very unhappy
There's no one anymore
To console me.

The bird sings for me
The bird cries for me
The bird sings for me
The bird cries for me.

I left my country
I left my little island
I left my family
I also left my heart.

—*Song composed and sung by Mimose Bancoult Furcy, posted on the office
wall of the Chagos Refugees Group, 2004*[19]

EXCLUDED, POWERLESS, CLOSETED

On the wall of their home on Diego Garcia, Marie Ange Pauline's family
had a photograph of the Queen of England. Arriving in the Seychelles as a
young girl she remembered being confused about her and her family's nationality. *Are we British? Are we Mauritian?* she wondered. "What are we?"
she and others, in Mauritius and the Seychelles, asked, as a people without
a country, without a homeland, without their "*ter natal*"—natal land.

Many like Marie Ange describe feeling excluded and isolated from
mainstream life in exile. As several in Mauritius put it, Chagossians are
"eksklu de lavi moris." They are excluded from Mauritian life.

Some of the sense of exclusion in Mauritius stems from feeling that
they are literally not part of the nation. Such feelings are rooted in the history surrounding Mauritian independence and the bargain by which the
"father of the nation," Sir Seewoosagur Ramgoolam, is understood to have
"sold" Chagos—and the Chagossians—to the British in exchange for independence. As a result, many feel that Mauritius is, as they say, "not a nation
for them." Like many Afro-Mauritians, many feel that Mauritius is "for the
Indians" or "for the Hindus," the majority ethnic and religious groups. The
nation is not, they believe, "for the Creoles," and it is especially not "for
Chagossians." The exclusion is double: first, as Chagossians who gave up
their homeland so the rest of Mauritius could have its independence, and
second, as people identified with the most marginalized elements of the
minority Afro-Mauritian Creole population.

In the Seychelles, similar feelings of exclusion are widespread. Unlike
Chagossians in Mauritius, who gained citizenship upon its independence,

those in the Seychelles were not granted automatic citizenship. Many lived in the country for decades as noncitizens and eventually had to buy citizenship. Again this literal form of exclusion combines with widespread feelings of being discriminated against as "foreigners" in access to jobs, housing, schooling, and other opportunities. Many point to their national identity cards in particular as a source of job and other discrimination: One of the eleven digits in the national identification number indicates a holder's place of birth. A "1" indicates the holder is from the capital, Victoria; "2" means you're from South Mahé; "3," from Praslin. The children of citizens born outside of the country and those naturalized, like many Chagossians in the Seychelles, carry the unusual numbers "5" and "6" respectively.[20]

Many in both countries also speak of never feeling "at home." And many non-Chagossians have treated them this way, as a people apart. Anthropologist Elizabeth Colson describes how home and a familiar environment generally provide a refuge that is crucial to people's sense of self and identity. Destroy people's home, take away their familiar environment, and people are likely to suffer, both materially and psychologically, becoming disoriented and insecure.[21]

While there is no automatic connection between home and psychological disorder among displaced peoples,[22] most Chagossians suffer painful feelings of homelessness and alienation. Marie Ange said she sometimes thinks about what life would be like if they had not been removed. *Maybe Diego would be like Seychelles is now,* she said, referring to the ways in which the Seychelles has developed economically since she arrived in 1972.[23]

I would be more at ease there, she continued. I've never felt comfortable here in Seychelles. We are treated as foreigners in Seychelles and in Seychelles they don't like foreigners. We have always been treated as foreigners here.

Like other victimized peoples and individuals, many have internalized blame for the expulsion, questioning how they could have allowed themselves to be exiled. Many in both the first and second generations have been left asking why the expulsion happened, why they were victimized, and why they cannot live in their homeland.

Why didn't we resist? Marie Ange often asks herself. Even though she remembers Chagossians on Diego Garcia being scared of U.S. military forces arriving on the island with their boats, planes, and heavy equipment, even though she remembers fearing they might be bombed if they did resist, even though she remembers her father protesting the removals, she can't get the question out of her head: *Why did we let it happen to us?*

Anthropologist Thayer Scudder explains that to have been moved against one's will is to have suffered a "terrible defeat." It is "hard to imagine a more dramatic way to illustrate impotence than to forcibly eject people from a preferred habitat against their will."[24] Colson likewise holds that expulsion causes increased dependence and, as importantly, an awareness among displacees of this increased dependence. Involuntary displacement, she says, is a clear demonstration to a group and its members that they have lost control over their own destiny, that they are literally powerless.[25]

Among women, this powerlessness has sadly expressed itself in a vulnerability to sexual assault and abuse. Josiane Selmour's Mauritian husband beat her for years until she finally went to the police and took him to court (which eventually fined him). For Josiane, abuse stems from the fact that *Mauritians don't like Chagossians.* She explained, Mauritians call Chagossians *"sovaz"* [savages] and say, *"Alle Zilwa!"* [Go away Ilois!]. Husbands too. . . . they take advantage of Chagossian women. They abuse them, they call them names, because Chagossian women are powerless.

Other women have echoed these feelings. Many have reported experiencing abuse from their husbands or domestic partners (especially from non-Chagossian men), as well as physical and sexual abuse at work. Some have described verbally or physically abusive relationships between Chagossian spouses as a result of stress and pressures in the home. When the islanders first arrived, some Mauritian public welfare officers raped or sexually abused Chagossian women, even suggesting that friends do the same: "Some Mauritian men who pretended to help," Botte writes, "were looking for other benefits."[26] Still, it's important to note that Josiane was able to go to the police and take her husband to court. And as we shall see, in political organizing, where women play a dominant role, they have proven themselves to be far from powerless.

Like other victims, many have also felt considerable shame. Some of this shame derives from the material poverty and discrimination they have faced. Many tell of the shame they felt attending school (or, like Rita, as parents sending children to school) barefoot when their classmates wore shoes. Marie Ange's sister Francine Volfrin felt deeply ashamed that her family couldn't afford fancy clothing to wear to church like other children; instead they wore secondhand and tattered clothing.

As a result of these and other accumulated forms of abuse, discrimination, and negative stereotyping, many have concealed their identity as Chagossians. While some, especially those who have been heavily involved in political organizing, have maintained a strong sense of Chagossian identity, many young people in particular have grown up with little sense of this identity at all.

Some stress too that they have been prevented from full cultural expression, and thus self-identification, as they have felt forced to adapt to the cultures of Mauritius or the Seychelles, especially in their styles of dance, music, and cuisine. Many describe having hidden their identity by concealing their accents and changing their linguistic practices shortly after arrival. While their Chagos Kreol is related to and mutually intelligible with Mauritian Kreol and Seselwa (Seychellois Kreol), Chagos Kreol is distinguishable in some of its vocabulary and the accent of its speakers. Islanders described to me trying consciously to change their accent. One man explained that people cannot express themselves as they would like: Chagossians have to change their language and their accent, he said. *Chagossians have to think twice every time they start to speak.*

For years after arriving in the Seychelles, Marie Ange hid her identity for fear of being deported by the government in a one-party state where she held no citizenship. For years she felt ashamed to identify herself as a Chagossian in school when teachers asked where she was born. For years, while an active protest movement was growing in Mauritius, she and others in the Seychelles felt powerless to argue for their rights in the one-party state. Finally in the late 1990s (after the start of a multiparty democracy), Marie Ange decided that she was no longer going to hide her identity. She described this as her "coming out." Although Marie Ange did not intend to compare her experience to that of nonheterosexuals in heterosexist societies, the parallels are strong. Like many who do not conform to heterosexual norms, Marie Ange experienced discrimination, stigmatization, and fear, giving her good reason to keep her identity secret.

COMPENSATION

In 1978 and again between 1982 and 1985, most Chagossians in Mauritius received financial and land compensation as a result of their expulsion. No one in the Seychelles received compensation. The 1978 compensation was payment from the £650,000 transferred by the British Government in 1972 to the Mauritian Government to resettle the islanders. Although when the Mauritian Government surveyed them, a majority requested that compensation come in the form of housing, eligible adult Chagossians received only cash payments of around $1,210 and around $200 for children 18 and under.[27]

Between 1982 and 1985, many but not all Chagossians in Mauritius received land and cash payments totaling around $4,620 for adults (around

Figure 9.1 "Try It and You're Stuck" (Mauritian Kreol proverb), Baie du Tombeau, Mauritius, 2002. Photo by author.

$8,750 in 2004 dollars). In part the cash was to pay for the government's construction of a home or to build one's own home. Since the expulsion, housing had been one of the islanders' most pressing problems, with most still living in "ramshackle houses and in dire conditions": By the early 1980s, more than 80 percent were living in two- or three-room "hovels," with 27 percent of households doubling up with other families.[28] Those who opted to accept land and housing received small plots and two-room concrete-block houses built by the Mauritian Government in what became known as a *Cité Ilois* in either the impoverished neighborhood of Baie du Tombeau or Port Louis's brothel district Pointe aux Sables. Others who opted not to receive these houses could use their compensation money to purchase new housing or to improve preexisting homes.

Many instead used both rounds of compensation and the sale of land and houses to pay off substantial debts. Unscrupulous brokers (Chagossians, among them, according to some) enabled many of the real estate sales, which are widely seen as having significantly undervalued the properties. Some real estate brokers preyed upon islanders desperate for cash, buying at low prices and quickly flipping the properties. Others offered the new homeowners loans, forcing them to put their property up as collateral and then charging high rates of interest; when they were unable to repay the loans, the lenders seized the property.

After leaving school for his job in a cologne factory, Alex eventually found work as a stevedore at the docks in Port Louis's main harbor. "But then the docks fired him," Rita said, and "he had no work." Before long, she recounted, "he wasn't working . . . *sagren* . . . he drank." In 1990, at the age of 38, Alex died, having ruined his body with alcohol and drugs, leaving behind a wife and five boys under the age of 15.

"The same as with Eddy," Rita said of one of her other sons. One day he "told me he was going out, that he was going to look for work. He went two days and he didn't come back—I was very worried and went looking all over for him. It was then that his friends from the streets drove him into drugs."

Eddy grew addicted to heroin and soon "he became like a bone," Rita said. He was a "skeleton. His insides were completely finished."

When Eddy died, Rita had to take a Rs7,000 loan to pay for the burial. Like other Chagossians she went to a local "*madam kredi*"—a money-lender who took Rita's government-issued pension card, withdrawing her monthly pension to collect the Rs7,000 and interest.

When Rénault died at 11 for reasons still mysterious to the family after selling water and begging for money at the cemetery, Rita buried him in the clothes he wore for his First Communion. "The same clothes, I got them out. The same clothes, I put on him," she said.

"I have suffered so much, David, here in Mauritius. I am telling you look at how many—three sons, one daughter, and my husband. Five people have died in my arms. It's not easy. . . . Not easy. It's not easy, David."

CHAPTER 10

DYING OF *SAGREN*

"*Sagren*, that's to say, it's *sagren* for his country. Where he came from, he didn't experience *mizer* like we were experiencing here. He was seeing it in his eyes, *laba*.* His children were going without, were going without food. They didn't have anything," Rita said of Julien's death. "And so he got so, so many worries, do you understand? That's *sagren*. Many people have died like that. You know, David?"

"Died from—" I started to ask, wanting to understand more about how people could die from *sagren*.

"*Sagren*! Yes! When one has *sagren* in your heart, it eats at you. No doctor, no one will be able to heal you! If you have a *sagren*, if you, even—you can't get it out. That's to say, David—*Ayo*! What can you do? Let it go—something that came on like that. There are many people that can't bear it."

"Mmm," I uttered, trying to take in what she was saying.

"Yes. Do you understand? Then, it goes, it goes, until at the end, you don't want to eat, you don't want anything. Nothing. You don't want it. . . . There's nothing that you do, that you have that's good. You've withdrawn from the world completely and entered into a state of *sagren*."

"Have you experienced *sagren*?" I asked.

"Yes. *Sagren*. Yes," Rita replied slowly.

"It's very hard," I said.

"Do you understand? You have *sagren* when in your country you haven't experienced things like this. Here you're finding food in the trashcan."

How do we understand Julien's dying of *sagren*, of profound sorrow? How do we understand the deaths of others that Chagossians likewise attribute

---

* Remember that Chagossians need only say *laba*, meaning "out there," to tell each other they are talking about Chagos.

to *sagren*? And how do we understand the islanders' comparisons of an almost disease-free, healthy life in Chagos to one filled with sickness and death in Mauritius and the Seychelles? And how are we to make sense of the comparisons people make between an idyllic life in Chagos and what Rita and others call the "hell" of exile?

To start, we must return to neighborhoods like Cassis and Pointe aux Sables where Chagossians have lived since the time when Rita and Julien arrived in Mauritius. Rita now lives in the *Cité Ilois*, the Ilois Plot, in Pointe aux Sables, where she received her small concrete block house and some land from the compensation provided in the 1980s. Her yard there is hedged in by a wall nailed together out of corrugated iron and wood. Three dogs patrol the inside, chained to a line allowing them to roam back and forth, barking at passersby. On one side of the house stand several trees: three mango, a bred murum, and two coconut—only one produces nuts. On the other side, Rita has allowed her youngest son Ivo to build a smaller three-room metal-sheeted home for his wife and two sons; they couldn't afford to buy a place of their own. Hanging on the wall inside her house, Rita proudly displays a sun-bleached poster of a fruit and vegetable still life—pineapple, broccoli, melons, grapes, green-hued oranges. Another print of a dew-spotted rose hangs nearby, alongside a poster of a coconut tree on a beach in the Seychelles. Rita told me it reminds her of beaches in Peros.

Housing conditions have improved to some extent for those like Rita who received and kept their compensation homes. For most who didn't get a home or had to sell theirs, however, conditions remain poor. A 1997 WHO-funded report described how housing varies "between the decent"—that is, compensation housing—"and the flimsy"—homes like those occupied since the earliest days in exile, usually built with a metal roof and walls of metal sheeting or perhaps some combination of wood and concrete block, with kitchen and sanitary facilities located outside the home and generally lacking running water and electricity.[1]

Even with the improvements some enjoyed when they obtained a concrete-block house, most still live in conditions that are among the worst in Mauritius and the Seychelles. Overcrowding remains a serious problem. Most are still concentrated in the poorest, least desirable, most disadvantaged, and most unhealthy neighborhoods. Many live with dangerous structural deficiencies and limited access to basic services: 40 percent are without indoor plumbing and more than one-quarter lack running water.[2] Generally housing problems are more critical for those in Mauritius than for those in the Seychelles, in line with wider national differences. In Mauritius, the islanders' housing conditions are broadly comparable to those found in the poor townships of South Africa.

Compounding their housing difficulties, most Chagossians still struggle to find work. At the time of my 2002–3 survey, just over a third (38.8 percent) of the able-bodied first generation and less than two-thirds (60.6 percent) of the second generation were working.[3] In many households, only a single adult had a job. Other households relied on multiple income earners, from teens working in factories to elderly women doing laundry for neighbors, to support a family.[4] Median monthly income was less than $2 a day: far below the median incomes for their Mauritian and Seychellois neighbors.[5]

Of those who are employed, many still have jobs at the bottom of the Mauritian pay scale, characterized by high job insecurity, temporary duration, and informal employment commitments. Chagossians are still primarily employed in manual labor: as dockers and stevedores in the shipping industry; as janitorial, domestic, and child care workers; as informal construction workers and bricklayers; as factory workers. Some find various piecework employment, often to supplement other jobs, including stitching shoes, assembling decorative furnishings, and weaving brooms from coconut palms.

In general, those born in Mauritius and the Seychelles or who left Chagos at a very young age seem to have been more successful in securing employment and better remunerated jobs than their elders. These groups have little if any memory of Chagos and experienced less disruption in their lives as a result of the expulsion (although I stress that this is a relative distinction). And in contrast to most of the first generation, which received little if any formal education in Mauritius or the Seychelles, this group has had at least some chance to benefit from the Mauritian and Seychellois education systems (however discriminatory they are).

In part because the group in the Seychelles is composed disproportionately of islanders who arrived in the first years of their lives, islanders in the Seychelles are, economically speaking, generally better off than their counterparts in Mauritius. While some are living in the most impoverished conditions in the Seychelles, significant numbers enjoy secure public sector employment as bureaucrats, teachers, and police officers. By contrast, the rare few that have government jobs or similarly stable employment in Mauritius are notable for having escaped the impoverishment facing the vast majority there.

The different economic outcomes in the two nations is a complicated matter that can only be understood with extensive comparative study. Some of the difference is surely attributable to higher standards of living enjoyed in the Seychelles (per capita GDP is roughly $7,500 higher), a better and more equitable education system, and lower levels of discrimination. At the same time, just as the relative economic success of some World War II–era Japanese-American internees has done little to negate their experiences of internment, any (relative) material comfort that *some* may have found in the Seychelles in no way negates other ways in which they have suffered and continue to face pain and discrimination.

Among many in both countries, in fact, there remains deep pessimism about their economic and employment prospects. The French aphorism, "Ceux qui sont riches seront toujours riches, ceux qui sont pauvres restent toujours pauvres"—the rich will always be rich; the poor will always be poor—is a kind of chorus in Mauritius among some young adult Chagossians.

I asked Jacques Victor, who was then working weekends as an informal clothing vendor, if he thought it would be possible to find a better paying job. "In Mauritius, no. In Mauritius, no," Mr. Victor responded in English—one of a very few islanders to speak at least some of the official national language, which is generally a marker of middle- or upper-class status. "Ilois have the qualifications," he explained, but Mauritian employers say, "'How can they have this kind of qualification?' They much prefer [us] lower than low. It's like that."

As we ended our conversation, I asked Mr. Victor if there was anything else he wanted to tell me. "I want to return to our land. Be there now—get our lives that we were living, yesterday," he said. "Maybe my children will get jobs."

SAGREN AS SYNECDOCHE

"It gave me such suffering, David, and to this day, I still have this suffering. In my heart, it's not at all gone. Not at all gone," Rita told me from her house in Pointe aux Sables. "Look at how many of my children have died. How can I explain it to you? If we were *laba*, Alex would be here, Eddy would be here, Rénault would be here. . . . Eddy died from drugs but *laba*, we didn't have them."

Rita continued, "They pulled us from there to come take us to hell. Drugs are ravaging people. The children aren't working, they're following friends to the side of having, to the side of having problems, understand? It's always the same, it's not easy."

"It's a very sad story," was all I could muster in response.

"There, in St. George's cemetery, I have three boys—three boys, two girls," she said. To the deaths of her own four children, Rita added the death of Alex's wife, who committed suicide in 2001, dousing herself with gasoline and setting herself afire. Their five boys—five of Rita's grandchildren—were left orphaned.

We return now to the deaths of Julien and others from *sagren* and the comparison of a disease-free, healthy life in Chagos to one of illness, drugs, and death in exile. Examining first the contrast between lives of health and lives of illness, we see that the islanders' diagnosis is an accurate one: The contrast they describe represents an accurate portrayal of changing health conditions before and after the expulsion. While Chagossian health was once better than that in Mauritius, it is now comparable to the low levels of health characterizing the poorest sectors of Mauritian society, a nation with one of the highest incidences of chronic disease in the world.[6]

The WHO-funded study found that Chagossians suffer from elevated levels of chronic colds, fevers, respiratory diseases, anemia, and transmissible diseases like tuberculosis, as well as problems with cardiovascular diseases, diabetes, hypertension, work accidents, and youth alcohol and tobacco abuse. The report found children and the elderly particularly vulnerable to disease, including water-borne diseases tied to poor hygiene and contaminated water supplies like infant diarrhea, hepatitis A, and intestinal parasites. The people also exhibited a large number of work accidents, most likely related to the physical labor and limited work protections many face.[7]

At the same time, the study found that Chagossians don't enjoy the same access to health care services as others in Mauritius because of their poverty, their limited knowledge of the health care system, and their limited confidence in both health care providers and the efficacy and quality of treatment.[8] Around 85 percent of the Chagossians that I surveyed reported needing more health care—more than any other reported social service need.[9]

Sandra Cheri is a Chagossian nurse and one of few people qualified to comment professionally on the state of Chagossian health (she is also one of the few islanders in Mauritius with a government or semiprofessional job). I asked Sandra about common health problems experienced by the islanders. She listed diarrhea and vomiting, gastroenteritis, fevers, and influenza—illnesses they share with people throughout Mauritius. But Sandra said Chagossians also suffer from a high incidence of diabetes and hypertension because of dietary changes experienced since arriving in Mauritius. In Chagos, she said, there was no stress and the food was different (fish even tasted better, she and others said). Nor was there hard alcohol, only wine and homemade brews like *baka* and *calou.*

In Mauritius, she said, there's rum and whiskey and "many, many Chagossians are alcoholics." She sees many at her hospital and in Cassis, where she finds them stumbling and drunk, shoeless and dirty along the road. Mauritians exploit many of them, Sandra added, knowing that they will work for a few rupees just to buy a Rs60 (around $2) bottle of rum.

Visibly intoxicated men are a common sight in Mauritius and the Seychelles, and most Chagossians attest to substance abuse as a serious problem in the community. In 2002 and 2003, we asked survey respondents if they needed help or treatment for an alcohol or drug problem, well aware that survey questions asking about substance abuse are renowned for underreporting actual use. The response was striking: One in every five volunteered having a problem. Less than two percent said they were receiving such treatment.[10]

"There wasn't sickness" like strokes or *sagren*, we remember Rita saying. "There wasn't that sickness. Nor diabetes, nor any such illness. What drugs?" she asked me rhetorically, having lost Alex and Eddy to drug and alcohol abuse. At worst, she said, "If by chance you got drunk" and fell asleep "and you went to get your money—your cash—you would find it untouched when you awoke. No one would take it. No one would steal anything from another Chagossian. This is what my husband remembered and pictured in his mind. Me too, I remember these things that I've said about us, David. My heart grows heavy when I say these things, understand?"

As Rita's words and the prevalence of substance abuse suggest, when people contrast a life filled with illnesses and drugs with a nearly disease-free life in Chagos, the comparison represents more than an accurate depiction of rising morbidity and declining health. The contrast also represents a commentary on and implicit critique of the expulsion. It represents a sign and recognition of the emotional and psychological damage the expulsion has caused.

"What must be heard" at the "emotional core" of stories of displacement, says psychiatrist Mindy Fullilove in the context of displacement caused by urban renewal in the United States, "is the howl of amputations, the anguish at calamity unassuaged, the fear of spiraling downward without cessation, and the rage at poverty imposed through repeated dispossession."[11]

For many Chagossians, the illnesses that they and their relatives and friends have experienced have come to represent all the difficulties of life in exile and the pain of being separated from their homeland. Illness, disease, and substance abuse have become metaphors, synecdoches—with one part representing the whole—for all the suffering of the expulsion.

EMBODIED ILLNESS

"So many troubles. My head went, went to a mental hospital. I already went before to a mental hospital, where I had shocks."

"Shocks?" I asked, fearing that Rita meant electroshock therapy.

"I had too many troubles."

"You got shocks?" I asked again.

"Yes."

"What happened?"

"The same, the same deal like before. I got the treatment. My children didn't have food in the house, and one by one they were dying like dead coconuts falling from the tree. So they gave me shocks."

When Chagossians like Rita describe people dying of *sagren*, they are not just speaking metaphorically. The Chagos Refugees Group, which represents the vast majority of the community in Mauritius, has an "Index of Deceased Chagossians" listing the names of Chagossians who have died in exile. For 396 of the deceased individuals, as of 2001, a cause of death was indicated. In 60 of these cases, the cause of death was listed as wholly or in part due to "sadness" or "homesickness."[12]

"The notion of *sagren* has an important place in the explanative system for illness," the WHO-funded study reports: *Sagren* "explains illness and even the deaths of members of the community." *Sagren* is "nostalgia for the Chagos islands. It is the profound sadness of facing the impossibility of being able to return to one's home in the archipelago." The WHO report cites the case of one elderly man who died after suffering from diabetes, hypertension, and paralysis for many years. Before his death he only left his home once every three months when an ambulance drove him to get treatment. After his death, one of his friends said he had died of *sagren*. "Knowing that he would never again return to the island of his birth, he had preferred to let himself die."[13]

Sagren is an example of what Fullilove has called the "root shock" of forced displacement.

> Root shock is the traumatic stress reaction to the destruction of all or part of one's emotional ecosystem. It has important parallels to the physiological shock experienced by a person who, as a result of injury, suddenly loses massive amounts of fluids. Such a blow threatens the whole body's ability to function. The nervous system attempts to compensate for the imbalance by cutting off circulation to the arms and legs. Suddenly the hands and feet will seem cold

and damp, the face pale, and the brow sweaty. This is an emergency state that can preserve the brain, the heart, and the other essential organs for only a brief period of time. If the fluids are not restored, the person will die. Shock is the fight for survival after a life-threatening blow to the body's internal balance.[14]

With other symptoms that include wasting and weakness, confusion and disorientation, sadness and depression, shaking and paralysis, often ultimately resulting in death, *sagren* also resembles the affliction of *nervos* found among many in the world, but especially among the poor and marginalized in the Mediterranean and Latin America. Medical anthropologist Nancy Scheper-Hughes has shown through work with the poor in northeast Brazil how nervos is far from a matter of somatization or malingering, at least as they are typically understood by medical professionals. Nervos is instead "a collective and embodied response" to poverty and hunger and to a corrupt, violent political system that colludes to entrap the poor in these conditions—what she calls everyday forms of violence.[15] The roots of such afflictions are not psychological, as those who administered Rita's electroshock therapy likely thought. The roots of such afflictions are social, political, and economic, with forms of violence like displacement becoming embodied by victims.

DYING OF *SAGREN*

As the sometimes fatal illnesses of root shock and nervos indicate, Chagossians are not alone in finding that forms of grief and sadness can cause death. "There is little doubt," Theodore Scudder and Elizabeth Colson explain, "that relocatees often believe that the elderly in particular are apt to die 'of a broken heart' following removal." Importantly, this belief appears to have medical support: "The evidence is highly suggestive" that sadness can cause death "for Egyptian and Sudanese Nubians . . . and the Yavapai. . . . Elderly persons forced into nursing homes or forcibly removed from one nursing home to another are reported to have high mortality rates in the period immediately succeeding the move."[16] Other research has shown that acute stress can bring on fatal heart spasms in people with otherwise healthy cardiac systems.[17] Among Hmong refugees in the United States who fled Laos in the 1970s, Sudden Unexpected Death Syndrome was the leading cause of death for years after their arrival. The syndrome is "triggered by cardiac failure, often during or after a bad dream. No one has been able to explain what produces the cardiac irregularity, although theories over the years have included potassium deficiency, thiamine deficiency, sleep apnea, depression, culture shock, and survivor guilt."[18]

In my own family, my grandmother, Tea Stiefel, reminded me recently how her mother, Elly Eichengruen, died of a broken heart. A German Jew who fled to the United States in 1939 just before the outbreak of World War II, Elly never recovered from the guilt she felt for sending her 13-year-old son, Erwin, to Amsterdam a year earlier, where he was ultimately deported to Auschwitz and murdered. After learning of his fate, Elly never talked about her son. In 1947 she had a major heart attack and spent six weeks in a hospital unable to move. For the next ten years she lived as an invalid under my grandmother's care until her death in 1957. When she died, her doctor said that she had died of a broken heart. "The guilt she carried with her ultimately just broke her heart," my grandmother said. "Yes. It's possible."

Ranjit Nayak's work with the Kisan of eastern India provides more evidence of the connections between the grief of exile and health outcomes, between mental and physical health. "The severance of the Kisan bonds from their traditional lands and environment is a fundamental factor in their acute depression and possibly in increased mortality rates, including infant mortality," Nayak writes. Like Chagossians grieving for their lost origins in Chagos, for the Kisan, "a continuous pining for lost land characterizes the elderly. Anxiety, grieving, various neuropsychiatric illness and post-traumatic stress disorders feature among the Kisan. In essence, they suffer from profound cultural and landscape bereavement for their lost origins."[19] This is what Scudder refers to among displacees as the "grieving for a lost home" syndrome.[20]

For many, the intimacy of their connection to Chagos is closely related to the fact that their ancestors are buried on the islands. Repeatedly since the expulsion, Chagossians have requested permission to visit the islands to clean and tend to the graves of their ancestors. In 1975, hundreds petitioned the British and U.S. governments for aid and the right to go back to their islands. If they were to be barred from returning they asked the governments to at least "allow two or three persons from among us to go clean the cemetery at Diego Garcia where our forefathers, brother, sisters, mothers and fathers are buried, and to enable us to take care of the Diego Church where we were baptised."[21]

Marie Ange Pauline, who was forced to leave Diego Garcia for the Seychelles as an adolescent, said she can see in her elders the pain of not going

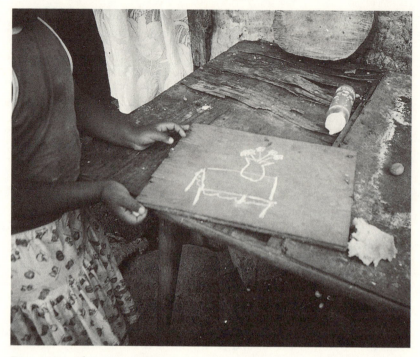

Figure 10.1 *Flowers on a Table*, drawing, Baie du Tombeau, Mauritius, 2002. Photo by author.

to the graves of their ancestors. Being barred from visiting their graves and bringing them flowers, she said, being separated from one's ancestors is yet another blow to their entire way of life. As Nayak writes of the Kisan, "In essence, they suffer from profound cultural and landscape bereavement for their lost origins."[22]

I ACCEPT MY MIZER

I've always had mizer,
I've always had mizer.
On the Earth, without end,
In the end, why am I on the Earth?

I've always had mizer,
I've always had mizer.
On the Earth, without end,
In the end, why will I be on the Earth?

I accept my own mizer, yes.
I accept my own mizer, here.
On the Earth, without end,
When it ends, why will I be on the Earth? . . . .

All my family had mizer, here.
All my friends had mizer, yes.
On the Earth, without end,
When it ends, why will we be in this life?

—*Excerpts from "Mizer" (2004) by Jean-Roy Bancoult and Toombo Bancoult, two of Alex Bancoult's five orphaned sons*[23]

"Stress and depression trickle up and down the generations, affecting people almost irrespective of age or gender," writes Nayak. "The children can narrate the expulsion and resettlement experience in minute detail as if they had themselves experienced the process."[24]

Among Chagossians born in exile there is this kind of intimate, experiential, almost bodily awareness of and about life in Chagos and the expulsion. Many born after the final removals narrate stories of the islands and the *derasinman* just as one who was born there. Ivo Bancoult is the only one of Rita and Julien's children to be born in Mauritius. He described for me how pained he is at not having been born in the islands and being unable to live there now. Often Ivo asks himself, and God, why he wasn't born *laba*. And yet in many ways he spoke as if he'd been born there too: It's a very different thing to come to Mauritius by force, he said about his life, compared to coming by choice. It's much harder to adapt when you come by force.

"My father came by force!" Ivo said emphatically. "By force he came" (indicating how many properly understand the experience of having been barred from returning to Chagos to be equally a matter of "force" as the experience of deportation).

Sitting behind the Chagossian community center in Pointe aux Sables, I asked Ivo if he, like others, distinguishes himself as being a *zanfan Chagossien*—a second-generation child born in exile to a Chagossian born in Chagos—as opposed to being a Chagossian proper. "I, truly, I am *Chagossian*," he replied. "I am Chagossian because my mother was born in Chagos. My father was born in Chagos. All my family was born in Chagos. I am a Chagossian. On paper perhaps" it says he was born in Mauritius, he continued, "but I am a Chagossian. Honestly. I am proud to be Chagossian."

I asked Ivo, who works on and off, mostly in construction, about his hopes for the future. "I would like to dream that one day I will be able to have a life definitely able to change in one sense—in one sense," he said, meaning the dream of returning to Chagos.

"It is difficult for me to forget my history, my origin. Because there is an enormous silence about it—a lot, a lot of silence. . . . All my family was born there—only I was born here. I would like to tell this story."

SAGREN, LATRISTES, MIZER

Sandrine Alexis, now in her early 30s, came to Mauritius as a young child with her parents and six siblings on one of the last voyages of the M.V. *Nordvær*. Sandrine explained that her family had to leave everything in Chagos. When they first arrived, the family lived on the streets of Port Louis's largest slum, Roche Bois. Often they had no food or water. When they came to Mauritius, her parents were healthy, she said. But once in Mauritius, her parents "*tombe malad*" with *sagren* and *latristes*—they fell ill with profound sorrow and sadness. They "*tombe dan mizer*," she continued. They fell into miserable abject poverty. Over time, three of her siblings died in Mauritius.

When Joseph Vindasamy told me how his father died of *sagren* in 1970 after he was prevented from returning to Diego Garcia, I asked him to define *sagren*. Joseph replied, *sagren* is "not having work." It's "lacking" food, water, education for yourself and your children. It's not becoming "*abitye*"—being unable to adjust—to life in Mauritius.

We notice here how Joseph made no mention of sorrow or sadness in his description of *sagren*. For Joseph and others, the sorrow connoted by *sagren* is so obvious it needs no mention. When Chagossians talk about *sagren*, we can see, they are talking about more than their deep sorrow. They are also talking about their experiences with what Sandrine and others call *mizer*—miserable abject poverty. Equally we can see, when people talk about *mizer*, they are referring to more than their experiences of deep impoverishment in exile. They are also talking about their feelings of *sagren* and *latristes*—their feelings of profound sorrow and sadness.

Sagren, *latristes*, and *mizer* have become three intertwined ways for Chagossians to talk about their suffering. In using any one of these words, people immediately refer to their common experience of having been *derasine*—deracinated, forcibly uprooted and torn from their birthplace—and the myriad ways—physical, economic, social, cultural, psychological—

that they have suffered as individuals and as a community as a result of their *derasinman*—their forced uprooting. *Sagren, latristes,* and *mizer* have come to represent the inseparable combination of Chagossians' profound sorrow over their expulsion and the profound material suffering the expulsion has caused.

ROOT SHOCK

I was thirteen years old,
When I was thirteen years old in Chagos,
I was thirteen years old, a worker's kuto dekoke** was in my hand.

The English arrived, Mr. Englishman arrived in Chagos,
The English arrived, the English uprooted us, cut off our food supply.
I will not forget,
Never, I will not forget my family,
The whistle blew three times to board the Mauritius,***
It dumped us in Mauritius.

I will not forget,
Never, I will not forget my mother,
I will not forget those we left there in the cemetery.

O ye li le, O li le, O li le la la la. . . .

> —*"I Was Thirteen Years Old," excerpt, composed and sung by*
> *Mimose Bancoult Furcy (2004)*[25]

If you're anything like me, it may be difficult to fully grasp the pain of having been *derasine*, of having been uprooted. Like me, you may live a far more transient life than Chagossians once did. Like me, you may be someone who expects to move several, perhaps many times in a lifetime, choosing to move from place to place following employment opportunities, education, family members, even romance. Still we can and must try to imagine what being forcibly uprooted and torn from Chagos felt like for the Chagossians who had been living there for generations, some never leaving the islands.

** Chagossians' coconut knife.
*** The M.V. *Mauritius*, a cargo ship, which, with the *Nordvær*, carried out parts of the expulsion.

"Imagine the victim of an earthquake, a hurricane, a flood, or a terrorist attack," suggests Mindy Fullilove in her discussion of root shock. "He suffers from root shock as he looks at the twisted remains of the known universe, searching for the road to the supermarket, which used to be there, but is now a pile of rubble. Imagining such a person—and knowing that these tragedies can happen to any of us—we open our hearts and our wallets to the Red Cross and other relief organizations that show up immediately to be . . . the transfusion of an environment to those who are naked to the elements." However, she adds, "The experience of root shock . . . does not end with emergency treatment, but will stay with the individual for a lifetime," potentially affecting "generations and generations."[26]

This experience of root shock and the way it affects not just individuals but whole communities across generations is an example of what medical anthropologists mean by "social suffering."[27] The concept is useful for the way the word *social* helps identify a distinct kind of suffering where causation resides in the social world rather than within individuals. "Social suffering," three prominent medical anthropologists explain, "results from what political, economic, and institutional power does to people." The phenomenon is also social because it affects specific populations as a result of their (vulnerable) positioning in the world—for example, Jews and other minorities in the Holocaust, Native Americans growing up on impoverished reservations, African Americans and Latinos consigned to urban poverty in the United States, Iraqi refugees fleeing their homes. Further, the phenomenon is social because it is a kind of suffering that is fundamentally experienced not just as an individual but socially, among a group or community of sufferers. This kind of suffering is so "profoundly social," they say, "that it helps constitute the social world."[28]

Yet unlike nervos, which is a form of social suffering that tends to obscure its own social, political, and economic sources, in Chagossians' use of the words *sagren*, *latristes*, and *mizer*, the islanders are continually, implicitly identifying the source of their suffering. They are placing the blame for their afflictions squarely on their expulsion and the actions of the governments responsible for their having been *derasine*. As Mimose's sega says, "The English arrived, Mr. Englishman arrived in Chagos. The English arrived, the English uprooted us, cut off our food supply."

And so "social suffering" captures important elements of the Chagossian experience: Their suffering was and is caused by the force and power of the U.S. and U.K. governments and by individuals within those governments who targeted the Chagossians as a vulnerable group. Likewise, as indicated by their common use of the words *sagren*, *latristes*, and *mizer* to describe their lives, their suffering has been experienced not just individually but socially. With their lives utterly transformed by exile, they have suffered as a community, sharing common experiences that have shaped a common social world.[29] *Sagren*, *latristes*, and *mizer* reflect this shared social reality; together they have come to serve as a kind of shorthand, among Chagossians and with outsiders, for the totality of their suffering and for the shared experience of having been *derasine*.[30]

"THE SAME AS WHEN I LOST ALETTE . . ."

"Enormous anguish. Enormous problems for me," replied Rita when I asked what she felt that day when she heard she couldn't return to her islands.

"How can I explain it—you know, there was a child that I breastfed. She grew all the way up to seventeen months. And despite it all, she died. It left me with enormous grief. The same grief. The same as when I lost Alette, when I lost . . . Eddy. The same suffering, David."

"The same suffering," I repeated.

"The same suffering. And how can I say it? When I have that suffering—there's a time when I remember, there's a time when I forget. But that moment, I turn it over. I turn it over in my mind. Because I've had so many problems, David. If my children and grandchildren were born there, it would be something different. They would have had a different house. They would have had a different everything. The same as I had."

"We have great difficulty grasping the full horror of the situation in which the Crow found themselves," Charles Taylor has commented about Native American lives radically overturned by displacement, death, and the destruction of their way of life.[31]

I agree. Yet we must try—we must struggle, really—with the lives of the Chagossians, the Crow, and too many others, to stretch ourselves empathically to understand, to begin to fully comprehend the horror. And then, with this knowledge, we must begin to act.

For now, let us turn to see how Chagossians have mobilized themselves to act.

CHAPTER 11

DARING TO CHALLENGE

In May 1973, the last boatload of haggard and hungry Chagossians deported from Chagos refused to disembark in Mauritius. The group of about 125 demanded that they be returned to Chagos or else receive compensation and housing in this "foreign country" where they had "no housing, no money, no work." For five days, the people resisted all entreaties to get off the boat, living and sleeping on a deck designed for less than half their number and in the ship's dark hold, in what a local newspaper called "deplorable conditions."[1]

After days of negotiations, the Mauritian Government finally convinced the group to disembark. The government paid adults Rs5, children Rs3, and gave nineteen families what turned out to be dilapidated apartments, amid pigs, cows, and other farm animals, in the slums of Port Louis. Twelve other families found their own housing, crowding into the shacks of relatives and friends.[2]

"In '72, I was deported," described Aurélie Lisette Talate, one of the last to go. "I left Diego—Diego was closed," in 1971. After that she was sent to Peros Banhos before her final deportation. "In '72, I left Peros. I went via Seychelles."

"I came to Mauritius with six children and my mother," Aurélie said. "I arrived in Mauritius in November. November '72 we got our house near the Bois Marchand cemetery, but the house didn't have a door, didn't have running water, didn't have electricity."

A stick-thin woman in her sixties, Aurélie eats little, smokes a lot, and speaks with a power that earned her the nickname *ti piman*—little chili pepper: In Mauritius the littlest chilies are the hottest and the fiercest.

"The way we were treated wasn't the kind of treatment that people need to be able to live. And then my children and I began to suffer. All my children started getting sick."

Within two months of arriving in Mauritius, two of Aurélie's children had died. The second was buried in an unmarked grave because she lacked the money to pay for a burial. "We didn't have any more money. The government buried him, and to this day, I don't know where he's buried."

In the first years in exile, most of the islanders' anger was directed at the Mauritian Government and Prime Minister Ramgoolam, who were understood to have "sold" Chagos and the Chagossians to Britain in exchange for Mauritian independence.

Mauritians "committed more than a crime," Aurélie said. They "deracinated us. Sold Diego so that Mauritius could get its independence. We lived there. We lost our houses," and suddenly in Mauritius "we had none. We were living like animals. Land? We had none. . . . Work? We had none. Our children weren't going to school. . . . I say to everyone, I say to them, 'Yes, the English deceived me.'"

A tradition of resistance among Chagossians started in 1968 when some of the first islanders prevented from returning to their homes protested to the Mauritian Government, demanding that they be returned to Chagos. From the beginning of what they came to call *lalit chagossien*—the Chagossian struggle—women have been at the forefront of the movement, protesting in the streets, rallying supporters, going on hunger strikes, confronting the police and getting arrested.

The 1975 petition delivered to the British and U.S. governments cited failed promises of compensation made by British agents in Chagos. "Here in Mauritius, everything has to be bought and everything is expensive. We don't have money and we don't have work." Owing to "sorrow, poverty, and lack of food and care," they said, "we have at least 40 persons who have died" in exile. The Chagossians asked the British Government to "urge" the Mauritian Government to provide land, housing, and jobs or return them to their islands. "Although we were poor" in Chagos, they wrote, "we were not dying of hunger. We were living free."[3]

The petition and numerous other pleas to the governments of Britain, the United States, Mauritius, and the Seychelles went unheeded. The U.S. Government declared it had "no legal responsibility" for the islanders;[4] the following year, a British official sent to investigate found the islanders "living in deplorable conditions." Both governments did nothing.[5]

In 1978, after years of protests and pressure, the Government of Mauritius finally paid compensation to some of the islanders from the £650,000 it had received from the British Government in 1972. When the money proved "hopelessly inadequate,"[6] Aurélie and several other Chagossian women went on what would be the first of five hunger strikes over four years to protest their conditions. The protesters demanded proper housing: "Give us a house; if not, return us to our country, Diego," proclaimed one of their flyers.[7]

The hunger strike lasted 21 days in an office of the Mauritian Militant Party (MMM), a leftist opposition party whose leaders had assisted the struggle since the first arrivals in 1968. Later that year, four Chagossians were jailed for resisting the police when Mauritian authorities tore down their shacks.[8] Both protests yielded few concrete results but added to mounting political momentum for the islanders.

In 1979, with MMM assistance, several Chagossians engaged a British lawyer, Bernard Sheridan, to negotiate with the British Government about providing additional compensation. Sheridan was already suing the United Kingdom on behalf of Michel Vincatassin, a Chagossian who charged that he had been forcibly removed from his and his ancestors' homeland.

British officials reportedly offered £1.25 million in additional compensation to the group on the condition that Vincatassin drop his case and Chagossians sign deeds "in full and final settlement," waiving future suits and "all our claims and rights (if any) of whatsoever nature to return to the British Indian Ocean Territory."[9]

Sheridan came to Mauritius offering the money in exchange for the renunciation deeds. Initially many impoverished Chagossians signed them—more precisely, given near universal adult illiteracy, most provided their thumbprints on deeds written in English. When Chagossian and MMM leaders heard the terms of the deal, they halted the process and sent Sheridan back to London. A support group wrote to Sheridan to explain that those who had "signed" the forms had done so without "alternative legal advice," and "as a mere formality" to obtain desperately needed money, rather than out of agreement with its conditions. No compensation was disbursed.

RANN NU DIEGO!

Before long Chagossians were back in the streets of Mauritius, launching more hunger strikes and their largest protests yet in 1980 and 1981. Along with Aurélie, Rita was part of a group of women who guided the movement. Together they repeatedly faced police intimidation, violence, and arrest, to lead hundreds marching on the British High Commission, protesting in front of government offices, and sleeping on the streets and sidewalks of the Mauritian capital. In one notorious incident, now recounted with embarrassed glee, a group of women faced off against a line of male riot police officers in downtown Port Louis. The police charged some of the women, hitting them with batons to get them to disperse and knocking them to the ground. Suddenly and spontaneously, a woman reached up and grabbed a cop by the testicles. "Grabbed his, grabbed his testicles, his balls! Yes!" said Aurélie. "She grabbed the cop's balls! She grabbed his balls and then he fell to his knees." Yelling in pain, he and other riot police ran off in full retreat.

"No one was afraid," Rita said of the women protesters. "We weren't afraid. They were shooting tear gas at us, so we hit back, threw rocks at them. We weren't afraid."

Led by women like Rita and Aurélie, the islanders demanded the right to return to Chagos as well as immediate compensation, decent housing, and jobs.[10] "We yelled, 'Give us back Diego! Give us back Diego that you stole, Ramgoolam! That you sold, Ramgoolam!'" Aurélie recounted. "We went and we yelled in the streets: 'Ramgoolam sold Diego! Ramgoolam, give us back Diego! Get a boat to take us to Diego!'"

For the first time, a broad coalition of Mauritian political groups and unions supported the people under the Kreol rallying cry *Rann Nu Diego*—Give Us Back Diego. The slogan served to unite the Chagossians' struggle with the demands of many Mauritians to return Chagos to Mauritian sovereignty and close the base.[11] Ambiguity in the Kreol phrase, however, also obscured key disagreements between the groups still visible today in what are at times difficult alliances: Does *rann nu* mean "give us back" or "return us to"? Does the *us* mean Chagossians or Mauritius and the Mauritian people? And does giving back Diego mean evicting the base or only a reversion of control over the island with the base allowed to stay?

During this moment of unity, though, the coalition soon won results. Following violent clashes and the arrest of six Chagossian women and two Mauritian supporters during another eighteen-day hunger strike, Mauritian Prime Minister Seewoosagur Ramgoolam left for London to meet British Prime Minister Margaret Thatcher. The two governments agreed to hold talks on compensation with Chagossian representatives.

After two rounds of negotiations, the British Government agreed to provide £4 million in compensation, with the Mauritian Government contributing land it valued at £1 million. In exchange, most signed or thumbprinted so-called "renunciation forms" to protect the U.K. Government from further claims for compensation and the right to return.

Many Chagossians have later disputed the legality of these forms and their knowledge of their contents, again written in English without translation. Rita explained, "I didn't make my thumbprint to renounce my right. I made my print to get money to give my children food. They had no food."

Rita continued insistently, "I never renounced my right. . . . You can show me my thumbprint, my thumbprint, my signing, there was Rs8,000 for me in the bank, but I don't know how to read. I don't know how to write. . . . I took it because my children were dying of hunger. I was pulling food out of the trashcan to give to them. I went to buy food so I could give them food," Rita said. "If I didn't sign, I would have been pulling food from the trashcan again to give to my children. . . . I did not renounce my right."

CHAGOSSIANS TAKE CHARGE

In the wake of the compensation agreement, many felt that their interests had not been well represented by some of their Mauritian allies and spokespeople. Several, including prominent Chagossian leaders and former hunger strikers Aurélie and Charlesia Alexis, created the first solely Chagossian support organization, the Chagos Refugees Group (CRG).[12] With Rita's help, they asked her last son born in Peros Banhos, eighteen-year-old Louis Olivier Bancoult, to join the organization. The women felt their illiteracy had allowed the community's manipulation in the past, and Olivier was one of the few community members who had gone to secondary school and was literate. "They needed a Chagossian who had some education," he explained.

The CRG, under the leadership of Aurélie, Charlesia, Rita, and Olivier, pressed for the right to return and additional compensation. They continued their work through the 1980s and 1990s but showed little progress. Gradually they lost support among the exiles.

Another organization, the Chagossian Social Committee (CSC), eventually took charge of the people's political struggle, led by CSC founders Fernand Mandarin and his Mauritian barrister Hervé Lassemillante. The group pursued out-of-court negotiations with the U.K., U.S., and Mauritian governments for compensation and the right to return. While the CSC had little success in pursuing substantive talks, the group gained recognition for Chagossians as an indigenous people before the UN.[13] A CSC leaflet showing Fernand participating in a session at the UN Working Group on Indigenous Populations proclaims, "To live on our land of origin: A sacred right, wherever our origin may be!"

NEW APPROACHES

In 1997, two Chagossian women approached Mauritian attorney Sivaku-maren Mardemootoo about bringing a lawsuit against the British Government challenging the legality of the expulsion. Mardemootoo discussed the matter with British solicitor Richard Gifford and on the strength of their case soon gained British legal aid to pursue the suit.[14] To expand the plaintiff class, Mardemootoo approached CSC leaders to ask about their joining the case. He explained to me that he heard no response from the CSC, and on the day he made his inquiry the two women instructed him to stop working on their behalf.

Gifford and Mardemootoo turned to the CRG, whose leaders had previously pursued the possibility of bringing a suit against Britain and the United States. Working closely with Olivier, who was now juggling the presidency of the CRG with his day job as an electrician for the Mauritius Central Electricity Board, the lawyers filed a 1998 lawsuit at the High Court in London.

Figure 11.1 Chagos Refugees Group (CRG) members outside office (Mimose Bancoult Furcy at front right), Cassis, Mauritius, 2002. Photo by author.

Initially the CRG, which by then only had the support of a handful of Chagossians, faced considerable opposition from the CSC's leadership and Mauritians concerned about the political and legal implications of the suit. Since Britain detached Chagos from Mauritius to create the BIOT in 1965, Mauritian political parties and citizens have criticized the detachment as illegal under the rules of decolonization and campaigned at the UN and other international forums in favor of a reversion to Mauritian sovereignty. Many Mauritians (and the CSC) believed that in suing the United Kingdom, the Chagossians were implicitly recognizing Britain's possession of Chagos and thus damaging Mauritius's sovereignty claim. Although Mauritian governments and political parties have at times offered various forms of high- and low-profile support to the Chagossians, they generally remained noncommittal on the issue of the suit.[15]

With little support in Mauritius and great skepticism there and abroad about the chances of their suit, the CRG and its lawyers pressed on. To the shock of many, on November 3, 2000, the British High Court in London found for the Chagossians, ruling their expulsion illegal under U.K. law. Olivier walked out of the court with his hands outstretched above his head, making the sign of "V" for victory.[16]

On that day, Olivier recalled, "the Chagossian community won a victory, winning its right that had been deliberately scorned years before by British authorities, winning what was a great acknowledgment from a hugely important institution in England recognizing our—Chagossians' rights."

"When I went outside the court," Olivier said, "I was making a 'V.' It was a 'V' for victory. It was a 'V'—it was a day that for me, I say, David finally defeated Goliath. David, the people, the people succeeded over that great Goliath, that great power, the British Government."

Almost immediately British Foreign Secretary Robin Cook, who as a backbencher had been one of the Chagossians' few supporters in Parliament since the 1970s, announced that the government would not appeal the judgment. "This Government has not defended what was done or said thirty years ago," Cook said. The government changed the laws of the BIOT to allow Chagossians to return to all of Chagos but continued the ban on a return to Diego Garcia. They also refused to assist with a return and resettlement, promising only to study its "feasibility."

Lacking the money to visit Chagos on their own let alone to resettle and reconstruct their society, the CRG was forced to file a second suit against the Crown for compensation and the funds to finance a return and reconstruction.[17]

Journalist John Pilger asked Cook why he didn't do more about an episode in British history that Cook had called "one of the most sordid and morally indefensible I have ever known."

"It was never a political possibility to return them," Cook explained. "The Americans were there, and they had an agreement with us."

But, Pilger asked, why had he not just told the U.S. Government, "The highest court in our country has said a great injustice has been done and we have to give these people the opportunity to go home and reconstruct their lives"?

"Well, I did say that, more or less," Cook replied.

"But you left out Diego Garcia?"

"Oh yes, because that was never achievable politically with the Americans."

"That's where it all stopped?" Pilger queried.

"Yes."[18]

NEW SUITS AND NEW DISPUTES

Turning to the empire across the Atlantic, the CRG and islanders organized in the Seychelles enlisted Michael Tigar to file the class action lawsuit that marked my introduction to the story. They sued the U.S. Government, Defense Secretaries McNamara and Rumsfeld, Melvin Laird and James Schlesinger, Admirals Thomas Moorer and James Holloway III, State Department officials George Churchill and Eric Newsom, the major oil and construction multinational Halliburton Company (whose Brown & Root subsidiary helped build the base), and the Mauritian recruitment firm for Diego Garcia (and former Arthur Andersen affiliate) De Chazal du Mée.[19]

In addition to demanding the right to return and proper compensation, the U.S. suit asked for an immediate end to employment discrimination on the base. While the U.K. court victory meant that almost every Chagossian now supported the CRG, this last demand proved somewhat divisive within the community: Indeed, for decades there have been divisions in the community over the legitimacy of the base, although the issue has always remained secondary to near total support for the right of return and compensation.[20] During the 1980–81 protests, Chagossians protested under the Rann Nu Diego slogan, which included the demand to close the base, and many still oppose the base on the grounds that it was the cause of their expulsion. Anthropologist Laura Jeffery quotes a Chagossian from

Diego Garcia saying, "I suffer because they took my country and made it into a base for war." Others oppose the base because they believe it would endanger resettlement. "If America can bomb Iraq from Diego Garcia," a second-generation Chagossian told Jeffery, "then Iraq could bomb Diego Garcia."[21]

Some are more tolerant or even supportive of the base. Despite the CRG's opposition to the war in Iraq, the group's position is, according to Olivier, "We have no problem with the military base on Diego Garcia."[22]

Chagossian feelings about the base must be understood within the context of their struggle to return and gain compensation. Many (mostly men) have been interested in working on the base—and thus finding one way to return to their homeland—since the base began employing non-U.S. or U.K. support personnel. Others see the base as essential to any resettlement effort, both as a source of employment and, given the only runways in the archipelago, as a regular air link with the outside world.

The intricacies of U.S. law have also played a role in shaping Chagossians' feelings about the base. Because U.S. law broadly prohibits suits against the U.S. Government that challenge the foreign policymaking power of the U.S. executive and legislative branches, the CRG and its lawyers have had to distance themselves from any positions appearing to oppose the legitimacy of the base. Instead, they have made clear that they are only challenging the legality of the removals. The leftist Mauritian party *Lalit de Klas* (Class Struggle) has described a resulting "chorus" from Chagossians having to repeat "again and again" that they are "*not* against the military base."[23]

CITIZENSHIP AND DEFEAT

As they waited for the result of their U.K. compensation suit, the islanders won a new victory in 2002, when most gained the right to full U.K. citizenship and passports. The background behind the triumph dated to 1968. At the time, Chagossians had been given Mauritian citizenship as part of the nation's independence agreement with Britain. But as British officials soon realized, any children born in the BIOT after Mauritian independence had "exclusive attachment" to the BIOT and "could not be disguised as Mauritians."[24] Putting the matter of the children aside, there was already a sizable population with both Mauritian and U.K. citizenship by virtue of their birth in a British colony. To avoid the possibility that Mauritius would resist resettling people who were in fact British citizens,

U.K. officials conspired to hide this fact from the Mauritian Government and the Chagossians. In the 1980s, the islanders realized the deception and began claiming BIOT citizenship, giving them the right to a British Dependent Territory (i.e., colonial) passport, although not residential rights in Britain (nor of course in the BIOT).

In May 2002, the British Government was in the process of changing its citizenship laws to extend full citizenship and passports to citizens of its few remaining colonies, newly renamed the U.K. Overseas Territories (Bermuda, the Falkland Islands, and Montserrat among them). Initially the government had not intended to include Chagossians in the law. With the help of a few parliamentary supporters, however, a special clause incorporated the people into the British Overseas Territories Act of 2002, on the grounds that their current residency outside a British territory was the result of their involuntary removal by the U.K. Government.[25] The change made most native-born Chagossians and their first-generation offspring, along with other citizens, eligible for the same citizenship as British nationals, including residential rights in Britain.[26]

In recent years more than 1,000 Chagossians, mostly from the second generation, have left Mauritius and the Seychelles in search of work and better lives in England,[27] where they have met with mixed success. In July 2003, around thirty arrived with little or no money and what they believed were promises of work. The group soon found themselves stranded and homeless, sleeping for more than a week on the floors of London's Gatwick Airport. Others have launched suits claiming the same social service benefits due other British citizens. So far the courts have rejected the claims on the grounds that the islanders have not met residency requirements in Britain. In 2007, a group staged a five-month sit-in on government property, only to have a judge force them off the land. While some have returned to Mauritius or the Seychelles, many in England have eventually found housing and low-wage service sector jobs, mostly in working-class cities and towns surrounding London. Some now have janitorial and other service jobs at Gatwick.

In late 2003, a year after they won citizenship, the tide of victories turned. In October, the British High Court denied the islanders' claim for compensation. Though the judge in the case admitted that Chagossians had been "treated shamefully by successive UK governments," he found against them on every major issue, ruling that there was no arguable tort of unlawful exile, that the statute of limitations had run out, and that officials had not been reckless in carrying out the removal, despite its unlawfulness. An appeal was similarly rejected.[28]

A year later, in December 2004, the Federal District Court for the District of Columbia dismissed the U.S. suit. Judge Ricardo Urbina found no wrongdoing on the part of the government, its officials, or contractors for what he described as the "improper misplacement of the plaintiffs."[29] Ultimately the suit failed to overcome two major legal hurdles: first, the "political question" doctrine, which gives near total authority over matters of foreign and military policy to the executive and legislative branches; and second, the "Westfall Act," which provides "practically impenetrable" immunity to government employees for any "negligent or wrongful act or omission," as long as they are acting within the scope of their employment—which the Attorney General certified the defendants had.[30] Far from the defeat being the result of the particular interpretation of a judge or conservative judicial activism, the case demonstrates how, as legal scholar Christian Nauvel says, "the deck is (almost impossibly) stacked against foreign parties wishing to obtain relief against either the U.S. or its employees."[31] An appeals court upheld the initial ruling in 2006, and in early 2007, the U.S. Supreme Court denied a petition for further appeal.

Undeterred, Chagossians filed suit against the U.K. Government in the European Court of Human Rights. They charged violations of their rights on grounds that the European Convention on Human Rights prohibits forced displacement, that international treaties like the UN Charter prohibit Britain from violating the right to self-determination, and that common law prohibits Britain from violating people's fundamental rights.

Before receiving a European hearing, the British Government made a stunning announcement. In the name of Her Majesty the Queen, the British Government again enacted two Orders in Council (another had created the BIOT in 1965) barring any Chagossian from returning to Chagos. Again the Queen rubber-stamped the decision of her ministers, which officials announced on June 10, 2004, a busy election day in Britain, "tucked away on a list of innocuous royal decrees between an amendment to the Royal Charter of Optometrists and the appointment of four of Her Majesty's education inspectors for Scotland." Pilger describes how it happened: "A Privy Councillor simply read out the fate of thousands of Her Majesty's most vulnerable, abused and wronged subjects and, in that curious high-pitched voice, she said, 'Agreed!'"[32]

In effect, without parliamentary debate or consultation, the British Government used the archaic power of royal decree to overturn the November 2000 High Court victory and Chagossians' briefly held right of return.

There are signs that the Orders were the result of "intense U.S. pressure."[33]

A RETURN?

Despite the setbacks in the U.S. and U.K. suits and the issuing of the Orders in Council reinstating their exile, the Chagossians continued their legal and political struggle, building international attention and support. In December 2005, they returned to the High Court with Richard Gifford and Nelson Mandela's lawyer Sir Sydney Kentridge to challenge the Queen's decree.

While they waited for a ruling, CRG leaders convinced the British Government to accede to a decades-old request to allow a contingent to visit Chagos to care for and pay respects to their ancestors' graves.[34] On March 30, 2006, after numerous postponements and repeated negotiations, British authorities finally let around one hundred Chagossians travel to Chagos for a ten-day "humanitarian" voyage to visit each of their islands (though not to stay overnight) and to tend to the cemeteries. The trip was widely seen as a concession by the U.K. Government and generated widespread international media coverage.

Upon arriving back in Mauritius, Olivier, CRG's vice president Aurélie Talate, and a few others rushed to London to hear the ruling in their case challenging the Orders in Council. For the second time, the High Court of Justice ruled their expulsion illegal. The Orders in Council were overturned.

"The suggestion," two judges wrote, "that a minister can, through the means of an Order in Council, exile a whole population from a British Overseas Territory and claim that he is doing so for the 'peace, order and good government' of the territory is, to us, repugnant."[35]

Outside the court, Olivier said, "We always believed in our struggle. We always believed that what was done to us was unlawful. It is not possible to banish our rights. . . . We will go back to our native land. It is now very clear that we have the right to do so."[36]

To the disappointment of Olivier and others, the government appealed the decision again, forcing the islanders to head back once more to the Court of Appeal. A year later, on May 23, 2007, the Court handed the people its third victory. The decision called the 2004 Orders in Council nothing less than an "abuse of power."[37]

Figure 11.2 Aurélie Talate addresses a Chagos Refugees Group general assembly with Olivier Bancoult in foreground, Mauritius, 2004. Photo by author.

"It has been held," said CRG lawyer Richard Gifford, "that the ties that bind a people to its homeland are so fundamental that no Executive Order can lawfully abrogate those rights." Hoping that this third victory would put an end to the litigation, Gifford and the CRG called on the government to start negotiations to return the "loyal British subjects to their homeland."[38]

After several months' delay and to the people's disappointment, British officials decided to issue their final appeal. The government would bring the case before the Law Lords of the House of Lords, the highest court in the United Kingdom. There would be a final legal showdown over the islanders' right to return. Again, though, the people would have to wait, this time more than a year before a June 2008 hearing.*

To now, both governments remain adamantly opposed to any return. U.K. officials claim that resettlement would be too expensive, citing a £5 million initial investment and £3–5 million contributed on a yearly basis until the islands reach self-sufficiency.[39] Some observers have speculated that officials are using every legal and logistical hurdle to drag the case out as long as possible. "There must be hope in London," one journalist writes, "that as more and more of the original 2000 inhabitants of the Chagos Islands grow old and die . . . the Chagossians' campaign to return to their homeland will lose momentum. By and large, elderly people don't make good campaigners and dead ones don't campaign at all."[40]

U.S. officials say they are opposed to a return on security grounds. "The use of the facilities on Diego Garcia in major military operations since September 11, 2001, has reinforced the United States' interest in maintaining secure long-term access to them," wrote Assistant Secretary of State for Political-Military Affairs Lincoln P. Bloomfield in a letter sent to British officials. "We believe that an attempt to resettle any of the islands on the Chagos Archipelago would severely compromise Diego Garcia's unparalleled security and have a deleterious impact on our military operations, and we appreciate the steps taken by Her Majesty's Government to prevent such resettlement."[41]

Even putting aside for a moment the CRG's position that nothing can override a people's right to its homeland, the scores of yachts anchoring at any given time in the archipelago as well as the hundreds of non-U.S. service workers on Diego Garcia would seem to make a mockery of such arguments.[42]

Responding to British officials' claims that the costs of resettlement are too high, the CRG has observed that the British Government collects sizable fees for commercial licenses to fish the waters of the BIOT and spends tens of millions of pounds annually on its other remaining colonies. "The British Government has the ability to rebuild—to put in place all the infrastructure, to work for the welfare of the Chagossian community," Olivier

* This book was completed several months before the court date. See http://www.chagossupport.org.uk for updates.

told me. "But we ask, where are the rights of the Chagossians?" Pointing to both governments, he said, "The money that they spend to buy arms, to destroy humanity—is it too expensive to resettle the Chagossians in our natal land?"

U.S. officials have calculated since the 1960s that there would be few if any costs of ignoring the Chagossians' welfare as long as British officials assumed the responsibility to deal with the political and economic ramifications of the removals. And to this point, U.S. officials have largely been correct: The U.S. Government has faced few political or economic costs as a result of ignoring the Chagossians' plight, while enjoying all the benefits of the base.

Equally, given the significance of the base to the U.S. military, the prospect that the United States, under pressure from the Chagossians or the international community, would voluntarily leave the island or that the United Kingdom would evict its closest ally appears dim in the short term. On the other hand, the Chagossians' multiple recent court victories, the 2006 visit to Chagos granted by both governments, and growing media attention focused on the case signal new momentum that might result in longer-term impacts on the U.S. and U.K. governments. With the islanders headed to the highest court in the United Kingdom, successive judicial rebukes are increasing pressure on British officials not only to allow the Chagossians' return but to finance some kind of rehabilitation of the islands, possibly as part of a wider reparations package.[43]

With the islanders' movement inflicting increasing costs and embarrassment on both nations, it is hard to know how the two governments will react. If Chagossians were to return even in small numbers to some of Chagos's outer islands, the financial and political costs of maintaining the BIOT as a militarized territory would increase. The presence of a non–self-governing population in Chagos should force the UN to give renewed attention to the islanders and the conditions under which the BIOT was created. With awareness of the case growing in the United States, pressure is already mounting on the U.S. Government to accept responsibility for the people, to assist with resettlement and compensation, and to allow them to work on the base.

"The great powers, they who control the world, they who make so many noble declarations" about human rights, they must "correct this error that they made with the Chagossian community," Olivier told me, his voice rising, the palm of his hand slapping against his thigh. "[We] were a people that was living in prosperity. A people that was living in a state of well-being. A people that had its own culture and that had its own traditions. A people that had a full life like everyone else."

The initial U.S.-U.K. agreement for Diego Garcia ends in 2016. Exercising an optional twenty-year extension written into the agreement once appeared automatic. Now growing momentum for the Chagossians coupled with the failure of the Anglo-American military project in the Middle East leaves the future for both the islanders and the "Footprint of Freedom" very much in the balance.

For now let us ponder the image of Rita Bancoult's son Olivier standing at a podium in Geneva, addressing a forum of the United Nations, speaking to a gathering of hundreds of indigenous groups from around the world: "How can a small people like us dare challenge the UK and the United States?" he asks. "It seems an impossible conflict to resolve, but we stand by our convictions that justice will prevail even if we know it will take a long, long process."[44]

CHAPTER 12

THE RIGHT TO RETURN AND A HUMANPOLITIK

While to now the Chagossians have been almost entirely forgotten in the United States, the responsibility of the United States for the people's fate is clear: Although the British Government and its agents performed most of the physical work involved in displacing the Chagossians, the U.S. Government ordered, orchestrated, and financed the expulsion. First, the U.S. Government developed and advanced the original idea for a base on Diego Garcia as part of the Strategic Island Concept. Next, U.S. officials solicited and then colluded with the British Government as its partner. In the process, the U.S. Government insisted on the removal of the Chagossians, a condition to which the British Government readily agreed. Subsequently, the United States secretly paid the British for the expulsion, for the silence of Mauritius and the Seychelles, and for other costs of establishing the BIOT as a military colony. Along the way, the Kennedy, Johnson, and Nixon administrations circumvented congressional oversight of military appropriations and base creation, censored media coverage of base plans, and took other steps to conceal the expulsion and the creation of the base from the U.S. public and the world.

After finally receiving a congressional appropriation for the base, the U.S. Government ordered the British Government to complete the removal of the islanders, refusing requests from the U.S. Embassy in London and British officials to allow the people to remain on Diego Garcia as base employees. U.S. officials then monitored the progress of the deportation process, ignoring warnings about the absence of a resettlement plan, as U.S. Seabees assisted in the last deportations on Diego Garcia and the extermination of Chagossians' pet dogs. Finally, since the expulsion, the U.S. Government has continually denied all responsibility for the islanders and their welfare and barred them from working as civilian employees on the base. In exile, most Chagossians quickly found themselves impoverished. Most to this day have remained impoverished as marginal outsiders in Mauritius and the Seychelles.

Given these facts, we must now step back to consider what we can learn from Diego Garcia and what we must do about it.

RACE AND RACISM

First and foremost, we cannot mince words. The expulsion was an act of racism. Because Chagossians were considered "black," because Chagossians were small in number and lacked any political or economic clout, they were an easy target for removal. Because they were considered black, planners could easily regard them as insignificant, as a "nitty gritty" detail. Planners could think of them (in the moments that officials gave them any thought), as the CIA once put it, as "NEGL"—NEGLIGIBLE.[1]

"The fact is that nobody cared very much about these populations," said former Defense Department official Gary Sick, who testified to Congress about the removals in 1975. "It was more of a nineteenth-century decision—thought process—than a twentieth- or twenty-first-century thought process. And I think that was the bind they got caught in. That this was sort of colonial thinking after the fact, about what you could do." And U.S. officials, Sick said, "were pleased to let the British do their dirty work for them."

In this way, the Chagossians' expulsion and the pattern of forcibly displacing numerically small, non-"white," non-European colonized peoples to build bases resembles many forms of violence that tend to afflict the poor, the dark, and the powerless, those who so often get treated as "rubbish people." Anthropologists Nancy Scheper-Hughes and Philippe Bourgois explain:

> The mad, the differently abled, the mentally vulnerable have often fallen into this category of the unworthy living, as have the very old and infirm, the sick-poor, and, of course, the despised racial, religious, sexual, and ethnic groups of the moment. Erik Eriksen referred to "pseudo-speciation" as the human tendency to classify some individuals or social groups as less than fully human.[2]

Mark Curtis has called the Chagossians "unpeople."[3]

Ultimately, however, race and racism played a different role in the displacement of the islanders and other victims of base displacement than

in older forms of empire. Whereas race and racism were the explicit ideologies of European imperialism,[4] in more recent history, race and racism
have played a prominent role in structuring the vulnerability of those who
will be displaced, while serving as a more subtle, internal ideological influence allowing officials to "assume the license" to displace the racialized.[5]

The Chagossian case illustrates this shift: As a people, the islanders have
been displaced twice—once as enslaved people and indentured laborers
taken to work on Chagos by the British and French empires and once
expelled from Chagos at the behest of the U.S. Empire. The result in both
cases has been the profound disruption and impoverishment of their lives.
Though racism played different roles in the two displacements, both are
examples of how, in different ways, as anthropologist Leith Mullings says,
"racism works through modes of dispossession," turning "perceived differences, generally regarded as indelible and unchangeable, into inequality."[6]

At another level, U.S. officials displaced the Chagossians and similar
groups because military officials prefer not to be bothered by local populations, and because a group of powerful officials had the power to make
it so—among them, Barber, Rivero, Burke, Komer, Nitze, Moorer, and
Zumwalt, as well as the Navy itself, pushing the base plan over fifteen
years. As sociologist Frances Fox Piven put it to me simply one day, U.S.
officials displaced the Chagossians "because they could." "Across history,"
writes Mark Gillem, "the hands of empire predictably travel past the same
markers: displacements and demolitions are the norm."[7]

And the displacement of locals for military bases continues. In South
Korea, the U.S. military has been expanding Camp Humphreys, which
already occupies two square miles, to seize 2,851 additional acres from
Daechuri village and other areas near the city of Pyongtaek. At the behest
of the United States, the South Korean Government used powers of emi-
nent domain to take farmers' land for the base. When the farmers resisted,
the South Korean Government sent police and soldiers to enforce the evic-
tions. From March to May 2006, riot police invaded Daechuri with bulldozers and backhoes, beating protestors, destroying a local school, and
tearing up farmers' rice fields and irrigation systems. When many still refused to leave, the government surrounded the village with police, soldiers,
and barbed wire. On April 7, 2007, the last villagers finally were forced to
go, carrying a symbolic Peace Boat as they walked out of town. "I can't stop
shedding tears," one older resident said. "My heart is totally broken."[8]

In the minds of many U.S. officials, whether consciously or not, removals were (and are) justified by what they saw as the limited impact
of removing a small number of people, especially when weighed against

the supposed gains to be realized from a base. Henry Kissinger once said of the inhabitants of the Marshall Islands, "There are only 90,000 people out there. Who gives a damn?"[9] Stu Barber's Strategic Island Concept was predicated on the same assumption. In fact, after the expulsion, Stu claimed he hadn't known the Chagossians "had a history of several generations there," but even if he had, he still would have recommended the creation of the base.[10] From the perspective of Chagossians and others, there was of course nothing limited about the effects of displacement.

While the Chagossians and other base displacement victims were certainly removed in part because they were small, isolated populations, another island comparison suggests the decisive role played by a people's socially defined race and ethnicity. In Iwo Jima and Japan's other Bonin-Volcano islands, there were before World War II roughly 7,000 inhabitants. The islanders were the descendants of nineteenth-century settlers who came both from Japan and in smaller numbers from the United States and Europe. In 1944, after the start of U.S. attacks on the islands, Japanese officials evacuated all the islanders to Japan's main islands. After the U.S. capture of the Bonin-Volcanos and the end of the war, U.S. officials prohibited the return of the local people, to allow unhindered military use of the islands. In 1946, U.S. officials "modified" the decision: They would "permit the return of those residents of Caucasian* extraction who had been forcibly removed to Japan during the war and who had petitioned the United States to return." Approximately 130 men were eventually repatriated with their families, becoming "the sole permanent residents of the islands."[11] The Navy helped establish self-government, a cooperative trading company to market agricultural products in Guam, and a Bonin-Volcano Trust Fund for financial support.[12]

MILITARY POWER, EMPIRE, AND THE CONTROL OF OIL: DIEGO GARCIA TO IRAQ

To understand why officials wanted a base on Diego Garcia in the first place and what this says about the nature of the United States as an empire, about current trajectories in U.S. foreign and military policy, and

---

* As I wrote earlier, there is no biological validity to the concept of "race" or to supposed racial groups like this one. They are as fictitious biologically and scientifically as the fictions invented about the Chagossians. At the same time, as we see in this case, race and the separation of peoples into supposed racial groups are deeply real social phenomena, engrained in the minds of most human beings the world over and shaping fundamental issues like who gets protected in their homes and who gets displaced.

about empire more broadly, we must now return to the history of the Cold War and to longer-term imperial trends. Remember that in the 1950s and 1960s, U.S. officials faced a swirling mixture of fears about decolonization, base access, rising Soviet and Chinese power, and appearing "soft" on "defense" before domestic political audiences. At the same time, they retained an understanding of the profound military superiority of the United States over its rivals and a powerful interest in maintaining U.S. economic and political domination in the Indian Ocean region, increasingly in the Persian Gulf, and around the world. In this context, the Strategic Island Concept provided an answer to both their anxieties and their interests: Strategically located remote island bases would protect the nation's "future freedom of military action" and its dominant position in the world.[13]

The history of Diego Garcia shows that much of the national security bureaucracy quickly adopted the Navy's concept as an important strategic framework. Although the costs of the Vietnam War reined in the most far-reaching plans and left Diego Garcia as the only major base created under the Strategic Island Concept, the strategy became an important argument for the retention and expansion of major preexisting island bases, including those in Guam, Micronesia, the Bonin-Volcano islands, British Ascension, the Portuguese Azores, and Okinawa (in the early 1970s Stu hoped to create another BIOT-like territory with the British in Micronesia).

Coupled with the first-ever buildup of U.S. naval forces in the Indian Ocean, moreover, Diego Garcia increasingly enabled the insertion of military power into a large and increasingly unstable portion of the world (made unstable in many ways by other U.S. actions). Fearing an unknowable and threatening future in the non-Western world and increasingly in the Persian Gulf and southwest Asia, officials in the 1950s and 1960s crafted a plan for Diego Garcia to control the future through military force. As was often the case in the Cold War, the easiest "solution" was the military solution.[14]

One reason the military solution was often the easiest has to do with gender: It is not surprising and yet still remarkable that, as far as my research has shown, every official involved in any significant way in the development of Diego Garcia was a man.[15] As in previous generations and elsewhere in the world, these gods of foreign policy were unquestionably male gods. And among these men, as we have seen, qualities of toughness, strength, efficiency, rationality, and hardness were most admired. These were "male" qualities best demonstrated by "tough" policies involving the use of military force and a fearless attitude in confronting the Soviet Union. Paraphrasing Adam Hochschild, when you came from a generation raised on war, violence, and toughness, and when war (cold and hot), violence, and toughness remained the unquestioned order of the day, wielding violence efficiently was regarded as a manly virtue.[16] Any signs of weakness, doubt, or concerns for human suffering were denigrated as weak, womanly, female. This generation of foreign policy leaders demonstrated its maleness through exterior displays of force, through a war in Vietnam, and through policies like that on Diego Garcia based on the seizure and cleansing of territory and the deployment of military power, rather than, as Halberstam points out, through more interior forms of strength that might have entailed "a good deal of domestic political risk."[17]

Still, the solution provided by Diego Garcia and the Strategic Island Concept was hardly about toughness and military force alone. The intent was always political, military, and economic: Diego Garcia allowed what strategists euphemistically call "intervention" and the threat of intervention in the affairs of other nations, while also, like eighteenth-century French and British bases, helping to protect U.S. economic interests in the region. As we have seen, protecting U.S., European, and Japanese access to Middle Eastern oil was initially just one of several motivations behind the military buildup. Within a few years of the base becoming operational, however, oil was at the core of Diego Garcia's mission.

After the Iranian Revolution and the Soviet invasion of Afghanistan in 1979, the base played a central role in the first large-scale thrust of U.S. military strength into the Middle East. To respond to any future threats to the oil supply, Presidents Carter and Reagan developed a "Rapid Deployment Force" at bases in the region, including a rapidly enlarging Diego Garcia.[18] In the years that followed, the Rapid Deployment Force transformed into the U.S. Central Command (CENTCOM), which came to lead three wars in Iraq and Afghanistan. As we saw in the introduction, Diego Garcia was a launchpad for bombers and prepositioned weaponry critical to each of these wars. In this evolution of the island's role, the base was one of the first major steps by the United States to deploy its military power to defend U.S. and global oil supplies. Indeed, Diego Garcia has been central to a more than half-century-long period during which, as Chalmers Johnson says, "the United States has been inexorably acquiring permanent military enclaves whose sole purpose appears to be the domination of one of the most strategically important areas of the world."[19]

The history of Diego Garcia thus suggests an important revision to how we think about the United States as an empire. Contrary to the idea stressed by some that the U.S. Empire has become an empire of economics, Diego Garcia and the Strategic Island Concept represent a reliance on traditional imperial tools of overseas bases and military power to maintain U.S. dominance. Clearly Diego Garcia and the Strategic Island Concept were not the only reactions to declining U.S. power during the Cold War—there were economic, political, and other military reactions as well. But they provided part of a solution to perceived threats while simultaneously answering the challenges posed by decolonization to the exercise of power through overseas bases.

That is, Diego Garcia and the Strategic Island Concept were part of the invention of a new form of empire in the postwar era, relying heavily on overseas bases and increasingly on discreet, isolated bases—often island bases—to exert power. Responding to decolonization, Diego Garcia helped initiate an ongoing shift of bases from locations near population centers to locations insulated from potentially antagonistic locals. Today one sees the realization of this model and this new kind of empire in the military's "lily pad" basing strategy: Under the strategy, the military is creating bases that are isolated from population centers, have limited troop deployments, and instead rely largely on prepositioned weaponry for future (un)anticipated conflicts. As Mark Gillem writes, "avoidance" is the new aim. "To project its power," the United States wants "secluded and self-contained outposts strategically located" around the world.[20]

In the words of some of the strategy's strongest proponents, the goal is "to create a worldwide network of frontier forts" with the U.S. military serving as "the 'global cavalry' of the twenty-first century."[21] With as many bases as possible, the military hopes always to be able to turn from one nation to another if it is denied base access in a time of war.

While the reliance on smaller bases may sound preferable to the huge bases that have caused so much harm and anger in places like South Korea and Okinawa, the construction of lily pads in an increasingly long list of nations including Ghana, Gabon, Chad, Niger, Equatorial Guinea, Senegal, Mali, Mauritania, Morocco, Tunisia, Algeria, India, Pakistan, Thailand, Aruba, and Poland, represents the growing militarization (and likely destabilization) of even larger swaths of the globe and a dramatic expansion of an imperial vision to dominate the world militarily.[22] And, as the once "austere" base on Diego Garcia shows, installations that might start out as lily pads can quickly grow into massive behemoths.

To be clear, the U.S. Empire has been characterized to a significant degree by economic forms of Open Door imperialism. However, the history of Diego Garcia shows that the U.S. Empire has relied in important ways on the continued use of military force and on increasingly discreet overseas bases in particular to maintain its dominance. This is not to deny the significance of economics to the U.S. Empire, only to shift the focus toward the relatively underexplored military dimensions. Diego Garcia suggests a more balanced perspective on U.S. Empire, highlighting how overseas bases, along with other military and political tools, have worked in tandem with and undergirded economic forms of power.

RUNNING THE WORLD

In the face of Chagossians' struggle to return (and to work on, not remove, the base), the intransigence of the U.S. and U.K. governments is striking for a facility that was a product of the Cold War. Interestingly as well, Diego Garcia only saw its first significant use as a base with the Cold War's end.[23] Since the fall of the Soviet Union, the base has indeed become a pivot point of U.S. strategy for the control of areas from the Persian Gulf to east Asia. Prior to the 2003 Iraq war and September 11, 2001, the U.S. military was in the process of turning Diego into one of four major "forward operating locations" for "expeditionary" Air Force operations. Along with Guam, the island was selected as a recipient of an eastward shift of materiel and weaponry from Cold War European bases. For many in the military (especially the Air Force) the dream is to be able to strike any location on the planet from Diego, Guam, and Barksdale Air Force Base in Louisiana. As I quoted military analyst John Pike at the outset, the military's aim is "to run the planet from Guam and Diego Garcia by 2015, even if the entire Eastern Hemisphere has drop-kicked us" from every other base in the hemisphere.

These trends suggest that Diego Garcia reveals something fundamental about U.S. Empire, beyond the Cold War era alone: While previous empires generally sought to dominate as much of the globe as possible through the direct control of territory, in the twentieth and twenty-first centuries, the U.S. Empire has increasingly accomplished the same not only through economic and political tools but also through a global network of extraterritorial U.S. military installations that allow the control of territory vastly disproportionate to the land actually occupied.

Viewed geographically, one sees how the small-scale acquisition of territory for island bases has allowed the United States, like empires before it, to dominate large swaths of *ocean territory* upon which global trade and economic expansion relies. Coupled with a powerful navy, an island base provides the force to effectively rule areas of ocean and transiting military or commercial traffic. In the Pacific, controlling bases from Okinawa and

Japan's main islands to Guam and Pearl Harbor has allowed the U.S. Navy to make the ocean an "American lake." Maintaining a base on Diego Garcia has helped the United States exert similar control in the Indian Ocean, particularly over oil traffic from the Persian Gulf. In the role that island bases and navies play in patrolling sea lanes and protecting oceangoing commerce, one sees a very direct way in which overseas bases undergird the economics of U.S. Empire.[24]

Bringing us back to Iraq and Afghanistan, the base helps show how these wars were not the aberrant actions of a single presidential administration but were instead, in important ways, the fulfillment of a strategic vision for controlling a large swath of Asia and, with it, the global economy, dating to at least World War II (and significantly advanced by Diego Garcia). As others have shown, the wars have significantly advanced the pursuit of U.S. control over Central Asian and Persian Gulf oil and natural gas supplies through the presence of hundreds of thousands of U.S. troops and private military contractors and the creation or expansion of bases in Pakistan, Kyrgyzstan, Uzbekistan, Bulgaria, Poland, Romania, Qatar, Bahrain, Kuwait, Oman, the United Arab Emirates, Afghanistan, and Iraq.

DIEGO GARCIA AND THE CARTER DOCTRINE GO GLOBAL

The strategic logic of Diego Garcia, of using bases to control resource-rich regions, becomes even clearer when one considers reports that the United States has been exploring plans to develop a new base off the oil-rich west coast of Africa, in the Gulf of Guinea, on one of the islands of São Tomé and Príncipe. Currently, oil imports from the Gulf of Guinea account for 15 percent of the U.S. total. Many predict that the share will grow to 20 percent by 2010 and 25 percent by 2015. Continent-wide, the *Council on Foreign Relations* has suggested, "By the end of the decade sub-Saharan Africa is likely to become as important as a source of U.S. energy imports as the Middle East."[25] Indeed, this may have already come to pass. Looking at São Tomé, at least one U.S. official has described the proposed base as "another Diego Garcia."[26]

The story sounds eerily familiar: In July 2002, the Deputy Commander-in-Chief of the U.S. European Command visited the islands. The next month, then-President of São Tomé and Príncipe, Fradique de Menezes, told Portuguese television that he "received a call from the Pentagon to tell me that the issue [was] being studied." He added, "It is not really a military base on our territory, but rather a support port for aircraft, warships, and patrol ships."[27] Since 2002, several U.S. companies, including Exxon-Mobil and Noble Energy, have won oil exploration concessions in the Gulf of Guinea.[28] At the end of 2006, the military built a radar installation on the islands. The following March, 200 U.S. marines conducted four days of military exercises. Months earlier, the U.S. military announced the creation of its first-ever "Africa Command" (AFRICOM) to oversee military operations on the continent. Elsewhere, U.S. officials are considering the creation of or have already established bases in Algeria, Djibouti, Gabon, Ghana, Kenya, Mali, Nigeria, Senegal, and Uganda.[29] Officials have repeatedly denied having any interest in a base on São Tomé.

IMPERIAL SHIFTS AND CONTINUITIES

The expansion of Diego Garcia into a major naval and air base fulfilled the hopes of many in the U.S. Navy and elsewhere in the national security bureaucracy, including Stu Barber, Horacio Rivero, Arleigh Burke, Robert Komer, Paul Nitze, and Elmo Zumwalt. So too the base was the realization of French lieutenant La Fontaine's vision from two centuries earlier for having "a great number of vessels" at anchor in Diego Garcia's lagoon.[30]

Viewed from this long-term perspective, Diego Garcia points to both shifts and continuities in the evolution of U.S. Empire and empire more broadly. On the one hand, Diego Garcia and the base network represent several long-standing imperial trends, including the persistence of traditional imperial tools of territorial acquisition and displacement, the development of modes of increasingly informal and indirect rule, and the continued use of a handful of remaining colonies and colonial relationships—Diego Garcia, Guam, Puerto Rico, Thule, Okinawa, South Korea among them—to exert dominance.[31] This suggests that there is more continuity between the U.S. Empire and previous empires than has been acknowledged.

Diego Garcia and much of the U.S. global basing network are to some extent a return to an earlier form of imperialism when Britain and France were first interested in colonizing Diego Garcia and other islands in the Indian Ocean. In the eighteenth century, islands were initially valued for their military and not their economic value. Bases in Mauritius and Réunion hosted warships used to secure trade with India and later to subdue the subcontinent.

Three centuries later, weapons and supplies from Diego Garcia were among the first arriving in the Persian Gulf to link with U.S. soldiers preparing for war in Iraq. Once the war was underway, B-1, B-2, and B-52 bombers based on Diego Garcia dropped hundreds of thousands of pounds of ordnance on Iraq's battlefields, killing thousands. From this perspective the Chagossians' expulsion is unsurprising: Their ancestors' enslaved arrival in Chagos was the result of a European empire's efforts to claim bases in a strategic ocean; their removal was the result of a similar search by a new empire two centuries later.

On the other hand, Diego Garcia shows us how the U.S. Empire is a dramatically new kind of empire. Unlike its predecessors, the United States exercises control over other nations and peoples not primarily through colonies but through its base network and a range of other military, economic, and political tools. Anthropologist Enseng Ho explains that the United States has become an empire symbolized by *invisibility* and *remote control*. "The passing of the baton" from previous empires, he writes, "is marked by the progress from gunboat diplomacy to aerial bombing." Now "remote control bombers fly ever higher out of sight, while military advisors disappear into the Filipino jungles, Yemeni mountains, and Georgian gorges. As well, security, military, and colonial functions are farmed out to private companies, removing them from political oversight."[32]

That the United States has become an empire of invisibility goes further: As the power of the United States has grown since World War II, the Chagossians and increasing numbers of people around the world have found themselves subject to the actions of the U.S. Government but lack legal recourse to challenge their treatment in U.S. courts. The government and its officials have thus increasingly conducted activities that, while illegal in the United States, are invisible to the U.S. Constitution and U.S. laws when conducted abroad. Recent examples include the decision to hold terrorist suspects at the U.S. naval base at Guantánamo Bay. At Guantánamo, the Bush administration and later Congress withheld from detainees the *habeas corpus* right to a trial and other rights generally due people on U.S. soil. Similarly, the CIA's use of "extraordinary rendition," sending detainees to nations known to use torture as an interrogation technique, allowed the agency and its employees to attempt to circumvent laws and treaties banning torture. "In consequence," Ho says, "the U.S. enjoys rights in [other] lands but owes no legally demandable obligation to foreigners there. . . . Without recourse to U.S. law, prisoners at Guantánamo are subject to the unchecked and therefore tyrannical power of the U.S. president."[33]

So it is for most U.S. military bases and troops abroad where status of forces agreements generally give the United States, its troops and civilians, broad powers little constrained by local, U.S., or international law.[34] Maintaining this immunity from prosecution overseas is precisely one of the reasons why the Bush administration prevented the United States from joining the International Criminal Court.

And so it is for the Chagossians, as well as for any prisoners currently or previously held on Diego Garcia: If such acts had taken place within the United States, the U.S. Government, its executive agencies or officials could likely be challenged for violating U.S. law and the Constitution. Because the acts that were committed against the Chagossians took place outside U.S. soil, however, courts have upheld total federal and individual immunity. "Living outside of direct colonial rule," the islanders have fallen "within the purview of its empire" but are "condemned to invisibility by the U.S. Constitution."[35] So far U.S. courts have allowed them no legal recourse whatsoever; those responsible for their expulsion have gotten off scot-free.

THE EFFECTS OF EMPIRE AND WHAT WE MUST DO

We are the descendants of slaves. Our skin is black. We don't have blue eyes. . . . Whether we are black, whether we are white, whether we are yellow, we all must have the same treatment. That is the treatment that the Chagossian community is asking for. At least give us our chance to live. Give us our chance to live like every other human being. Stop all the injustices that have been committed against us.

—*Olivier Bancoult, President, Chagos Refugees Group, 2004*

As we consider the empire that the United States has become, we must face the damage that the nation has inflicted on families like Rita Bancoult's and so many others. We cannot allow the harmful effects of U.S. Empire, too often ignored or given short shrift by empire's proponents and others, to continue. We cannot continue to allow claims of "national interest" to justify the destruction of the lives of others.

The story of Diego Garcia is in many ways a story of just that: how we have allowed empire and militarism to trump human lives.[36] "The military expansionists in our Defense and State Departments push on inexorably like a giant bulldozer," Iowa Senator John Culver testified on the one day Congress has ever thought about the Chagossians, "oblivious to diplomatic options, oblivious to violations of human rights. . . . What happens is the means become the end and military expansionism in effect assumes command of our foreign policy."[37]

To unmake the ways in which our ability to make both war and money has trumped human lives, we must shift U.S. foreign policy and the national security bureaucracy that runs it away from deep-seated imperial instincts, away from the pursuit of economic and military interests benefiting the few, away from engrained hierarchical notions that some human lives are more valuable than others. We must shift our foreign policy toward a consideration of people's lives and the impact of the nation's actions on human beings above all else. We must begin to pursue a "humanpolitik"—a human-centered foreign policy based around international cooperation and diplomacy that places human lives, regardless of nation, above perceived and shortsighted notions of national interest and security. Self-described "realists" will say that such an approach isn't realistic. The Chagossians and more than half a century of this aggressive and tragic form of U.S. Empire, which has brought death and destruction abroad and helped create unparalleled inequality and bankruptcy at home, demand that we ask, "Realistic for whom?"

As a start, here is some of what we should do to redress the damage and prevent future harm.

The Chagossians

As with other victims of base displacement, the United States and the United Kingdom must immediately restore the right to return, in this case to all of Chagos including Diego Garcia. Because this is a largely symbolic right without the infrastructure to support life on the islands or the means to return, the two nations should, under the direction of the islanders, commence reconstruction of inhabitable islands and finance resettlement for those wishing to return.

Consultants working with the people as well as four decades of military habitation on Diego Garcia have already demonstrated the feasibility of restoring and maintaining life in Chagos. The islanders are exploring plans for tourism, fishing, and coconut industries; with lodging in private island hotels and beachside resorts going for upwards of $7,000 a night in Mauritius and the Seychelles just imagine the possibilities in the even more exclusive Chagos.

Making resettlement feasible would necessitate the cooperation of the U.S. Government and the base. In line with long-term Chagossian demands, the U.S. military and its contractors should immediately cease all employment discrimination barring islanders from civilian employment on the base. The military and its contractors should take further compensatory steps to hire any members of the community interested in working on the base, to establish a permanent employment preference for Chagossians, and to create a comprehensive training program to prepare islanders for skilled base and other employment.

To enable the importation of materials necessary for reconstruction of the islands' infrastructure, the U.S. military should allow use of the airport on Diego Garcia or finance the creation of a civilian runway elsewhere in the archipelago. In addition to opening up existing civilian housing on the base to newly employed Chagossian workers, both the U.S. and U.K. governments should enable the resettlement of parts of the eastern arm of Diego Garcia that are unused by base operations and far from the base itself. In an ironic and unintended monument to the expulsion, base employees already groom and maintain much of the islanders' village at East Point for the recreation of off-duty troops.

A return to Diego Garcia and the rest of Chagos raises questions about islander self-determination and the life of the base. As in its other "overseas territories" and as mandated by the UN, the United Kingdom should assist with the creation of forms of local self-governance. As democratic rule develops, the continued tenancy of the base, and any conditions thereof, as well as the islands' sovereignty, should be matters of local self-determination.

While the above steps are crucial to enable a return, resettlement should be treated as only one part of a proper reparations agreement. Given the responsibility of both governments for orchestrating and carrying out the expulsion and for the impoverishment that has followed, both nations should finance a significant compensation fund. This should include a lifetime pension and a comprehensive lifetime social services package for all Chagossians, whether born in Chagos or in exile.[38] Like any resettlement program or reparations effort (and in contrast to previous compensation), the people themselves should determine how monies will be distributed and spent and what social services (education, housing, health care, training, employment assistance, and others) will help guarantee their long-term security.

Indeed, as recently as 2004, British and U.S. officials have secretly discussed the creation of a "compensatory trust fund to alleviate the poverty of the most needy former Islanders." In response to a British proposal, however, a recently declassified State Department letter indicated that while the U.S. Government shared British "concern for the plight of the former Chagos Islanders. . . . we must respectfully decline participation in this fund because, after careful review, we are unable to resolve complications this initiative would cause in our budget process and our own equities relative to this complex issue."[39] British officials have never discussed the proposal publicly.

For too long both governments have denied and hid from their responsibility. For too long they have allowed the Chagossians to languish in exile. Now is the time for both governments to rectify the injustice they have done to the Chagossians. Now is the time when both governments, both nations must bring the cruel irony that is the Footprint of Freedom to an end.

Overseas Bases

The Chagossians and the fifteen other cases of base displacement are but an extreme example of a larger well-documented pattern of damage that overseas bases inflict on local populations. The harmful impacts of bases include economic, social, cultural, health, and environmental harms, the exploitation of women, increased crime, loss of self-determination, and support for dictators and repressive undemocratic regimes. In too many recurring cases, soldiers overseas have raped, assaulted, or killed locals, most prominently of late in South Korea, Okinawa, and Italy.[40]

These and other forms of harm that the Chagossians and hundreds of other local populations suffer on a daily basis should force us to question the legal, political, and moral legitimacy of maintaining many, if not all, of the United States' overseas bases. A first step would be to properly redress the damage caused by the United States during the development of its base network. As the Chagossians show, such damage is generally ongoing—which makes it possible and necessary for the United States to prevent future harm. This should come in the form of some kind of independent congressional investigation to expose past harms caused by overseas bases and current impacts on host communities. While the issue of financial reparations would be the most contentious, some kind of limited claims tribunal might satisfy locals and improve the accountability of extraterritorial facilities.

Just as critically, we must acknowledge how bases like Diego Garcia and occupying U.S. troops have become a major "face" of the United States, damaging the nation's reputation, engendering grievances and anger, and generally creating antagonistic rather than cooperative relationships between the United States and others. Most dangerously, as we have seen in Saudi Arabia and Yemen and as we are seeing in Iraq and Afghanistan, the existence of foreign bases creates breeding grounds for radicalism, anti-Americanism, and attacks on the United States, reducing, rather than improving, U.S. national security.

With the withdrawal of U.S. troops from Iraq hopefully underway by the time this book goes to press, now is the time for Congress to initiate a major reassessment of global troop deployments and our 1,000 overseas bases. Now is the time for Congress to demand the closure and consolidation of bases abroad that have silently spread around the world, causing harm to local peoples like the Chagossians and undermining U.S. and global security.

Indeed, the United States undermines its own international legitimacy and ultimately its own security so long as the bases claimed to be so critical to the nation's security continue to depend on the insecurity of others.

HOPE

When the Chagossians finally return to Chagos, there will be jubilation but there will be no storybook ending. Too many have died in exile. Too many lives, like those of Julien, Alex, Eddy, and Rénault Bancoult, have been cut short. Too many have suffered the *sagren* of expulsion for too long.

Still, taking in the whole of the history of the Chagossians as a people, the islanders' struggle represents a challenge not just to U.S. imperial power but to more than five centuries of injustice tied to the global expansion of European empires. In the words of their 1975 petition proclaiming, "Our ancestors were slaves on those islands, but we know that we are the heirs of those islands," the Chagossians' struggle says that the governments of Great Britain and the United States can't get away with just one of the most recent injustices befalling non-European peoples.

"We are reclaiming our rights, our rights like every other human being who lives on the Earth has rights," Olivier told me. "A right to liberty, a right—I was born on that land, my umbilical cord is buried on that land, I have a right to live on that land. It cannot be that a foreigner profits from all my wealth, profits from my sea, profits from my beaches, profits from my coconuts, profits from it all, while I'm left with nothing."

"Chagossians are not asking for charity," Olivier explained. "Chagossians are asking for our due for what has happened since we were deracinated. . . . For all the damages that we've suffered. To recognize, to give reparation. To give reparation for all the suffering that we have experienced during these years." But, he added, "We are not only asking for money. . . . We are also asking for our islands, our fundamental rights, and our dignity."

Although the task before us of restraining the power of the military and U.S. Empire may sound daunting; although guaranteeing fundamental rights for all human beings may sound difficult; although realizing the highest ideals of the United States may sound like blind idealism; although restoring the true meaning of freedom—freedom for all, not just for some—may sound like a dream, the Chagossians can give us hope: five thousand people. Five thousand abused people in the Indian Ocean, led by a group of determined women and one of their sons, every day taking on the distant power of the United States and Great Britain. And winning. Five thousand people.

"I will never give up the struggle!" Rita told me. "I've suffered, suffered, suffered so much. And I'm still suffering." But when they finally do win, she said, she'll write a sega so that everyone can remember the victory.

In 1991, the *Washington Post* received the following strongly worded letter:

> It seems to me to be a good time to review whether we should now take steps to redress the inexcusably inhuman wrongs inflicted by the British at our insistence on the former inhabitants of Diego Garcia and other Chagos group islands. The costs would be trivial compared with what we invested in construction and what we gained. . . . It is my firm opinion that there was never any good reason for evicting residents from the Northern Chagos, 100 miles or more from Diego Garcia. Probably the natives could even have been safely allowed to remain on the east side of Diego Garcia atoll. . . . It would be safe to let them go back, to North Chagos certainly. Such permission, for those who still want to return, together with resettlement assistance, would go a long way to reduce our deserved opprobrium. Substantial additional compensation for 18–25 past years of misery for all evictees is certainly in order. Even if that were to cost $100,000 per family, we would be talking of a maximum of $40–50 million, modest compared with our base investment there, with the value derived from it, and with the costs of Philippine bases. If we are too poor to pay it, perhaps the Japanese or Germans or Saudis might suggest *they* would like to allocate some of their Persian Gulf contributions to it.

The letter's author was Stu Barber.[1]

During the course of my research I tried several times to find Stu but had no success. I suspected that he had died but could find no living relatives. A small reference to his having written a memoir about his Navy career encouraged me to keep looking. A week before I was to finish this book my research assistant, Naomi Jagers, found a 2007 obituary for an Anna Barber that we suspected was his wife. The article mentioned two surviving sons. An internet search produced a phone number and an address just two miles from my old apartment in Brooklyn. Although it was after 8 p.m. on a Friday night, I rushed to call.

With the sounds of dishes being washed in the background, I found Richard Barber. He said he was Stu's son. Trying to contain my excitement as well as nervousness about how he might react, I told him about the book. Richard remembered his late father's talking about the base and being "dismayed" to discover what had happened to the people after reading a copy of the Minority Rights Group's 1985 report, "Diego Garcia: A Contrast to the Falklands."[2]

Over the next two days Richard emailed several remarkable typewritten letters his father had written on the subject. After trying to interest the *Washington Post* in picking up the story again, Stu had written an admiral who was a former Navy superior, the British Embassy in Washington, and Human Rights Watch, to implore them to help return the Chagossians to Chagos. The "cessation of the Cold War," he wrote, "would certainly permit the return of those natives so desiring to at least the northern islands of the group, 100 miles from the U.S. base."[3]

In another letter, he made an astonishingly honest admission: The expulsion, he said, "wasn't necessary militarily."[4]

According to his son, Stu received no response to his requests for help.

"As far as I know," Richard wrote in an email, "the after-the-fact concerns expressed by the guy who thought up the idea in the first place didn't have much impact. To me this is a poignant reminder of the extent to which many of us are more or less complicit in powerful organizations that act on imperatives ultimately beyond our individual control."[5]

Indeed, beyond Stu Barber and the other officials in this story, aren't most of us complicit in the Chagossians' exile and the suffering they experience to this day? Don't we all share responsibility, beginning with the tax dollars that U.S. and British citizens paid to expel the islanders and build the base? Don't the people and governments of countries like Japan, Germany, and Saudi Arabia share responsibility through financial and other contributions that assist U.S. domination of Diego Garcia and the Persian Gulf? Don't we all share responsibility through our silence? And while the base has mostly brought militarization, war, and death to the region, has it not, through U.S. domination of oil supplies and the global economy, in some ways helped support the lives that so many of us enjoy? While culpable government actors must be held responsible for the crimes they commit, each of us must ask ourselves every time we pay our taxes, pump our gas, or return to the safety and comfort of our homes how we too are part of this story of empire and exile, and what we're going to do about it.

MY THANKS

I am deeply grateful to so many friends who helped me with this work. First I want to thank all the Chagossians in Mauritius, the Seychelles, and England who greeted me so warmly, answered my many questions, and made so much of this research possible. Thanks especially to so many who graciously took time out of their lives to sit down for an interview or who invited me into their homes, making me always feel so much at home. I owe the same deep thanks to many former government officials and others who granted me interviews in the United States. Many invited me into their homes and offices, and I thank each of my interviewees for the time, hospitality, and thoughtful conversation you offered to someone who usually came to you as a stranger. Thank you to Michael Tigar for writing the foreword and even more importantly, for making this life-changing work possible. Thanks to Simon Winchester for generously suggesting the book's title, one serendipitous day on a Manhattan street corner.

Profound thanks are due to several groups and individuals that helped to coordinate and make possible my work in Mauritius and the Seychelles. There is no way to thank you enough: the Chagos Refugees Group, Olivier Bancoult, Lisette Aurélie Talate, Elena Rabouine, and CRG's executive and delegate committee members; Rita Bancoult, Mariline Bancoult, Oliver, Jessica, and Evelyna Bancoult, Mimose and Cyril Furcy, Ivo Bancoult, Marie-Ange Bancoult, Jean-Roy and Toombo Bancoult; the Chagos Committee (Seychelles), Jeannette Alexis, Jean-Guy Alphonse, Bernadette Dugasse, Pierre Prosper, and other committee members; the American University UNROW Human Rights Law Clinic, Meghan Colloton, Emily Creighton, and all its other incredibly dedicated students; Robin Mardemootoo, Dick Kwan Tat, Frances Kwan Tat and the Kwan Tat family, Satyendra Peerthum and the Peerthum family, Satinder Ragobur, Jean-Claude Mahoune, Julienne Barra; the committed and incredibly helpful members of the Kamarad de Resers research advisory group who oversaw and assisted with so much of my research in Mauritius: Eddy Bégue, Jenny Rabouine Bertrand, Isabelle France, Louis Rene France, Martin France, Louis Raphael Louis, Cynthia Othello, Piangnee Sweetie, Corinne Uranie, Linley Uranie; those who worked so hard on the "Kestyoner avek Chagossiens": Daniel Anacooa, Dinesh Appayya, Micheline Arlando, Martine Ballaram, Candice Bonnefin, Dominique Percy Catherine, Tarkeeswarsing

Hurrynag, and Komadhi Mardemootoo; amazingly dedicated transcribers Diana Bablee, Micheline, and Dominique; Vijaya Teelock and Melville Molle; Diego Garcia Islanders Council and Allen Vincatassin; Chagos Social Committee, Fernand Mandarin, and Hervé Lassémillante; the University of Mauritius and the Government of Mauritius; Seychelles National Heritage Research Section, Patrick Nanty, the Seychelles Ministry of Local Government, Sports and Culture, and the Government of Seychelles; Richard Gifford and Sheridans Solicitors.

I am also extremely grateful to all the former U.S. Government officials and the many others who participated in interviews or assisted with my work in the United States. They include Ken Bacon, Jeffery Barlow, Monoranjan Bezboruah, James Bishop, Bill Brewer, Abby Brown, John Dalton, Paul Davis, Robert Estabrook, Peter Findlay, Robert Harkavy, Stuart Johnson, Jennifer Jones, Robert Murray, James Noyes, David Ottaway, John Pike, Robin Pirie, Henry Precht, Earl Ravenal, Gary Sick, Ronald Spiers, David Stoddart, John Stoddart, George Vest, Jerry Wever, Simon Winchester, William Wishon, and others who chose not to be identified. To Richard Barber, special thanks for sharing your father's letters and your insights, especially under such a time crunch. A huge thank you also goes to Michael Tigar, Richard Gifford, and David Stoddart for graciously giving me access to critical collections of documents and for providing invaluable support and encouragement all along the way.

I will always be deeply indebted to Shirley Lindenbaum for the phone call that initiated this incredibly life-enriching and life-changing work. Thank you for your guidance, care, and support throughout my time in graduate school. Thanks also to Leith Mullings and Neil Smith, for being treasured intellectual guides, and for all your time, interest, and help in shaping this work. Phil Harvey and Wojtek Sokolowski have been dedicated teachers and colleagues; I look forward to continuing our work together. Thanks to Michael Cernea, Donald Robotham, and Lesley Sharp for taking an interest in my work and for your support. I am grateful to Catherine Lutz for agreeing to assist with this project and for being so thoughtful and encouraging at every stage. Thanks to Rob Rosenthal for being my mentor, friend, and general life guide since I took my first steps on the court. Brooke, thanks for always being there for me as a writer, friend, and confidant—and for seeing me through it all.

Thanks as well to so many others at the Graduate Center, where this work primarily took shape, including Louise Lennihan and the Ph.D. Program in Anthropology, Ellen DeRiso, Janet Kaplan, Frances Fox Piven, David Harvey, Mitch Duneier, Ida Susser, Kate McCaffrey, Michael Blim,

Mark Edelman, Kay Powell and the staff of the Institutional Review Board, and so many others who make the Graduate Center such a wonderful institution. Thanks to Julian Brash and Susan Falls for their tireless data entry work that made the Chagossian Survey possible, as well as for being great friends and colleagues. Thanks to friends from classes and the department, who created such a stimulating, fun, and supportive environment at the Graduate Center.

I want to note the debt that I (like many others) owe to Paul Farmer (whom I have never met). His work, passion, and ideas move and inspire me in the deepest parts of my mind and heart.

In Washington, DC, thank you to so many who have welcomed me and helped make American University a new home. They include all the terrific, committed faculty, staff, and students in and around the Department of Anthropology, who I thank here as a collective group of true friends and colleagues. Thanks to Marta Portillo, Jacki Daddona, and the work study students; to Naomi Jagers, who helped with so much work at the last minute, including the breakthrough that led me to the Barber family; and to my "Writing Ethnography for Social Change" class, which so generously offered critical help and encouragement with my writing and my heart and the connection between the two. Thanks also to new friends in DC who provided great writing help and so much additional support, including Andy Bickford, Melissa Fisher, Hugh Gusterson, Susan McDonic, Susan Terrio, and Salvador Vidal-Ortiz.

I would also like to acknowledge and thank those responsible for the financial support that made my research and writing possible, including the CUNY Graduate Center's Gilleece and Dissertation Year fellowships; the Mellon Foundation and the Ralph Bunche Institute's Inter-University Consortium for Security and Humanitarian Action at the Graduate Center; the John F. Kennedy Library in Boston, Massachusetts; the Lyndon B. Johnson Library in Austin, Texas; and the Gerald R. Ford Library in Ann Arbor, Michigan.

My thanks as well for careful assistance from the staffs of the Graduate Center's Mina Rees Library, JFK Library, LBJ Library, Library of Congress, Mauritius Archives, Mauritius National Library, Musée et Archives de la Photographie, Public Records Office, Seychelles National Archives, Seychelles National Library, U.S. National Archives, and Tim Pettit and the U.S. Navy Historical Center Operational Archives Branch. I am continually impressed and amazed by the dedicated, considerate, and tireless work of librarians and archivists around the world. I also owe a great debt to all those who helped make the production of this book possible at

Princeton University Press. Thanks to everyone at the Press for believing in the book and helping it come into print. I especially want to thank Fred Appel for guiding me through every step of the process. Thanks also to the book's cartographer Chris Brest, Elizabeth Byrd, David Campbell, Nathan Carr, Maria denBoer, Dimitri Karetnikov, Heath Renfroe, Jennifer Roth, and Claire Tillman-McTigue. A huge thanks to Jodi Beder for her extraordinarily careful and thoughtful editing that helped improve both the style and substance of the book.

There are many, many other friends and family who have supported, sustained, and assisted me through this process. Although I will surely forget some (sorry!), they include Roberto Abadie, Dan Aibel, Tick Ahearn, Sue Barrow, Jorge Baxter, Lisa Braun, Fuphan Chou, Patricia Cogley, the Gan, the Goobs, Sam Goodstein, Alex Goren, the Greenbaum family, Hugh Gusterson, Christine Hegel, Claire Hirsch, Dan Hirsch, Rudy Hirsch, Sue Hirsch, Kim Hopper, Lynn Horridge, Alison Ince, Laura Jeffery, Josh Kletzkin, Lynn and Morris Kletzkin, Linda Kolodner, Sarah Kowal, Linda Kuzmack, Nicole Laborde, Ilisa Lam, Willow Lawson, Rae Linefsky, Emma Sofía Madrazo Borboa, Carola Mandelbaum, the McNeil family, Trisha Miller, Kellye Nakahara, Alix Olson, Sascha Paladino, Joe Perpich, Claudine Pied, David Rappaport, Roee Raz, the Rosenthals, Cliff Rosky, Rebecca Ross, Caroline Simmonds, the Singer-Vine West-Side crew, Cathy Sulzberger, Carlitos Tevez, Maureen Tong, Neil Tonken, Meredith Trainor, Elly Truitt, Mauricio Tscherny, Dylan Turner, Ellis Turner, Ilana Umansky, Hugh and Lydia Vine, Joanne Vine, Lee Ving, David Vise, and Deb Yurow. Thanks especially for the generous and timely last-minute editing help of my mom, dad, Joanne, Rachel, Adam, Sam, Ally, Cliff, Sofía, Josh, and Alix.

Above all, to my parents and siblings: thank you for your loving support of everything that has ever been important to me, a quality perhaps never more on display than with this work.

This work is dedicated to Tea and Erwin Stiefel, Gloria and Theodore Vine, for their love, and to the memory of Marty Pinson, who played the role of stepfather as well as anyone could but who will always be so much more.

FURTHER RESOURCES

The Chagossians and Their Struggle

Chagos Refugees Group: obancoultcrg@intnet.mu; 62 Cassis Road, Port Louis, Mauritius

UK Chagos Support Association: http://www.chagossupport.org.uk
The UK Chagos Support Association is a nonprofit organization dedicated to supporting the Chagossians. The group's website includes updates about the Chagossians' lawsuits, recent news coverage, history and photographs, ways for concerned individuals to get involved, and links to many other relevant websites.

Stealing a Nation: A Special Report by John Pilger
This is a 56-minute documentary film about the Chagossians and Diego Garcia by award-winning investigative journalist John Pilger. See http://www.bullfrog films.com/catalog/steal.html. The film is also available for free on Google Video and YouTube.

U.K. Lawsuits
The web addresses below link to U.K. court rulings, including the Chagossians' three victories (2000, 2006, 2007) and their compensation case defeat (2003).

2000: http://www.bailii.org/ew/cases/EWHC/Admin/2000/413.html
2003: http://www.bailii.org/ew/cases/EWHC/QB/2003/2222.html
2006: http://www.bailii.org/ew/cases/EWHC/Admin/2006/1038.html
2007: http://www.bailii.org/ew/cases/EWCA/Civ/2007/498.html

U.S. Lawsuit: *Bancoult et al. v. McNamara et al.*
The following web page, created by Charles Judson Harwood Jr., provides links to most of the court filings and decisions in the case, as well as links to information about some of the defendants and lawyers, legal analysis, the U.K. cases, and media coverage. See: http://homepage.ntlworld.com/jksonc/docs/bancoult -docket.html

Diego Garcia and Other Base Information

U.S. Navy Support Facility, Diego Garcia: http://www.dg.navy.mil/web
This is the official base website.

GlobalSecurity.org: http://www.globalsecurity.org/military/facility/diego-garcia.htm
This site provides independent information and analysis about the base on Diego Garcia, including extensive satellite and other photographic imagery.

http://www.globalsecurity.org also offers information about other U.S. bases globally.

"Department of Defense Base Structure Report Fiscal Year 2007"
The Base Structure Report provides the DOD's official yearly accounting of U.S. military installations globally. Note that the report omits numerous well-known bases, including all those in Iraq and Afghanistan. Subsequent years' reports should be available online after this book has been published. For the 2007 report, see: http://www.defenselink.mil/pubs/BSR_2007_Baseline.pdf

The Anti-Bases Movement

No Bases (International Network for the Abolition of Foreign Military Bases)
    See: http://www.no-bases.org

Interactive Google Earth map of the world's foreign bases created by the Transnational Institute:
    See: http://www.tni.org/detail_page.phtml?act_id=17252

"Outposts of Empire: The Case against Foreign Military Bases" (Transnational Institute, March 2007)
    This booklet, available at the web address below, is a primer on the harmful effects of foreign military bases and a resource for the global anti-bases movement. See: http://www.tni.org/detail_pub.phtml?&know_id=60&menu=11e

NOTES

Archival Sources

JFK   John F. Kennedy Presidential Library, Boston, MA
LBJ   Lyndon B. Johnson Presidential Library, Austin, TX
MA   Mauritius Archives, Cormandel, Mauritius
NARA   NARA and Records Administration II, College Park, MD
NHC   Naval Historical Center, Operational Archives Branch, Washington, DC
PRO   National Archives, Public Records Office, Kew Gardens, England
SNA   Seychelles National Archives, Victoria, Mahé, Seychelles
UKTB U.K. Trial Bundle, Sheridans Solicitors, London [U.K. litigation documents]

Introduction

1. Chagossians born in Chagos spoke Chagos Kreol, one of a group of Indian Ocean French Kreol languages, including Mauritian Kreol and Seselwa (Seychellois Kreol). Their vocabulary is largely French while also incorporating words from English, Arabic, and several African, Indian, and Chinese languages; the underlying grammar for the Kreols appears to come from Bantu languages. Speakers of the various Kreols can understand each other, but Chagos Kreol is distinct in some of its vocabulary and pronunciation. Most Chagossians have lost most of the distinctive features of the language over four decades in exile. See Philip Baker and Chris Corne, *Isle de France Creole: Affinities and Origins* (n.p.: Karoma, 1982); Robert A. Papen, "The French-based Creoles of the Indian Ocean: An Analysis and Comparison" (Ph.D. diss., University of California, San Diego, 1978). Throughout I use the word *Kreol* to identify languages and the word *Creole* when used to identify people of generally African ancestry who are socially categorized as such in Mauritius and Seychelles.

2. Auguste Toussaint, *History of the Indian Ocean*, trans. June Guicharnaud (London: Routledge and Kegan Paul, 1966), 110.

3. David Vine, "The Former Inhabitants of the Chagos Archipelago as an Indigenous People: Analyzing the Evidence," report for Washington College of Law, American University, Washington, DC, July 9, 2003.

4. Robert Scott, *Limuria: The Lesser Dependencies of Mauritius* (Westport, CT: Greenwood Press, 1976[1961]), 242.

5. Stuart B. Barber, letter to Paul B. Ryan, April 26, 1982, 3. My thanks to Richard Barber for his help with many important details about his father's life and for providing this and other invaluable documents.

6. Ibid., 3.

7. Horacio Rivero, "Long Range Requirements for the Southern Oceans," enclosure, memorandum to Chief of Naval Operations, May 21, 1960, NHC: 00 Files, 1960, Box 8, 5710, 2. Admiral Horacio Rivero credited Barber with doing most of the writing for the Long Range Objectives Group that produced this document.

8. Rivero, "Long Range Requirements," 2.

9. Horacio Rivero, "Assuring a Future Base Structure in the African-Indian Ocean Area," enclosure, memorandum to Chief of Naval Operations, July 11, 1960, NHC: 00 Files, 1960, Box 8, 5710; see also Monoranjan Bezboruah, *U.S. Strategy in the Indian Ocean: The International Response* (New York: Praeger Publishers, 1977), 58.

10. Barber, letter to Ryan, April 26, 1982, 3.

11. Roy L. Johnson, memorandum for Deputy Chief of Naval Operations (Plans & Policy), July 21 1958, NHC: 00 Files, 1958, Box 4, A4-2 Status of Shore Stations, 2–3. See also Bezboruah, *U.S. Strategy in the Indian Ocean,* 58; Vytautas B. Bandjunis, *Diego Garcia: Creation of the Indian Ocean Base* (San Jose, CA: Writer's Showcase, 2001), 2.

12. Massimo Calabresi, "Postcard: Diego Garcia," *Time,* September 24, 2007, 8.

13. GlobalSecurity.org, "Diego Garcia 'Camp Justice,'" http://www.global security.org/military/facility/diego-garcia.htm.

14. See, e.g., Peter Hayes, Lyuba Zarsky, and Walden Bello, *American Lake: Nuclear Peril in the Pacific* (Victoria, Australia: Penguin Books, 1986), 439–46.

15. Michael C. Desch, *When the Third World Matters: Latin American and United States Grand Strategy* (Baltimore, MD: Johns Hopkins University Press, 1993), 152–53.

16. GlobalSecurity.org, "Diego Garcia 'Camp Justice.'"

17. Neil Hinch, "A Time of Change," *Chagos News* 24 (August 2004), 6.

18. Times Online, "The Secret Downing Street Memo," May 1, 2005, available at http://timesonline.co.uk/tol/news/uk/article387374.ece.

19. Stephen Grey, *Ghost Plane: The True Story of the CIA Torture Program* (New York: St. Martin's Press, 2006); Ian Cobain and Richard Norton-Taylor, "Claims of a Secret CIA Jail for Terror Suspects on British Island to Be Investigated," *Guardian,* October 19, 2007; Council of Europe, Parliamentary Assembly, "Secret Detentions and Illegal Transfers of Detainees Involving Council of Europe Member States: Second Report," explanatory memorandum, June 7, 2007, Strasbourg, 13.

20. Democracy Now, "CIA Admits Used UK Territory for Rendition Flights," February 22, 2008, http://www.democracynow.org/2008/2/22/headlines#6.

21. Kevin Sullivan, "U.S. Fueled 'Rendition' Flights on British Soil," *Washington Post,* February 22, 2008, A16; Cobain and Norton-Taylor, "Claims of a Secret CIA Jail"; Duncan Campbell and Richard Norton-Taylor, "US Accused of Holding Terror Suspects on Prison Ships," *Guardian,* June 2, 2008; Reprieve,

"US Government Must Reveal Information about Prison Ships Used for 'Terror Suspects,'" press release, June 2, 2008, available at http://www.reprieve.org.uk.

22. See Vine, "The Former Inhabitants"; David Vine, S. Wojciech Sokolowski, and Philip Harvey, "*Dérasiné*: The Expulsion and Impoverishment of the Chagossian People [Diego Garcia]," expert report for American University Law School, Washington, DC, and Sheridans Solicitors, London, April 11, 2005.

23. I have never been employed or paid by Tigar or anyone connected with the suits. The American University law clinic that Tigar supervises paid for some of my research expenses in 2001–2 and in 2004.

24. This book builds on David Vine, "Empire's Footprint: Expulsion and the U.S. Military Base on Diego Garcia" (Ph.D. diss., Graduate Center, City University of New York, 2006). Despite the significant role that the British Government and its officials played in carrying out the expulsion, I focus on the U.S. role for three reasons: First, nearly all the literature on Diego Garcia has focused on the role of the British Government in organizing the removal process. The literature has not, other than in passing, examined the role of the U.S. Government in ordering and orchestrating the expulsion. This neglect has left some confusion about the role of the U.S. Government in creating the base and ordering the expulsion. Frequent historical and factual inaccuracies have also appeared in the journalistic and scholarly literature (e.g., to whom the base and the territory belong: as it should be clear by now, while the territory is technically controlled by Britain the base is controlled by the United States, with Diego Garcia *de facto* U.S. territory). These shortcomings have made a scholarly exploration of the history of the U.S. role long overdue. Second, because I have found that the U.S. Government ordered the expulsion, I believe any analysis of why the Chagossians were exiled must focus on the U.S. role. Third, on a personal level, as one who was born and lives in the United States, I was more immediately concerned about the U.S. Government's role in the exile.

25. Because I think social scientists have an obligation to ensure that people participating in and assisting with our research directly benefit from the research—we certainly benefit through grant money, book contracts, articles, speaking engagements, prestige, jobs—I made small contributions of food or money to families with whom I stayed. As thanks to the Chagos Refugees Group for helping to enable my research, I periodically worked in the group's office, primarily providing English translation and clerical assistance.

26. In this I was guided by the work of Hugh Gusterson, *Nuclear Rites: A Weapons Laboratory at the End of the Cold War* (Berkeley, CA: University of California Press, 1996); Carole Cohn, "'Clean Bombs' and Clean Language," in *Women, Militarism, and War: Essays in History, Politics, and Social Theory*, ed. Jean B. Elshtain and Sheila Tobias (Savage, MD: Rowman & Littlefield, 1990), 33–55, Jennifer Schirmer, *The Guatemalan Military Project: A Violence Called Democracy* (Philadelphia: University of Pennsylvania Press, 1998); Lesley Gill, *The School of the Americas: Military Training and Political Violence in the Americas*, (Durham, NC: Duke

University Press, 2004); James Mann, *Rise of the Vulcans: The History of Bush's War Cabinet* (New York: Penguin Books, 2004).

27. In total, I conducted in-depth semi-structured interviews with 18 former and 2 current U.S. Government officials. They included officials from the U.S. Navy, the U.S. departments of Defense and State, and the U.S. Congress. The interview sessions sought to elicit detailed histories of the decision-making process leading to the development of the base and the expulsion. Throughout, I continually asked interviewees to describe their thinking at the time of the events under discussion to identify their contemporaneous interests, motivations, assumptions, and understandings. I conducted more than 10 additional interviews of a similar nature with journalists, academics, military analysts, a scientist, and others who were involved in the history of Diego Garcia or who were knowledgeable about the base.

28. I used these sources and interviews not just to understand the history of Diego Garcia and the dynamics of U.S. Empire but also to understand more about the actors in the national security bureaucracy themselves. As Derek Gregory points out, the actions of states are not produced "through geopolitics and geoeconomics alone"; they are also produced by cultural, social, and psychological processes and practices, especially those that "mark other people as irredeemably 'Other'" and locate both the self and others spatially. Derek Gregory, *The Colonial Present: Afghanistan, Palestine, Iraq* (Malden, MA: Blackwell Publishing, 2004), 16, 20. The aim is not to demonize or blame particular individuals but to empathetically understand their involvement within the context in which they were living, while identifying processes and practices that conditioned their actions.

29. Stuart B. Barber, letter to Ryan, April 26, 1982.

30. Henri Marimootoo, "The Diego Files," *Week-end*, serial, May–September 1997.

31. Exchange of Notes between the Government of the United Kingdom of Great Britain and Northern Ireland and the Government of the United States of America concerning a limited United States Naval Communications Facility on Diego Garcia, British Indian Ocean Territory (The Diego Garcia Agreement 1972), London, October 24, 1972, 3.

32. "Guidelines for Visits to Diego Garcia," memorandum, August 21, 1992, UKTB 3.

33. Calabresi, "Postcard," 8. Having filed such a story when he was one of the first journalists to visit the island in at last 25 years, Calabresi calculated "the equivalent in 2007 media dollars" as "probably a box of Chablis."

34. Letter to author, May 12, 2004.

35. Simon Winchester, *The Sun Never Sets: Travels to the Remaining Outposts of the British Empire* (New York: Prentice Hall Press, 1985); "Diego Garcia," *Granta* 73 (2001): 207–26.

36. See, e.g., La Barca: Blog, available at http://labarcaatsea.spaces.live.com/Blog/cns!SCEFC52FCBOE5896!167; Diane Stuemer, "Caught in a Net of Colourful Neighbours," *The Ottawa Citizen*, February 5, 2001.

37. The Department of Defense defines a "facility" as a building, structure, or utility. Department of Defense, "Base Structure Report," 8.

38. Global Security.org, "Iraq Facilities," http://www.globalsecurity.org/military /facility/iraq.htm; "Afghanistan Facilities," http://www.globalsecurity.org/military/ facility/afghanistan.htm; Patrick Cockburn, "Revealed: Secret Plan to Keep Iraq under US Control," *Independent,* June 5, 2008; Joseph Gerson, "'Enduring' U.S. Bases in Iraq," CommonDreams.org, March 19, 2007; Alexander Cooley, "Base Politics," *Foreign Affairs* 84, no.6 (2005): 79–92; James Bellamy Foster, "A Warning to Africa: The New U.S. Imperial Grand Strategy," *Monthly Review* 58, no. 2(2006), available at http://www.monthlyreview.org/0606jbf.htm; Ann Scott Tyson, "Gates, U.S. General Back Long Iraq Stay," *Washington Post,* June 1, 2007, A11.

39. Guy Raz, "U.S. Builds Air Base in Iraq for Long Haul," *All Things Considered,* National Public Radio, October 12, 2007, http://www.npr.org/templates/ story/story.php?storyId=15184773]; Tom Engelhardt, "Baseless Considerations," Tom Dispatch.com, November 5, 2007.

40. Mark Gillem, *American Town: Building the Outposts of Empire* (Minneapolis: University of Minnesota Press, 2007), xvi.

41. Engelhardt, "Baseless Considerations."

42. See, e.g., Theresa Hitchens, Michael Katz-Hyman, and Victoria Samson, "Space Weapons Spending in the FY 2007 Defense Budget," report, Center for Defense Information, Washington, DC, March 6, 2006.

43. E.g., David Harvey, *The New Imperialism* (Oxford, UK: Oxford University Press, 2003); Neil Smith, *American Empire: Roosevelt's Geographer and the Prelude to Globalization* (Berkeley, CA: University of California Press, 2003); Niall Ferguson, *Colossus: The Price of America's Empire* (New York: Penguin Press, 2004); Chalmers Johnson, *The Sorrows of Empire: Militarism, Secrecy, and the End of the Republic* (New York: Metropolitan Books, 2004).

44. G. John Ikenberry, "Illusions of Empire: Defining the New American Order," *Foreign Affairs* 83, no. 2(2004): 144.

45. See, e.g., Ferguson, *Colossus*; Michael Ignatieff, "The Burden," *New York Times Magazine,* January 5, 2003.

46. David Ottaway, "Islanders Were Evicted for U.S. Base," *Washington Post,* September 9, 1975, A1; *Washington Post,* "The Diego Garcians," editorial, September 11, 1975.

47. U.S. Congress, House, "Diego Garcia, 1975: The Debate over the Base and the Island's Former Inhabitants," Special Subcommittee on Investigations, Committee on International Relations, June 5 and November 4, 94th Cong., 1st sess. (Washington, DC: U.S. Government Printing Office, 1975).

48. Catherine Lutz's *Homefront,* an ethnography of Fayetteville, North Carolina and the Fort Bragg U.S. Army base, has provided a particularly effective model for exploring the costs of militarization and U.S. Empire in the United States; in many ways I sought to replicate her study with a base abroad. Catherine Lutz, *Homefront: A Military City and the American 20th Century* (Boston: Beacon,

2001). See also Katherine T. McCaffrey, *Military Power and Popular Protest: The U.S. Navy in Vieques, Puerto Rico* (New Brunswick, NJ: Rutgers University Press, 2002); Gill, *School of the Americas*.

49. With few exceptions, anthropologists have been absent from the debates on empire. Amid earlier imperial arguments in the 1960s, Kathleen Gough criticized anthropology, "the child of Western imperialism," for having "virtually failed to study Western imperialism as a social system, or even adequately to explore the effects of imperialism on the societies we studied." More than three decades later, Catherine Lutz found there was still almost no anthropological analysis of empire. (Kathleen Gough, "New Proposals for Anthropologists," *Current Anthropology* 9, no. 5 (1968): 403, 405; Catherine Lutz, "Making War at Home in the United States: Militarization and the Current Crisis," *American Anthropologist* 104, no. 3 [2002]: 732.)

While there has been some progress in recent years, there should be little surprise that a discipline rooted in the imperialism and colonialism of Europe and the United States has shied away from making empire and imperialism its immediate subject of study (see Talal Asad, "Introduction," in *Anthropology and the Colonial Encounter*, ed. Talal Asad [London: Ithaca Press, 1973]). Notwithstanding Mina Davis Caulfield's critique of anthropologists' inattention to empire and Laura Nader's still largely ignored exhortations to study the powerful, most anthropologists have continued to study the lives of the powerless, the poor, and those whose lives have suffered the impact of large-scale forces like imperialism (Mina Davis Caulfield, "Culture and Imperialism: Proposing a New Dialectic," and Laura Nader, "Up the Anthropologist—Perspectives Gained from Studying Up," both in *Reinventing Anthropology*, ed. Dell Hymes [New York: Pantheon Books, 1969]).

In recent years, there has been progress toward the investigation of empire, paralleling important new research on elites, policymaking, and policymakers. Catherine Lutz has called for the production of "ethnographies of empire" as a way to ethnographically explore the particularities, practices, shifts, and contradictions in empire, as well as its costs. In her ethnography of Fayetteville, North Carolina, home to the Fort Bragg U.S. Army base, Lutz illustrates the domestic costs of militarization and U.S. Empire, providing an important model for investigating the international effects of militarization and empire in the lives of the Chagossians. (See Lutz, "Making War at Home"; "Empire Is in the Details," *American Ethnologist* 33, no. 4 (2006); *Homefront*. See also McCaffrey, *Military Power and Popular Protest*; Gill, *School of the Americas*.)

Too often, however, many anthropological analyses treat large-scale forces and sources of power like imperialism and the U.S. Government, which shape and structure people's lives, as abstract givens, without subjecting them to detailed analysis of any kind (Michael Burawoy, "Introduction: Reaching for the Global," in *Global Ethnography*, ed. Michael Burawoy et al. [Berkeley, CA: University of California Press, 2000], 1–40). To say, as many do, that structural forces shape lives, constrain agency, and create suffering is one thing. To demonstrate how these things happen is another.

This book then is an attempt to build on the need to subject extralocal forces to ethnographic investigation and to realize a model for understanding widespread suffering developed by Paul Farmer: With suffering, "structured by historically given (and often economically driven) processes and forces that conspire . . . to constrain agency," the task is to detail what the historically given, economically (and politically) driven processes and forces are, how they operate, and how they have shaped Chagossians' lives. As Michael Burawoy says, forces "become the topic of investigation." (See Paul Farmer, "On Suffering and Structural Violence: A View from Below," in *Social Suffering*, ed. Arthur Kleinman, Veena Das, and Margaret Lock [Berkeley, CA: University of California Press, 1997], 261–83; William Roseberry, "Understanding Capitalism—Historically, Structurally, Spatially," in *Locating Capitalism in Time and Space*, ed. D. Nugent (Palo Alto, CA: Stanford University Press, 2002), 61-79; Michael Burawoy, "Manufacturing the Global," *Ethnography* 2, no. 2 [2001]: 147–59; Burawoy, "Introduction: Reaching for the Global"; Michel-Rolph Trouillot, "The Anthropology of the State in the Age of Globalization," *Current Anthropology* 42, no. 1 [2001]: 125–38; Eric R. Wolf, *Europe and the People without History* [Berkeley, CA: University of California Press, 1982].)

At the same time, this corrective would go too far to focus, like many traditional foreign policy scholars, only on the structural dynamics or even the actors of U.S. foreign policy while ignoring the effects of foreign policy. I began to see that a bifocaled approach offering roughly equal study of the Chagossians and U.S. Empire would offer the best way to understand Diego Garcia (see also Gill, *School of the Americas*). The book aims to contribute to scholarship on empire, militarization, and foreign policy by subjecting U.S. Empire and its actors to the same kind of ethnographic scrutiny most often reserved for imperialism's victims, while still attending to the lives affected by the U.S. Empire so often ignored by most non-anthropologist scholars. Ultimately the book attempts to do justice anthropologically to both sides of Diego Garcia, both sides of U.S. Empire, by seeking to investigate ethnographically the experience of U.S. Government officials and the Chagossians while attending to the larger structural context in which the base was created. Bringing the two sides "into the same frame of study," I aim to "posit their relationships on the basis of first-hand ethnographic research." See George Marcus, *Ethnography through Thick and Thin* (Princeton University Press, 1998), 84.

Chapter One
The Ilois, The Islanders

1. On the history of Chagos, see especially former governor of colonial Mauritius Sir Robert Scott's *Limuria: The Lesser Dependencies of Mauritius*, and former commissioner of the British Indian Ocean Territory Richard Edis, *Peak of Limuria: The Story of Diego Garcia and the Chagos Archipelago*, new ed. (London:

Chagos Conservation Trust, 2004). The most important primary sources are those available in the Mauritius Archives and the Public Records Office (National Archives), in Kew, England.

2. Scott, *Limuria*, 68, 42–43, 48–50; Vijayalakshmi Teelock, *Mauritian History: From Its Beginnings to Modern Times* (Moka, Mauritius: Mahatma Gandhi Institute, 2000), 16–17.

3. Robert L. Stein, *The French Slave Trade in the Eighteenth Century: An Old Regime Business* (Madison: University of Wisconsin Press, 1979), 9.

4. Larry Bowman, *Mauritius: Democracy and Development in the Indian Ocean* (Boulder, CO: Westview Press, 1991), 13. See also Teelock, *Mauritian History*, 104–5; Stein, *The French Slave Trade in the Eighteenth Century*, 119.

5. Alfred J. E. Orian, "Report on a Visit to Diego Garcia," *La Revue Agricole et Sucrière* 38 (1958): 129; Scott, *Limuria*, 76.

6. Iain B. Walker, "British Indian Ocean Territory," in *The Complete Guide to the Southwest Indian Ocean* (Argelès sur Mer, France: Cornelius Books, 1993), 562; Scott, *Limuria*, 63, 69; Charles Grant, *The History of Mauritius or the Isle of France and the Neighboring Islands from Their First Discovery to the Present Time* (New Delhi: Asia Educational Services, 1995[1801]), 359.

7. It is possible that other enslaved people arrived as early as 1770.

8. H. Ly-Tio-Fane and S. Rajabalee, "An Account of Diego Garcia and its People," *Journal of Mauritian Studies* 1, no. 2 (1986): 91–92; I. Walker, "British Indian Ocean Territory," 563; Scott, *Limuria*, 20; B. d'Unienville, "Notes on the Chagos Archipelago." Mauritiana Collection, University of Mauritius, n.d.; Edis, *Peak of Limuria*.

9. "Diego Garcia Expedition 1786," India Office Records, Bombay Secret and Political Consultations, Vol. 73, 1786. See also Edis, *Peak of Limuria* , 30–31.

10. Edis, *Peak of Limuria*, 31; Scott, *Limuria*, 75, 20; I. Walker, "British Indian Ocean Territory," 562; "Diégo Garcia," report, n.d. [1825–29], MA: TB 3/2.

11. Europeans had previously referred to the Indian Ocean as an "Arab Lake." See Enseng Ho, "Empire through Diasporic Eyes: A View from the Other Boat," *Comparative Study of Society and History* 46 (2004): 219.

12. Permits to Slave Holders to Transport Slaves between Islands, 1828, MA: IA 32. See also MA: IA 32; IG 59; IG 112/5052, 5117, 5353, 5355, 5448.

13. See Herbert G. Gutman, *The Black Family in Slavery and Freedom, 1750–1925* (New York: Vintage, 1976), 185–201, on naming practices during slavery reflecting the maintenance of kinship ties among African Americans.

14. Scott, *Limuria*, 112, 119; Donald Taylor, "Slavery in the Chagos Archipelago," *Chagos News* 14 (2000): 3; Dulary Peerthum and Satyendra Peerthum, "'By the Sweat of Their Brow': A Study of Free and Unfree Labourers in the Chagos Archipelago, c. 1783–1880," preliminary paper abstract, 2002; MA: IB 12/47.

15. M. N. Lucie-Smith, "Report on the Coconut Industry of the Lesser Dependencies, Mauritius," Department of Agriculture, Port Louis, Mauritius, June 1959, 6.

16. Ly-Tio-Fane and Rajabalee, "An Account of Diego Garcia and Its People," 92; d'Unienville, "Notes on the Chagos Archipelago"; "Diégo Garcia" (report [1825–29]); I. Walker, "British Indian Ocean Territory," 563; Orian, "Report on a Visit to Diego Garcia," 129. Cyclones are only known to have hit Chagos in 1891 and 1944. See Edward P. Ashe, letter to Sir A. W. Moore, November 26, 1903, PRO: ADM 123/34, 2; Edis, *Peak of Limuria*. "Dauquet" was perhaps spelled "Danguet" or "Dauget." Six Islands actually includes a seventh.

17. Bowman, *Mauritius*, 17–18. British oversight in Mauritius and to an even greater extent in the isolated dependencies like Chagos was weak at best. The British sent the first government agent to investigate conditions in Chagos 10–15 years after taking possession of the archipelago, but otherwise simply encouraged the production of oil to supply the Mauritian market. See Scott, *Limuria*, 128; Ly-Tio-Fane and Rajabalee, "An Account of Diego Garcia and Its People," 92–93.

18. Lapotaire et al., "Mémoire," letter, October 8, 1828, MA: TB 1/41828, 13. For descriptions of life under slavery, also see Scott, *Limuria*, 99, 104–5, 149.

19. Lapotaire et al., "Mémoire," 13. Scott confirms that by law, slave owners were technically required to provide basic food rations, clothing, housing, and medical care, and that "slaves were usually supplied with various vegetables . . . [and] encouraged to rear small livestock . . . either by way of incentives to good work or to place on the slaves themselves as much as possible of the onus of providing a balanced diet." Scott, *Limuria*, 105.

20. Also known as the "plantation complex." See Sidney W. Mintz, "The Caribbean as a Socio-cultural Area," in *Peoples and Cultures of the Caribbean: An Anthropological Reader*, ed. Michael M. Horowitz (Garden City, NY: Natural History Press, 1971), 17–46; Mintz, *Caribbean Transformations* (Chicago: Aldine Publishing, 1974); Philip D. Curtin, *The Rise and the Fall of the Plantation Complex: Essays in Atlantic History* (New York: Cambridge University Press, 1990); Michael Craton, *Empire, Enslavement and Freedom in the Caribbean* (Kingston, Jamaica: Ian Bandle, 1997).

21. Curtin, *The Rise and Fall of the Plantation Complex*, 11–13; Mintz, *Caribbean Transformations*, 46.

22. Mintz, *Carribean Transformations*, 52, 54.

23. This was the case in the isolated Out Islands of the Bahamas, where similar conditions prevailed. See Howard Johnson, *The Bahamas from Slavery to Servitude, 1783–1933* (Gainesville: University of Florida Press, 1996), 50.

24. See W. J. Eccles, *The French in North America, 1500–1783* (East Lansing: Michigan State University Press, 1998), 172–74; William F. S. Miles, *Elections and Ethnicity in French Martinique: A Paradox in Paradise* (New York: Praeger Publishers, 1986), 32–34; Deryck Scarr, *Seychelles since 1770: History of a Slave and Post-Slavery Society* (Trenton, NJ: Africa World Press, 1999).

25. Scott, *Limuria*, 136; Craton, Empire, *Enslavement, and Freedom in the Caribbean*, 3; Eccles, *The French in North America, 1500–1783*, 172.

26. Eccles, *The French in North America, 1500–1783*, 172.

27. Scott, *Limuria*, 140–41.

28. L. B. Büehmüller and André Büehmüller, census record, April 8, 1861, MA: TB 3/1. The extent and rate at which Indian labor was introduced in Chagos is unclear. A visiting magistrate's report from 1880 says that there were on the order of 10 Indians in all of Chagos, a figure almost certainly far too low. See J. H. Ackroyd, "Report of the Police and Stipendary Magistrate for the Smaller Dependencies 1880," Magistrate for Lesser Dependencies 1880, Port Louis, Mauritius, March 22, MA: RA 2568, 11. Some claim a figure of 40 percent Indian descent by the 1960s, which may accurately reflect the percentage tracing at least some Indian ancestry. See Francoise Botte, "The 'Ilois' Community and the 'Ilois' Women," unpublished MS, 1980; Iain B. Walker, *"Zaffer Pe Sanze": Ethnic Identity and Social Change among the Ilois in Mauritius* (Vacoas, Mauritius: KMLI, 1986).

29. Marina Carter and Raymond d'Unienville, *Unshackling Slaves: Liberation and Adaptation of Ex-Apprentices* (London: Pink Pigeon Books, N.D), 57.

30. See Thomas V. Bulpin, *Islands in a Forgotten Sea* ([no city], Netherlands: Howard Timmins, 1958), 314; H. Labouchere, letter to Governor Higginson, February 26, 1957, MA: SA 57/47, and letter to Governor Higginson, August 20, 1957, MA: SA 59/19; Scott, *Limuria*, 263; Ackroyd, "Report of the Police and Stipendary Magistrate," 8.

31. Charles Anderson to Colonial Secretary, September 5, 1838, MA: RD 18.

32. G. Meyer, "Report on Visit to Chagos Archipelago," Port Louis, Mauritius, Labour Office, May 23, 1949, PRO: CO 859/194/8, 1.

33. Bulpin, *Islands in a Forgotten Sea*, 28, 314; Ackroyd, "Report of the Police and Stipendary Magistrate," 11; Scott, *Limuria*, 162.

34. Scott, *Limuria*, 162–65.

35. Ackroyd, "Report of the Police and Stipendary Magistrate," 11. Without hearing from Chagossians at the time, however, one must be careful about drawing conclusions based on these uncorroborated official reports.

36. Scott, *Limuria*, 253; Warner, "Report of Mr. Warner on the Dependencies of Mauritius," Port Louis, Mauritius, MA: TB 1/3.

37. H. J. Holland, letter to Colonial Secretary, February 7, 1887, MA: SA 167/25.

38. Ivanoff Dupont, "Report of the Acting Magistrate for the Lesser Dependencies of Mauritius on Diego Garcia," Bambous, Mauritius, June 4, 1883, MA: SA 142/9, 2–5; Scott, *Limuria*, 169–78.

39. Papen, "The French-based Creoles of the Indian Ocean"; John Holm, *Pidgins and Creoles*, vol. 2: *Reference Survey* (Cambridge: University of Cambridge Press, 1989), 403–4.

40. Also *Ilwa*. See Roger Dussercle, *Archipel de Chagos: En mission, novembre 10, 1933–janvier 1934* (Port Louis, Mauritius: General Printing and Stationery, 1934), 9; John Madeley, "Diego Garcia: A Contrast to the Falklands," The Minority Rights Group Report 54, London: Minority Rights Group Ltd, 1985 [1982], n. 5.

41. Ly-Tio-Fane and Rajabalee, "An Account of Diego Garcia and Its People," 105; Scott, *Limuria*, 182.

42. For a concise description of copra processing, see I. Walker, "British Indian Ocean Territory," 563.

43. The account and all quotations in this section come from W. J. Hanning, "Report on Visit to Peros Banhos," parts I and II, March 29, 1932. PRO: CO 167/879/4 102894. Unfortunately I was unable to ask Rita and other older Chagossians about the events described.

44. Ibid., I:6.

45. Ibid., I:5.

46. Ibid., I:6.

47. Ibid., I:8.

48. Ibid., I:8–9.

49. Ibid., I:9–10.

50. Ibid., attachment.

51. Ibid., II:1–3.

52. John Todd, "Notes on the Islands of the British Indian Ocean Territory," report, January 10, 1969. SNA, 33; "Notes on a Visit to Chagos by the Administrator, British Indian Ocean Territory," report, July 30, 1969, PRO, 3; Dalais 1935:18.

53. R. Lavoipierre, "Report on a Visit to the Mauritius Dependencies: 16th October–10th November, 1953," Port Louis, Mauritius, December 7, 1953, PRO: CO 1023/132 1953:5; Mary Darlow, "Report by Public Assistance Commissioner and Social Welfare Advisor," Port Louis, Mauritius, December, PRO: CO 1023/132 1953; Scott, *Limuria, 7.*

54. The plantation company had the power—and at times exercised it—to deport workers that management considered troublesome. Otherwise, everyone living on the islands was guaranteed work. The following description of working and living conditions comes from many sources, including interviews and conversations with Chagossians and other plantation employees. See also Scott, *Limuria*; I. Walker, *Zaffer Pe Sanze*, "British Indian Ocean Territory"; the reports of J. R. Todd; and a series of magistrate reports on Chagos dating to the nineteenth century.

55. See, e.g., Todd, "Notes on the Islands of the BIOT."

56. Scott, *Limuria*, 285.

57. Ibid., 266–67.

58. Ibid., 242.

59. Hilary Blood, "The Peaks of Lemuria," *Geographical Magazine* 29 (1957): 522.

60. Scott, *Limuria*, 184, 24.

61. Auguste Toussaint, *Histoire des Iles Mascareignes* (Paris: Editions Berger-Levrault, 1972), 18.

62. Scott, *Limuria*, 293. Scott meant his description to apply also to the people of the other Lesser Dependencies like Agalega.

Chapter 2
The Bases of Empire

1. Interview with U.S. Navy historian Jeffery Barlow, August 2005. This chapter's title owes a debt to *Monthly Review*, "U.S. Military Bases and Empire," March 2002, http://www.monthlyreview.org/0302editr.htm. There are few histories of how the U.S. and U.K. governments created the base on Diego Garcia and expelled the Chagossians. Works by Bandjunis (*Diego Garcia*) and Bezboruah (*U.S. Strategy in the Indian Ocean*), based in part on interviews with some of the key U.S. Government officials involved, provide the best accounts. The latter, by a retired naval officer who participated in the development of the base and who also had access to relevant Navy documents, is a detailed insider's account of the history. The self-published book has been indispensable to my reconstruction of the history but is not the work of a professional historian.

2. The idea is indicated by a curious three-sentence memorandum from shortly before the 1960 elections, found in the Navy archives without its originally attached proposal. The first and key sentence reads, "The attached proposal by Stuart Barber was intended as an idea to be fed, somehow, to both Presidential candidates." The memorandum's subject line reads "South Atlantic and Indian Ocean Monroe Doctrine and Force." See Op-61, "South Atlantic and Indian Ocean Monroe Doctrine and Force," memorandum to Chief of Naval Operations, August 2, 1960, NHC: 00 Files, 1960, Box 8, 5710. I am inferring the contents of the proposal from the subject line.

3. Long-Range Objectives Group, Director, "Annual Statement of Long-Range Navy Objectives," report to Chief of Naval Operations, 1956, NHC: 00 Files, 1956, Box 1, A1 Plans, Projects, and Developments, 1.

4. U.S. Naval Institute, "Reminiscences of Admiral Horacio Rivero, Jr., U.S. Navy (Retired), oral history vol. 3," Annapolis, MD, U.S. Naval Institute, May 1978, 300–301.

5. R. L. Johnson, memorandum for Deputy Chief of Naval Operations (Plans & Policy), 2. All signs indicate that Barber drafted the memo.

6. Bandjunis, *Diego Garcia*, 2.

7. *Monthly Review*, "U.S. Military Bases and Empire."

8. The Department of Defense acknowledges having 909 bases outside the 50 states and Washington, DC. This list strangely omits many well-known bases, including all those in Iraq and Afghanistan, as well secret bases unacknowledged by the DOD. An estimate of around 1,000 thus seems fair. The definitions and even the terminology surrounding bases (forts, camps, stations, etc.) are notoriously elusive. I generally use the term *base* and generally call anything the DOD refers to as a *site* a base. See Department of Defense, "Base Structure Report Fiscal Year 2007 Baseline (A Summary of DoD's Real Property Inventory)," 2007; C. Johnson, *The Sorrows of Empire*.

9. I define imperialism as the creation and maintenance of hierarchical relationships of formal or informal rule, domination, or control by one people or

sociopolitical entity over a significant part of the life of other peoples or sociopolitical entities such that the stronger shapes or has the ability to shape significant aspects of the ways of living (political, economic, social, or cultural) of the weaker. Empire is then the designation reserved for states and other entities practicing imperialism.

10. E.g., Harvey, *The New Imperialism*; Smith, *American Empire*; Ferguson, *Colossus*; C. Johnson, *The Sorrows of Empire*.

11. Ferguson, *Colossus*; Ignatieff, "The Burden."

12. Ferguson is ultimately skeptical that the nation has the proper will and "imperial cast of mind" to play such a role. See Ferguson, *Colossus*, 2, 25, 29.

13. Ignatieff, quoted in Chalmers Johnson, *Nemesis: The Last Days of the American Republic* (New York: Metropolitan Books, 2007), 73–74.

14. E.g., William Appleman Williams, *The Tragedy of American Diplomacy*, rev. ed. (New York: Delta, 1962); Lloyd C. Gardner, Walter F. La Feber, and Thomas J. McCormick, *Creation of the U.S. Empire*, vol. 1: *U.S. Diplomatic History to 1901*, 2nd ed. (Chicago: Rand McNally College Publishing, 1976); Lloyd C. Gardner, Walter F. La Feber, and Thomas J. McCormick, *Creation of the U.S. Empire*, vol. 2: *U.S. Diplomatic History since 1893*, 2nd ed. (Chicago: Rand McNally College Publishing, 1976); Smith, *American Empire*.

15. Smith, *American Empire*, 360.

16. See e.g., Williams, *The Tragedy of American Diplomacy*; Gardner et al., *Creation of the U.S. Empire*, vols. 1–2; Harvey, *The New Imperialism*.

17. Sydney Lens, *Permanent War: The Militarization of America* (New York: Schocken Books, 1987); Michael S. Sherry, *In the Shadows of War: The United States since the 1930s* (New Haven, CT: Yale University Press, 1995); C. Johnson, *The Sorrows of Empire*; C. Johnson, *Nemesis*; *Monthly Review*, "U.S. Military Bases and Empire"; Tom Engelhardt, "Gunboat Diplomacy," *Mother Jones*, April 1, 2004, http://www.motherjobes.com/news/dailymojo/2004/04/03_667.html 2004; and even Smith, *American Empire*, 349.

18. James R. Blaker, *United States Overseas Basing: An Anatomy of the Dilemma* (New York: Praeger, 1990), 29.

19. Scholars in the basing literature may have underestimated the number of pre–World War II bases. Given the frequency of major U.S. military interventions in Latin America before the war and occupations in Nicaragua, Panama, Cuba, Haiti, and the Dominican Republic, bases and garrisons (as well as U.S. naval power) likely played a key role in the maintenance of U.S. dominance in the region. See, e.g., Carolyn Hall and Héctor Pérez Brignoli, *Historical Atlas of Central America*, cartographer John V. Cotter (Norman, OK: University of Oklahoma Press, 2003), 288.

20. William Earl Weeks, *Building the Continental Empire: American Expansion from the Revolution to the Civil War* (Chicago: Ivan R. Dee, 1996), ix; Richard W. Van Alstyne, *The Rising U.S. Empire* (New York: Norton Library, 1960), 8; see also Reginald Horsman, *Expansion and American Indian Policy, 1783–1812* (East Lansing: Michigan State University Press, 1967), viii, 5–6.

21. Horsman, *Expansion and American Indian Policy,* 141, 157; Gillem, *American Town,* 18–19.

22. Anni P. Baker, *American Soldiers Overseas: The Global Military Presence* (Westport, CT: Praeger, 2004), 4; Gillem, *American Town,* 19.

23. Francis Paul Prucha, *A Guide to the Military Posts of the United States 1789–1895* (Madison: State Historical Society of Wisconsin, 1964), 10–11.

24. Dee Brown, *Bury My Heart at Wounded Knee: An Indian History of the American West* (New York: Henry Holt, 1970).

25. Alan Brinkley, *American History: A Survey,* vol. 1: *To 1877,* 10th ed. (New York: McGraw-Hill, 1999), 306.

26. D. Brown, *Bury My Heart at Wounded Knee,* 7.

27. In 1853, Commodore Matthew Calbraith Perry purchased a $50 plot of land on what is now called Chi Chi Jima, near Iwo Jima in the western Pacific, which he intended to become a U.S. coaling station. A. M. Jackson, memorandum for the Chief of Naval Operations, December 7, 1964, NHC: 00 Files, 1965, Box 26, 11000/1B, 2; Richard D. Challener, *Admirals, Generals, and American Foreign Policy: 1898–1914* (Princeton, NJ: Princeton University Press, 1973), 5.

28. Philip A. Crowl, "Makers of Modern Strategy from Machiavelli to the Nuclear Age," ed. Peter Paret (Princeton, NJ: Princeton University Press, 1986), 455.

29. Ibid., 444–77; see also Hall M. Friedman, *Creating an American Lake: United States Imperialism and Strategic Security in the Pacific Basin, 1945–1947* (Westport, CT: Greenwood Press, 2001), 2–3.

30. Stephen A. Kinzer, *Overthrow: America's Century of Regime Change from Hawaii to Iraq* (New York: Times Books, 2006), 86–87.

31. Ibid., 48.

32. See Williams, *The Tragedy of American Diplomacy;* Gardner et al., *Creation of the U.S. Empire,* vols. 1–2; Smith, *American Empire.*

33. For an interesting discussion of how the United States learned the value of a more discreet, indirect form of imperialism avoiding sovereignty over dependent lands, see Christina D. Burnett, "The Edges of Empire and the Limits of Sovereignty: American Guano Islands," *American Quarterly* 57, no. 3 (2005): 779–805.

34. John Lindsay-Poland, *Emperors in the Jungle: The Hidden History of the U.S. in Panama,* (Durham, NC: Duke University Press, 2003), 16–17; Hall and Pérez Brignoli, *Historical Atlas of Central America,* 209; Brinkley, *American History,* 767.

35. Hall and Pérez Brignoli, *Historical Atlas of Central America,* 228.

36. Ibid., 228; Lindsay-Poland, *Emperors in the Jungle,* 27.

37. C. T. Sandars, *America's Overseas Garrisons: The Leasehold Empire* (Oxford: Oxford University Press, 2000), 140.

38. Friedman, *Creating an American Lake,* 3.

39. See Desch, *When the Third World Matters;* Sandars, *America's Overseas Garrisons;* Blaker, *United States Overseas Basing,* 29.

40. Blaker, *United States Overseas Basing*.

41. Desch, *When the Third World Matters*, 183 n.123; Lindsay-Poland, *Emperors in the Jungle*, 45.

42. Sandars, *America's Overseas Garrisons*, 4–5.

43. Ibid., 4–6.

44. Hayes et al., *American Lake*, 18–19.

45. David Hanlon, *Remaking Micronesia: Discourses over Development in a Pacific Territory 1944–1982* (Honolulu, HA: University of Hawai'i Press, 1998), 24–26.

46. Although U.S. histories of this and other battles in the Pacific always note the "bloody" nature of the fighting, the attention is almost always on the (relatively few) U.S. soldiers who died, not on the Japanese and certainly not on the Marshallese.

47. Jonathan Weisgall, *Operation Crossroads: The Atomic Tests at Bikini Atoll* (Annapolis, MD: Naval Institute Press, 1994), 43.

48. Blaker, *United States Overseas Basing*, 23, 9.

49. Sandars, *America's Overseas Garrisons*, 59.

50. Hayes et al., *American Lake*, 23–24.

51. Donald F. McHenry, *Micronesia: Trust Betrayed* (New York: Carnegie Endowment for International Peace, 1975), 67, 66.

52. Friedman, *Creating an American Lake*, 1–2.

53. Hayes et al., *American Lake*, 28.

54. Stanley de Smith, quoted in Roy H. Smith, *The Nuclear Free and Independent Pacific Movement: After Mururoa* (London: I. B. Tauris, 1997), 42.

55. Blaker, *United States Overseas Basing*, 32.

56. George Stambuk, *American Military Forces Abroad: Their Impact on the Western State System* (Columbus: Ohio State University Press, 1963), 9.

57. Sandars, *America's Overseas Garrisons*, 21, 101.

58. Hayes et al., *American Lake*, 25.

59. Smith, *American Empire*, 2, 14–16, 21.

60. Carole McGranahan, "A Nonviolent History of War: Global Politics, Refugee Activism, and Forgetting Tibet," conference paper, "Forgotten Conflicts, Permanent Catastrophes?" Colgate University, Hamilton, NY, April 2007.

61. Smith, *American Empire*; Chalmers Johnson, *Blowback: The Costs and Consequences of U.S. Empire* (New York: Metropolitan/Owl, 2004[2000]), "America's Empire of Bases," http://www.tomdispatch.com/ index.mhtml?pid1181, January 15, 2004; *Monthly Review*, "U.S. Military Bases and Empire."

62. *Monthly Review*, "U.S. Military Bases and Empire."

63. Joseph Gerson, "The Sun Never Sets," in *The Sun Never Sets: Confronting the Network of Foreign U.S. Military Bases*, ed. Joseph Gerson and Bruce Birchard (Boston: South End Press, 1991), 14; see also *Monthly Review*, "U.S. Military Bases and Empire."

64. Lutz, "Empire Is in the Details."

65. Smith, *American Empire*, 349, 360.

66. Blaker, *United States Overseas Basing*, 32. For military and civilian leaders, the war further cemented the importance of maintaining large bases in the eastern Pacific, on Okinawa and elsewhere in Japan, on Guam, and in South Korea—a pattern that remains in place to this day. Hayes et al., *American Lake*, 29–30, 45.

67. Blaker, *United States Overseas Basing*, 32.

Chapter Three
The Strategic Island Concept and a Changing of the Imperial Guard

1. Edis, *Peak of Limuria*, 63, 109 n.1; Bandjunis, *Diego Garcia*, 13.

2. Edis, *Peak of Limuria*, 62–64, 68; Ashley Jackson, *War and Empire in Mauritius and the Indian Ocean* (Hampshire, UK: Palgrave, 2001), 42, 44–47.

3. See John Lewis Gaddis, *Strategies of Containment: A Critical Appraisal of Postwar American National Security Policy* (Oxford: Oxford University Press, 1982).

4. Ibid., 90–91.

5. Claude Ricketts, Study on Strategic Requirements for Guam, memorandum for the Chief of Naval Operations, February 21, 1963, NHC: 00 Files, 1963, 11000/1, Tab B.

6. Stambuk, *American Military Forces Abroad*, 13.

7. Baker, *American Soldiers Overseas*, 49.

8. Lutz, *Homefront*, 86.

9. Ibid., 47–48.

10. Sherry, *In the Shadows of War*; Lens, *Permanent War*.

11. Lens, *Permanent War*, 22.

12. Sherry, *In the Shadows of War*, 235.

13. Lutz, *Homefront*, 9.

14. Bezboruah, *U.S. Strategy in the Indian Ocean*, 59, 83, 227; Bandjunis, *Diego Garcia*, 1.

15. Barber, letter to Ryan, April 26, 1982, 2.

16. Ibid., 2.

17. Stuart B. Barber, letter to Senator Ted Stevens, October 3, 1975.

18. Bezboruah, *U.S. Strategy in the Indian Ocean*, 58.

19. The United States had major advantages in bombers, air defenses, submarines, and intercontinental ballistic missiles (ICBMs), and thus in first and second strike nuclear capabilities. The United States had its unparalleled system of bases, a navy with uncontested control of the seas, and a related ability, unmatched by any other competitor, to deploy its military power almost anywhere in the world. Gareth Porter, *Perils of Dominance: Imbalance of Power and the Road to War in Vietnam* (Berkeley, CA: University of California Press, 2005), 14, 4–10.

20. Ibid., vii–1. Although my interviewees almost all stressed the importance of the Cold War to understanding Diego Garcia, strikingly absent from their comments and the archival record is any concern among officials about the reaction

of the Soviet Union or China to U.S. plans for Diego. Government officials were unworried that the Soviets or Chinese would respond militarily by creating bases of their own, increase their naval presence, or make other military moves to resist the creation of a base in a neighboring region. The only fear expressed was that the Soviets and others might inflict some political or propaganda damage on the United States for militarizing a previously peaceful ocean.

21. Thomas H. Moorer, memorandum for Chief of Naval Operations, January 2, 1962, NHC: 00 Files, 1962, Box 12, 11000, 2.

22. Rivero, "Assuring a Future Base Structure," 5. Stu's memory and Bandjunis's history are in disagreement about the timing of the survey. Bandjunis says it took place in the summer of 1957, when the Navy sent Admiral Jerauld Wright, Commander in Chief of the U.S. Atlantic Fleet and Supreme Allied Commander for the Atlantic, to the island. Stu's recollection is that he began work on the idea in 1958. See Bandjunis, *Diego Garcia*, 2.

23. Weisgall, *Operation Crossroads*, 32.

24. Naval Historical Center, "Admiral Horacio Rivero, United States, Navy, Retired," biographies, July 26, 1972 NHC: Operational Archives Branch.

25. Weisgall, *Operation Crossroads*, 32, 328 n. 41.

26. Ibid., 32–33.

27. Ibid., 106–7.

28. Ibid., 107–8.

29. Ibid., 308–9.

30. Ibid., 309–14.

31. Hanlon, *Remaking Micronesia*, 186.

32. See Weisgall, *Operation Crossroads*, 302–5.

33. E.g., Robert C. Kiste, *The Bikinians: A Study in Forced Migration* (Menlo Park, CA: Cummings Publishing, 1974); Catherine Lutz, "Introduction," in *Micronesia as Strategic Colony: The Impact of U.S. Policy on Micronesian Health and Culture*, ed. Catherine Lutz, Cultural Survival Occasional Papers, 12 (Cambridge, MA: Cultural Survival, 1984).

In 1968, President Johnson allowed the Bikinians to return to their islands after a cleanup. They returned in 1969, although they were shocked to find the islands decimated, many parts having disappeared altogether. In 1978, medical tests revealed that the cleanup had been inadequate and that "the people may have ingested the largest amounts of radioactive material of any known population." They were again moved. After fifteen years of lawsuits and negotiations, the Bikinians received a $75 million settlement for the taking and use of their islands. $110 million was put into a trust for the decontamination and resettlement of the islands. After an extensive cleanup, some have now returned. Weisgall, *Operation Crossroads*, 314–15.

34. U.S. Naval Institute, "Reminiscences of Admiral Horacio Rivero, Jr.," 302–3.

35. See also Vine, "Empire's Footprint," for a full discussion of these dynamics.

36. Kinzer, *Overthrow,* 15. I have recently learned of land expropriations and possible displacements in the Waikane and Makua valleys.

37. Cheryl Lewis, "Kaho'olawe and the Military," ICE case study, Washington, DC, Spring 2001, http://www.american.edu/ted/ice/hawaiibombs.htm.

38. Globalsecurity.org, "Guam," 2003, http://www.globalsecurity.org/military /facility/guam.htm; James Brooke, "Threats and Responses: U.S. Bases," *New York Times,* March 10, 2003.

39. Lindsay-Poland, *Emperors in the Jungle,* 28–29, 42–43, 192.

40. McCaffrey, *Military Power and Popular Protest,* 9; Anna Piatek, "Displacement by Military Bases," unpublished paper, George Washington University, April 2006; Roland G. Simbulan, *The Bases of Our Insecurity* (Manila: BALAI Fellowship, 1985).

41. Barbara Rose Johnston, "Reparations and the Right to Remedy," contributing paper, World Commission on Dams, July 1, 2000.

42. McCaffrey, *Military Power and Popular Protest,* 38–39.

43. Ibid., 70–72.

44. By 1995, about 800 remained in Bolivia with their offspring. Okinawa remains home to 75 percent of U.S. bases in Japan, though it represents only 1 percent of Japanese land. It also remains the poorest of Japan's prefectures. C. Johnson, *The Sorrows of Empire,* 50–53, 200; C. Johnson, *Blowback,* 11; Kensei Yoshida, *Democracy Betrayed: Okinawa under U.S. Occupation* (Bellingham, WA: Western Washington University, n.d.[2001]); Kozy K. Amemiya, "The Bolivian Connection: U.S. Bases and Okinawan Emigration," in *Okinawa: Cold War Island,* ed. Chalmers Johnson (n.p.: Japan Policy Research Institute, 1999), 63.

45. Aqqaluk Lynge, *The Right to Return: Fifty Years of Struggle by Relocated Inughuit in Greenland* (n.p: Atuagkat Publishers, 2002); D. L. Brown, "Trail of Frozen Tears," *Washington Post,* October 22, 2002, C1; J. M. Olsen, "US Agrees to Return to Denmark Unused Area near Greenland Military Base," Associated Press Worldstream, September 24, 2002.

46. Lynge, *The Right to Return,* 10, 27, 32–36.

47. Hanlon, *Remaking Micronesia,* 189–91, 201–2.

48. Ibid., 193; Peter Marks, "Paradise Lost; The Americanization of the Pacific," *Newsday,* January 12, 1986, 10.

49. PCRC, "The Kwajalein Atoll and the New Arms Race: The US Anti-Ballistic Weapons System and Consequences for the Marshall Islands of the Pacific," *Indigenous Affairs* 2 (2001): 38–43. U.S. Representative John Seiberling, visiting the atoll in 1984, summed up the conditions in Ebeye by comparing them to those on the base: "The contrast couldn't be greater or more dramatic. Kwajalein is like Fort Lauderdale or one of our Miami resort areas, with palm-lined beaches, swimming pools, a golf course, people bicycling everywhere, a first-class hospital and a good school; and Ebeye, on the other hand, is an island slum, over-populated, treeless filthy lagoon, littered beaches, a dilapidated hospital, and contaminated water supply, and so forth." Hanlon, *Remaking Micronesia,* 201.

50. Andrew Bell-Fialkoff, *Ethnic Cleansing* (New York: St. Martin's Press, 1996), 54, 3–4.

51. McCaffrey, *Military Power and Popular Protest,* 9–10.

52. In the case of Fayetteville, North Carolina's Fort Bragg Army base, the location of the base was determined in no small part by the ease with which the government could evict black, Scotch, and Native American farmers and sharecroppers, as well as smallholders and renters, the majority of the population in the area. Lutz, *Homefront,* 26–27.

53. U.S. Naval Institute, "Reminiscences of Admiral Horacio Rivero, Jr.," 301.

54. Barber, letter to Ryan, April 26, 1982, 3.

55. U.S. Naval Institute, "Reminiscences of Admiral Horacio Rivero, Jr.," 302–3.

56. Attachment to Rivero, "Assuring a Future Base Structure."

57. Claude Ricketts, "Memorandum of Understanding Resulting from the CNO-First Sea Lord Discussions of October 31 and November 1," memorandum to Chief of Naval Operations, 1960, NHC: 00 Files, 1960, Box 8, 5710.

58. Bezboruah, *U.S. Strategy in the Indian Ocean,* 58–59; see also P. B. Ryan, "Diego Garcia," *Proceedings* 110, no. 9/979 (1984): 133.

59. Bezboruah, *U.S. Strategy in the Indian Ocean,* 58. See also Bandjunis, *Diego Garcia,* 1–3; Michael A. Palmer, *Guardians of the Gulf: A History of America's Expanding Role in the Persian Gulf, 1833–1992* (New York: Free Press, 1992), 95; Ryan, "Diego Garcia," 133; P. S. Mewes, letter to Mr. Gwynn, April 22, 1971, PRO.

60. F. J. Blouin, memorandum for the Director, J-5, November 23, 1960, NARA: JCS, 4920, November 1960.

61. Bandjunis, *Diego Garcia,* 3.

62. Barber, letter to Ryan, April 26, 1982. See also Ryan, "Diego Garcia," 133.

63. Black, memorandum to William Lang, April 15, 1961, NARA: R6330/490 ASD/ISA Decimal File, 1961, 680.1 January–March, 471.6-821, Box 27.

64. Henry S. Rowen, memorandum for Bundy, Rostow, McGhee, Amory, Bissell, and Nitze, March 31, 1961, NARA: RG 330/490, ASD ISA Decimal Files 1961, 680.1 January–March, Box 27.

65. Thomas H. Moorer, memorandum for Chief of Naval Operations, January 2, 1962, NHC: 00 Files, 1962, Box 12, 11000, 1.

66. William P. Bundy, memorandum for Chairman, Joint Chiefs of Staff, May 5, 1962, enclosure, NARA: RG 330/490, ASD ISA Decimal Files 1962, 680.1 January–July, Box 72:1–2.

67. The following quotations come from a 1970 oral history interview conducted from Komer's RAND Corporation office in Santa Monica, California.

68. Robert W. Komer, Sixth Oral History Interview, Dennis J. O'Brien, interviewer, JFK, Boston, MA, January 30, 1970, 28.

69. CINCPACFLT, memorandum to CINCPAC, August 13, 1964, NHC: 00 Files, 1964, Box 20, 11000/1A, Tab-B.

70. Ibid.

71. Paul H. Nitze, memorandum for record, October 2, 1962, NARA: RG 330/490, ASD ISA Decimal Files 1962, Box 106, UK 333 September–December.

72. Joint Chiefs of Staff, "Decision on JCS 570/548, a Report by the J-5 on Base Rights in the Indian Ocean Area," report, January 11, 1962, NARA 1962, 3930–3933.

73. *Foreign Relations of the United States, 1961–1963,* vol. 19: *South Asia,* ed. Louis J. Smith (Washington, DC: United States Government Printing Office, 1996), 565.

74. Ibid., 19:623–24.

Chapter Four
"Exclusive Control"

1. David Halberstam, *The Best and the Brightest,* new ed. (New York: Modern Library, 2001), 42–44.

2. Ibid., 48, 69–70.

3. Ibid., 70.

4. Tim Weiner, "Robert Komer, 78, Figure in Vietnam, Dies," *New York Times,* April 12, 2000, A29.

5. Robert W. Komer, Oral history interview, interviewer Joe B. Frantz, January 30, 1970, LBJ: AC 94-1, 1–2.

6. Komer, Oral history interview, January 30, 2–3.

7. Robert W. Komer, Oral history interview, interviewer Joe B. Frantz, August 18, 1970, LBJ: AC 94-1, 71.

8. Weiner, "Robert Komer." In the words of Halberstam, Komer, "anxious to show everyone in town how close he was to the President (six photographs of Lyndon Johnson on his office wall, a Saigon record), had gone around to dinner parties telling reporters that he had assured the President that the war would not be an election issue in 1968. It was not one of his better predictions." Halberstam, *The Best and the Brightest,* 738.

9. Komer, Sixth Oral History Interview, 29.

10. Ibid., 28–34.

11. Robert W. Komer, memorandum for the President, June 19, 1963, JFK: NSF, Komer, Box 422, India Indian Ocean (IOTF) 1963.

12. Ibid.

13. Robert W. Komer, *Maritime Strategy or Coalition Defense* (Cambridge, MA: Abt Books, 1984), xvi.

14. Robert W. Komer, Fourth Oral History Interview, interviewer Elizabeth Farmer, October 31, 1964, JFK; Komer, Sixth Oral History Interview, 32.

15. John F. Kennedy, letter to Robert S. McNamara, July 10, 1963, LBJ: NSF, Komer, Indian Ocean Dec 63-Mar 66 (including IOTF), Box 26, #75.

16. Komer, Sixth Oral History Interview, 29.

17. Dean Rusk, letter to Robert S. McNamara, August 17, 1963, JFK: NSF, Komer, Box 422, India Indian Ocean (IOTF) 1963, 2–3.

18. Bandjunis, *Diego Garcia*, 3–5; Bezboruah, *U.S. Strategy in the Indian Ocean*, 58–59.

19. *Foreign Relations of the United States, 1961–1963*, 19:653–54.

20. U.S. Embassy London, telegram to Secretary of State, August 26, 1963, NARA: RG 59/250/5/13/6, Subject Numeric Files 1963, Box 3745.

21. Ibid.

22. Robert W. Komer, letter to McGeorge Bundy, September 6, 1963, JFK: NSF, Komer, Box 422, India Indian Ocean (IOTF) 1963 [White House Memoranda].

23. *Foreign Relations of the United States, 1964–1968*, vol. 21: *Near East Region Arabian Peninsula*, ed. N. D. Howland (Washington, DC: United States Government Printing Office, 2000), 83–86.

24. Ibid., 85.

25. ADMINO CINCUSNAVEUR, telegram to RUECW/JCS, February 25, 1964, NHC: 00 Files, 1964, Box 20, 11000/1B.

26. U.K. Colonial Office, "Defence Interests in the Indian Ocean," memorandum, October 20, 1964, PRO.

27. David Bruce, memorandum to Secretary of State, February 27, 1964, NHC: OAB, 00, 1964, Box 20, 11000/1B.

28. U.S. Embassy London, telegram to Secretary of State, February 27, NHC: 00 Files, 1964, Box 20, 11000/1B, 1–2.

29. John Pilger, *Freedom Next Time: Resisting the Empire* (New York: Nation Books, 2007), 25.

30. U.S. Embassy London, telegram to Secretary of State, March 3, 1964, enclosure, "U.S. Defence Interests in the Indian Ocean," NARA: RG 59/250/6/23/3–4, Subject-Numeric Files 1964–1966, Box 1638:2–3.

31. "Defence Interests in the Indian Ocean" [author unknown], memorandum, 1965?. PRO: FO 371/184522, 37868.1965.

32. UK Foreign Office 1966: para. 10–11.

33. U.K. Foreign Office, "Steering committee on international organisations presentation of British Indian Ocean Territory in the United Nations," September 8, 1966, PRO: para. 10–12.

34. Alan Brooke-Turner, "British Indian Ocean Territory," memorandum, March 18, 1966, UKTB. John Pilger says, "Winston Smith in George Orwell's *1984* could not have put it better." See Pilger, *Freedom Next Time*, 23.

35. S. J. Dunn, "Shore up the Indian Ocean," *Proceedings* 110, no. 9/979 (1984): 131.

36. U.S. officials suggested that facilities for the islands might include prepositioned military stockpiles; an air base for 2–4 air squadrons and supporting cargo

planes, troop carriers, air tankers, antisubmarine patrols, and air logistics operations; an anchorage for an aircraft carrier task force; a communications station; an amphibious staging area; a space tracking facility; fuel and ammunition storage; and secondary support anchorages and logistics runways. U.S. Embassy London, telegram to Secretary of State, March 3, 1964.

37. Jeffery C. Kitchen, memorandum to the Secretary [of State], March 3, 1964, NARA: RG 59/250/6/23/3–4, Subject-Numeric Files 1964–1966, Box 1638, 3.

38. USUN, telegram to RUEHCR/SECSTATE, May 30, 1964, NARA: RG 59/250/6/23/3–4, Subject-Numeric Files 1964–1966, Box 1551, 1–4.

39. *Foreign Relations of the United States, 1964–1968,* 21:91–93; see also Bandjunis, *Diego Garcia,* 10–11.

40. Emphasis in original. A supporting document underlined this point further: "We have carefully chosen areas where there is a limited number of transients or inhabitants (e.g. 100–200 people)." See *Foreign Relations of the United States, 1964–1968,* 21:91, 93.

41. Bandjunis, *Diego Garcia,* 14.

42. CINCUSNAVEUR, telegram to RUECW/CNO, August 4, 1964, NHC: 00 Files, 1964, Box 20, 11000/1B.

43. Bandjunis, *Diego Garcia,* 14.

44. Robert Newton, "Report on the Anglo-American Survey in the Indian Ocean," 1964, PRO: para. 25.

45. Robert H. Estabrook, "U.S., Britain Consider Indian Ocean Bases," *Washington Post,* August 29, 1964, A1, A6.

46. U.S. Embassy London, telegram to Department of State, August 28, 1964, NARA: RG 59/250/6/23/3–4, Subject-Numeric Files 1964–1966, Box 1638.

47. U.S. Department of State, "Memorandum of Conversation, Islands in the Indian Ocean," April 15, 1965, LBJ: NSF, Country File, Box 207, UK Memos vol. III 2/65–4/65.

48. United Nations Declaration 1514 (XV), "Declaration on the Granting of Independence to Colonial Countries and Peoples," December 14, 1960, sec. 6.

49. E. H. Peck, "Defence Facilities in the Indian Ocean," May 7, 1965, PRO.

50. U.S. Embassy London, telegram to RUEHCR/Secretary of State, May 10, 1965. LBJ: NSF, Country File, Box 207, UK Memos vol. IV 5/65–6/65.

51. U.S. Embassy London, telegram to RUEHCR/Secretary of State, May 15, 1965, NARA: RG 59/250/6/23/3–4, Subject-Numeric Files 1964–1966, Box 1638.

52. Llewellyn E. Thompson, memorandum to the Secretary [of State], May 1, 1965, LBJ: NSF, Komer, Box 26, Indian Ocean, December 1963–March 1966.

53. *Foreign Relations of the United States, 1964–1968,* 21: 97; Jeffery C. Kitchen, memorandum to the Secretary [of State], August 17, 1965, NARA: RG 59/250/6/23/3–4, Subject-Numeric Files 1964–1966, Box 1638, 1–3.

54. See Marimootoo, "Diego Files."

55. James Calvert, memorandum for the Secretary of the Navy, September 29, 1965, NHC: 00 Files, 1965, Box 40, 5710/1–2.

56. Pilger, *Freedom Next Time*, 25.

57. The British Indian Ocean Territory Order 1965, statutory order, No. 1920, 1965.

58. Pilger, *Freedom Next Time*, 24–25.

59. United Nations General Assembly Resolution 2066, "Question of Mauritius," December 16, 1965.

60. Robert W. Komer, memorandum to Jeffery Kitchen, 10 November 1965, LBJ: NSF, Files of Robert W. Komer, Box 26.

61. James Calvert, memorandum for the Secretary of the Navy, January 10, 1966, NHC: 00 Files, 1966, Box 23, 5710.

62. Thomas D. Davies, memorandum for the Secretary of the Navy, January 27, 1966, NHC: 00 Files, 1966, Box 32, 11000/1.

63. Paul H. Nitze, memorandum for the Secretary of Defense, February 4, 1966, NHC: 00 Files, 1966, Box 32, 11000/1.

64. Catherine Lutz suggested this might be called "casino militarism" (email to author August 2006). Investment banking and of course hedge funds—not so far removed from the world of the casino—also make good analogies.

65. Nitze memorandum for the Secretary of Defense.

66. Ibid.

67. John T. McNaughton, memorandum for the Secretary of the Navy, February 19, 1966, NHC: 00 Files, 1966, Box 32, 11000/1.

68. Bandjunis, *Diego Garcia*, 20.

69. The previous year McNamara had denied an initial Air Force request for funding. See *Foreign Relations of the United States, 1964–1968*, 21:94–96.

70. Lyndon B. Johnson, Recording of Telephone Conversation between Lyndon B. Johnson and Robert McNamara, July 29, 1966, 10:51 AM, LBJ: Citation #10446, Recordings and Transcripts of Conversations and Meetings.

71. Bandjunis, *Diego Garcia*, 20.

72. Agreements governing every detail of an overseas military facility, from their use in times of war to peacetime criminal prosecution of soldiers, were standard practice for overseas bases and the specialty of the Kitchen's Bureau of Politico-Military Affairs in the State Department.

73. U.S. Embassy London, telegram to Secretary of State, November 16, 1966, NARA: RG 59/250/7/11/7, Central Foreign Policy Files 1964–1966, Political and Defense, Box 1695, Def UK-US.

74. United Kingdom of Great Britain and Northern Ireland, "Availability of Certain Indian Ocean Islands for Defense Purposes," exchange of notes, December 30, 1966, 1–2.

75. T. J. Brack, letter to Mr. Barratt and Mr. Unwin, April 20, 1971, PRO. Emphasis in original.

76. "British Indian Ocean Territory," memorandum, December 14, 1966, PRO, 2. Emphasis in original.

77. Chalfont, letter to David K. E. Bruce, December 30, 1966, NARA: RG 59/150/64–65, Subject-Numeric Files 1964–1966, Box 1552.

Chapter Five
"Maintaining the Fiction"

1. McCaffrey, *Military Power and Popular Protest*; Monthly Review, "U.S. Military Bases and Empire."

2. A comparative study of maritime empires notes, "navies, like their governments, regard any political upheaval as dangerous to imperial stability. Rebels cannot be tolerated if order (or 'peace') is to prevail." Clark G. Reynolds, *Command of the Sea: The History and Strategy of Maritime Empires* (Malabar, FL: Robert E. Krieger Publishing, 1983), 7.

3. Bezboruah, *U.S. Strategy in the Indian Ocean*, 52, 54, 58, 60.

4. Ryan, "Diego Garcia," 133.

5. UKTB 4-132.

6. Secretary of State for the Colonies, telegram to Commissioner, British Indian Ocean Territory, February 25, 1966, UKTB.

7. Brooke-Turner, "British Indian Ocean Territory."

8. Ibid.

9. *Queen v. Secretary of State ex parte Bancoult 2006*: para. 27, emphasis in original.

10. Ibid., para. 27.

11. Anthony Aust, "Immigration Legislation for BIOT," memorandum, 16 January 1970.

12. The British Government also acquired the islands of Desroches from Paul Moulinie (the primary owner in Chagos), and Farquhar from another private owner (Aldabra was already Crown territory belonging to the Queen).

13. Some may have been prevented from returning prior to this date.

14. The contract also established the number of workers allowed on the islands, working hours, and wages.

15. See also Mauritius Ministry of Social Security, letter, July 19, 1968, PRO: FCO 31/13. This history of the expulsion process builds on Vine et al., *Dérasiné*, and is drawn from several sources. Many published accounts of the expulsion exist: see, e.g., Ottaway, "Islanders Were Evicted for U.S. Base"; Winchester, *The Sun Never Sets*; Madeley, "Diego Garcia." Most provide a broad overview of the expulsion. To document the expulsion accurately and verifiably and with more detail than previous histories, this history draws almost exclusively on primary sources: interviews and conversations with Chagossians and others in Mauritius and the Seychelles who witnessed events; court documents; and contemporaneous British Government documents describing many of the events of the expulsion as

they occurred. Although I have relied on Chagossians' eyewitness accounts, I have tried to verify their accounts with published sources as cited.

16. UKTB 5-578. In January 1969, a joint State Department–Defense Department message indicated the U.S. Government's displeasure with a new request by the BIOT administrator to rehire fifty "Chagos-born laborers" in Mauritius for work on Diego Garcia. See William P. Rogers, telegram to the U.S. Embassy London, January 31, 1969, NARA: RG 59/150/64–65, Subject-Numeric Files 1967–1969, Box 1551, 4.

17. A. Wooler, letter to Eric G. Norris, August 22, 1968, attachment to Eric G. Norris, note to Mr. Counsell, September 9, 1968, PRO: FCO 31/134.

18. John Todd, "Tour Report—Chagos May 1967," report, May 1967, British Indian Ocean Territory, PRO. 5.

19. John Todd, "Chagos," report, British Indian Ocean Territory, September 1968, PRO, 4.

20. Todd, "Tour Report—Chagos May 1967," 3; Todd, "Chagos."

21. The school later seems to have briefly reopened before closing permanently.

22. Todd, "Tour Report—Chagos May 1967," 3; Todd, "Notes on the Islands of the British Indian Ocean Territory," 33; "Notes on a Visit to Chagos by the Administrator, British Indian Ocean Territory," 3; "Notes on a Visit, July 17th to August 2nd," 1970, PRO, 2.

23. Draft contract between the Crown and Moulinie and Company (Seychelles) Limited, 1968, PRO: WO 32/21295.

24. See, e.g., Madeley, "Diego Garcia," 4.

25. K. R. Whitnall, letter to Mr. Matthews, Miss Emery, May 7, 1969, UKTB: 6-755.

26. David Greenaway and Nishal Gooroochurn, "Structural Adjustment and Economic Growth in Mauritius," in Rajen Dabee and David Greenaway, eds., *The Mauritian Economy: A Reader* (Houndsmill, UK: Palgrav, 2001), 67; Ramesh Durbarry, "The Export Processing Zone," in Dabee and Greenaway, *The Mauritian Economy,* 109.

27. Wooler, letter to Norris, August 22, 1968.

28. E.H.M. Counsell, "Defence Facilities in the Indian Ocean; Diego Garcia," letter to Mr. Le Tocq, 1969, PRO: FCO 31/401.

29. *Foreign Relations of the United States, 1964–1968,* 21:103–5.

30. Fred Kaplan, *The Wizards of Armageddon* (Stanford, CA: Stanford University Press, 1991), 254–55.

31. Ibid., 257.

32. Cohn, "'Clean Bombs' and Clean Language"; also Gusterson, *Nuclear Rites.*

33. *Foreign Relations of the United States, 1964–1968,* 21:108.

34. James W. O'Grady, memorandum for the Secretary of the Navy, September 19, 1967, NHC: 00 Files, 1967, Box 74, 11000/2.

35. F. Pearce, "An Island of No Importance," *New Scientist,* February 7, 2004, 48.

36. Ibid. Stoddart has long been troubled by his role in saving Aldabra and inadvertently helping to clear the way for the Diego Garcia removals. Since the 1970s, he has expended large amounts of his time and money collecting documents about the creation of the base and the expulsion, provided assistance to the Chagossians' struggle to return, and written detailed letters to politicians in the United States and United Kingdom advocating on their behalf. See also Charles Douglas-Home, "Scientists Fight Defence Plans for Island of Aldabra," *Times* (London), August 16, 1967.

Chapter Six
"Absolutely Must Go"

1. Kaplan, *Wizards of Armageddon*, 138.

2. Ibid., 140, 139.

3. Ibid., 141; Bob Thompson, "Arsenal of Words," *Washington Post,* 29 October 2007, C2.

4. *Foreign Relations of the United States, 1964–1968,* 21:92–93, 109–17; Bandjunis, *Diego Garcia*, 30.

5. FRUS, *Foreign Relations of the United States, 1964–1968,* 21:109–12; James W. O'Grady, memorandum to Op-002, May 2, 1968, NHC: 00 Files, 1967, Box 74, 11000/3.

6. O'Grady, memorandum to Op-002, 3.

7. Alain Enthoven, memorandum for Secretary of Defense, May 10, 1968, NHC: 00 Files, 1967, Box 74, 11000/3.

8. *Foreign Relations of the United States, 1964–1968,* 21:113–14.

9. Earl C. Ravenal, "American Strategy in the Indian Ocean: The Proposed Base on Diego Garcia," Hearings before the Subcommittee on the Near East and South Asia of the Committee on Foreign Affairs, House of Representatives, 93rd Congress, March 14, 1974.

10. Bandjunis, *Diego Garcia,* 35–36.

11. U.S. Department of State, "Senior Interdepartmental Group, Chairman's Summary," December 24, 1968, NARA: CIA records, 7.

12. Ravenal, "American Strategy in the Indian Ocean."

13. Dean Rusk, telegram to U.S. Embassy London, August 7, 1968, NARA: RG 59/150/64–65, Subject-Numeric Files 1967–1969, Box 1552.

14. Ibid. At times the U.S. Government has argued that it did not know there was an indigenous population in Chagos and that it thought the population was composed of transient workers. This argument is difficult to believe. Any cursory inspection of writings on Chagos (most importantly Scott, *Limuria;* Blood, "The Peaks of Lemuria") would have revealed the existence of generations of Chagossians living on the islands. Even without reading a word, it is hard to imagine that the Navy's first reconnaissance inspection of Diego Garcia in 1957 would have overlooked hundreds of families (unusual in the case of migrant workers) and a fully

functioning society complete with nineteenth-century cemeteries and churches and people tracing their ancestry back as many as five generations in Chagos. The British were clearly well aware of the indigenous population, as their extensive discussions on the subject in memos and letters throughout the 1960s reveal. A secret 1969 letter from the U.S. Embassy in London to the British Foreign and Commonwealth Department confirms U.S. knowledge of "Chagos-born laborers" (Gerald G. Oplinger, letter to Richard A. Sykes, February 3, 1969, PRO).

15. U.S. Embassy London, telegram to Secretary of State, August 9, 1968, NARA: RG 59/150/64–65, Subject-Numeric Files 1967–1969, Box 1551, 1.

16. R. S. Leddick, memorandum for the Record, November 11, 1969, NHC: 00 Files, 1969, Box 98, 11000.

17. R. S. Leddick, memorandum for the Record, December 3, 1969, NHC: 00 Files, 1969, Box 98, 11000; Bandjunis, *Diego Garcia*, 37.

18. Tazewell Shepard, memorandum for Harry D. Train, January 26, 1970, NHC: 00 Files, 1970, Box 111, 11000.

19. Robert A. Frosch, memorandum for the Deputy Secretary of Defense, February 27, 1970, NHC: 00 Files, 1970, Box 111, 11000; John H. Chafee, memorandum for the Secretary of Defense, January 31, 1970, NHC: 00 Files, 1970, Box 111, 11000.

20. Throughout the development of Diego Garcia and BIOT, U.S. and U.K. government officials sought at least in public to describe the military activities there not as a "base" but as a "station," a "facility," or a "post." They usually linked these terms with adjectives like "austere," "limited," or "modest." From early in the development of Diego Garcia, however, the Navy and later the Department of Defense and the Air Force had large visions for the island: first, for naval communications in the Indian Ocean (including the coordination of nuclear submarines newly deployed there to strike the Soviet Union and China); second, as a large harbor for Navy warships and submarines, with enough room to protect an aircraft carrier task force; and third, as an airfield intended first for Navy reconnaissance planes and later for nuclear-bomb-ready B-52 bombers and almost every other plane in the Air Force arsenal (see Bandjunis, *Diego Garcia*, 8–14; U.K. Colonial Office; J. H. Gibbon et al., "Brief on UK/US London Discussions on United States Defence Interests in the Indian Ocean," memorandum, March 6, 1964, PRO: CAB 21/5418, 81174, 1–2). Faced with the potential for growing opposition, U.S. and U.K. officials insistently avoided describing plans for Diego Garcia as a "base." With the British soon committing to withdraw its troops east of the Suez Canal by 1971, the U.K. Government did not want to be involved in any development perceived to be a new base. See Mewes, 1. U.S. officials faced opposition to their expansion into the Indian Ocean in Congress, from nations around the Indian Ocean like India, and even within the Pentagon. This opposition was especially intense in reaction to the escalating war in Vietnam; as in southeast Asia, this would also be a move into a region almost entirely without a prior U.S. presence.

21. See attachment, Op-605E4, "Proposed Naval Communications Facility on Diego Garcia," briefing sheet, [January] 1970, NHC: 00 Files, 1970, Box 111, 11000.

22. Walter H. Annenberg, telegram to the Secretary of State, July 12, 1970, library of David Stoddart (see also NARA: RG 59, Subject-Numeric Files, 1970–1973 1970); Greene, telegram to the Secretary of State, December 16, 1970, library of David Stoddart (see also NARA: RG 59, Subject-Numeric Files, 1970–1973).

23. F. J. Blouin, memorandum for the Chief of Naval Operations, December 28, 1970, NHC: 00 Files, 1970, Box 115, 11000.

24. William P. Rogers, telegram to the U.S. Embassy London, June 19, 1970, library of David Stoddart (see also NARA: RG 59, Subject-Numeric Files, 1970–1973).

25. Ibid.

26. Walter H. Small, memorandum for the Chief of Naval Operations, December 11, 1970, NHC: 00 Files, 1970, Box 115, 11000.

27. William P. Rogers, telegram to the U.S. Embassy London, June 19, 1970, library of David Stoddart (see also NARA: RG 59, Subject-Numeric Files, 1970–1973).

28. Greene, telegram to the Secretary of State, December 16, 1970, library of David Stoddart (see also NARA: RG 59, Subject-Numeric Files, 1970–1973).

29. Bandjunis, *Diego Garcia*, 46.

30. William P. Rogers, telegram to the U.S. Embassy London, December 14, 1970, NARA: RG 59/150/67/1/5, Subject-Numeric Files 1970–1973, Box 1744.

31. Elmo R. Zumwalt, Jr., *On Watch: A Memoir* (New York: Quadrangle, 1976), 17–19. Matching his own elite background, Zumwalt married Mouza Coutelais-du-Roche, a woman of French and Russian parentage, whom he met at the end of World War II among the White Russian community-in-exile in Harbin, Manchuria.

32. Ibid., 203–4.

33. Ibid., 27–29.

34. Ibid., 34.

35. Ibid., 28.

36. U.S. Naval Institute, "Reminiscences by Staff Officers of Admiral Elmo R. Zumwalt, Jr., U.S. Navy, vol. I," Annapolis, MD, U.S. Naval Institute, 1989, 311–12.

37. Ibid., 313.

38. J. H. Dick, memorandum for the Chief of Naval Operations, December 18, 1970, NHC: 00 Files, 1970, Box 115, 11000.

39. I. Watt, letter to Mr. D.A. Scott, Sir L. Monson, and Mr. Kerby, January 26, 1971, PRO: T317/162, 1–2.

40. Blouin, memorandum for the Chief of Naval Operations, December 28, 1970.

41. Attachment to Walter H. Small, memorandum for the Chief of Naval Operations, January 11, 1971, NHC: 00 Files, 1971, Box 172, 11000. See also Walter H. Small, memorandum for the Vice Chief of Naval Operations, January 28, 1971, NHC: 00 Files, 1971, Box 172, 11000.

42. Small, memorandum for the Chief of Naval Operations, January 11, 1971, 1.

43. Attachment to Small, memorandum for the Chief of Naval Operations, January 11, 1971.

44. John Todd, letter to Allan F. Knight, February 17, 1971, PRO: T317/1625.

45. According to Madeley, "One Ilois woman, Marie Louina, died on Diego when she learned she would have to leave her homeland." Madeley, "Diego Garcia," 5. I have been unable to confirm this account.

46. See also Sunday Times, "The Islanders that Britain Sold," September 21, 1975, 10.

47. Marcel Moulinie, statement of Marcel Moulinie, application for judicial review, *Queen v. The Secretary of State for the Foreign and Commonwealth Office, ex parte Bancoult*, 1999.

48. Small, memorandum for the Vice Chief of Naval Operations, January 28, 1971, 1.

49. U.S. Department of State, telegram to U.S. Embassy Port Louis, U.S. Embassy London, February 4, 1971, library of David Stoddart. See also NARA: RG 59, Subject-Numeric Files 1970–1973.

50. Bruce Greatbatch, FCO Telno BIOT 52, telegram to Foreign and Commonwealth Office, August 26, 1971, PRO.

51. Attachment to E. L. Cochrane, Jr., memorandum for the Deputy Chief of Naval Operations (Plans and Policy), March 24, 1971, NHC: 00 Files, 1971, Box 174, 11000, 2.

52. Ibid., 1.

53. Ibid.

54. Ibid. The Deputy Chief of Naval Operations for Plans and Policy explained to Zumwalt that Diego's inhabitants were a mix of Ilois, Mauritians, and Seychellois. He also explained the Navy's position on employing any locals: "The decision not to hire local labor, even for domestic work, was made on the basis that no local economy dependent on the facility should be created. To do so would make it more difficult to remove the workers when the facility becomes operational. If a native community of bars, laundries, etc. grew and then was required to be disbanded, the resultant publicity could become damaging. Another important factor is that presentations to Congress have stressed that there will be no indigenous population and no native labor utilized in the construction." Zumwalt scrawled

the following in response: "Better than I had hoped." See Blouin, memorandum for the Chief of Naval Operations, December 28, 1970.

Chapter Seven
"On the Rack"

1. Bandjunis, *Diego Garcia*, 47.

2. Ibid., 47–49.

3. See also Marimootoo, "Diego Files," 46, 48.

4. Ottaway, "Islanders Were Evicted for U.S. Base."

5. D. D. Newsom, letter to James K. Bishop, Jr., February 1, 1972, NARA: RG 59/150/67/1/5, Subject-Numeric Files 1970–1973, Box 1715, 1.

6. Bruce Greatbatch, FCO Telno BIOT 52, telegram to Foreign and Commonwealth Office, August 26, 1971, PRO.

7. U.S. Congress, House, "Diego Garcia, 1975," 61.

8. See also Marcel Moulinie, "Statement of Marcel Moulinie," application for judicial review, *Queen v. The Secretary of State for the Foreign and Commonwealth Office*, ex parte Bancoult [1999], para. 14; Pilger, *Freedom Next Time*, 26–27, 35.

9. Moulinie, "Statement," para. 14. See also Madeley, "Diego Garcia," 4–5.

10. Some of the voyages to the Seychelles took as many as six days. Pilger, *Freedom Next Time*, 28.

11. Moulinie "Statement," para. 16.

12. Greatbatch, FCO Telno BIOT 52, August 26, 1971; Dale, telegram to Foreign and Commonwealth Office, Telno personal 176, September 23, 1971, PRO.

13. William D. Brewer, memorandum to Department of State, December 20, 1971, NARA: RG 59/150/67/27/6, Subject-Numeric Files 1970–1973, Box 3010, 4.

14. Ibid., 1, 4.

15. Ibid., 1, 3.

16. Ibid., 5, 1.

17. William D. Brewer, letter to Herman J. Cohen, January 5, 1972, NARA: RG 59/150/67/1/5, Subject-Numeric Files 1970–1973, Box 1715, 2, 5. Although Brewer's State Department superiors knew the Air Force undersecretary was being "intemperate and at times illogical," they chose not to challenge him (and the Air Force) on an issue they considered minor and which they perceived might harm other departmental priorities. See Herman J. Cohen, letter to David D. Newsom, January 20, 1972, NARA: Subject-Numeric 1970–1973, 59/150/67/1/5.

18. Brewer, letter to Cohen, January 5, 1972.

19. Ibid., 1.

20. Adam Hochschild, *King Leopold's Ghost: A Story of Greed, Terror, and Heroism in Colonial Africa* (Boston: Houghton Mifflin, 1999), 121–22. The possibility that others might have challenged the expulsion becomes more improbable when

one considers that to challenge any policy of the U.S. Government is not simply to challenge one's immediate superior or an office within the Government, but to challenge one's entire department, the department's secretary, and to a significant extent the U.S. Government as a whole. This lesson is communicated explicitly in most telegrams, which, in the case of the State Department, for example, deliver most orders and instructions not in the name of a State Department superior but in the name of the "Department of State," under the signature of the Secretary of State. This contributed to the feeling among many officials that they were carrying out the policy dictates of the U.S. Government writ large, matters about which they generally believed they had no input.

21. Charles Lemert, *Social Theory: The Multicultural and Classic Readings* (Boulder, CO: Westview Press, 1993), 119.

22. U.S. Department of State, telegram to U.S. Embassy London, February 5, 1972, NARA: RG 59/150/67/27/6, Subject Numeric Files 1970–1973, Box 3010.

23. Anthony Lake and Roger Morris, "Pentagon Papers (2): The Human Reality of Realpolitik," *Foreign Policy* 4 (1971): 159. See Samantha Power, *"A Problem from Hell": America and the Age of Genocide* (New York: Perennial, 2002), 365.

24. PRO: Foreign & Commonwealth Office, Overseas Development Administration, London, 1972; Henry Precht, airgram to Department of State, May 2, 1972, NARA: RG 59/150/67/1/5, Subject-Numeric Files 1970–1973, Box 1715, 2.

25. John Todd, letter to Allan F. Knight, June 17, 1972, PRO.

26. UKTB: M. T. Mein, 2002, para. 14.

27. C. A. Seller, Letter to Morris, June 20, 1967, PRO: T317/1347.

28. Bandjunis, *Diego Garcia*, 49, 58.

29. Ibid., 62.

30. C. S. Minter, Jr., memorandum for Chief of Naval Operations, July 20, 1972, NHC: 00 Files, 1972, Box 161, 11000.

31. Bandjunis, *Diego Garcia*, 64–71.

32. U.S. Congress, House, "Diego Garcia, 1975," 12

33. See Bandjunis, *Diego Garcia*, 309.

34. U.S. Congress, House, "Diego Garcia, 1975," 41.

35. Ibid., 42.

36. Ibid., 42–45.

37. Ibid., 79.

38. Ibid., 66.

Chapter Eight
Derasine: The Impoverishment of Expulsion

1. Anahita World Class Sanctuary Mauritius, "Paradise Found," available from http://www.anahitamauritius.com/anahita_location.php?langue=uk.

2. Susan Hack, "Butlers, Beaches, and Bubble Baths," *Condé Nast Traveler*, August 2004, 93. Elsewhere Hack unconsciously captures some of the colonialist tinge of the tourist industry when she remarks, "Encountering a butler in the flesh, I savor the strange power of making demands on a man who lives to obey my orders."

3. Madeley, "Diego Garcia," 5.

4. *Sunday Times* (London), "The Islanders that Britain Sold," September 21, 1975, 10.

5. U.S. Congress, House, "Diego Garcia, 1975," 114–21. The persistence of poor housing standards left Chagossians vulnerable to new displacements and renewed homelessness, especially to the cyclones that periodically strike Mauritius with especially ferocious effects on the homes of poor families. A 1975 interview with a Chagossian from Diego Garcia describes the damage of the cyclone on a family of nine: "The five [chickens] that were left and the coop were lost in February in Cyclone Gervaise. She also lost during the cyclone her two coconut-straw mattresses that she brought from Diego. She tried to save them, but the wind became too strong and she and the children had to flee to a neighbor's house. When she returned, the mattresses, and most of the iron sheets from the house, were gone. Now she has to gather grass for the children to sleep on." Ibid., 111.

6. Richard M. Titmuss and Brian Abel-Smith, *Social Policies and Population Growth in Mauritius* (London: Frank Cass, 1968).

7. V. S. Naipaul, *The Overcrowded Barracoon* (New York: Vintage, 1984).

8. Titmuss and Abel-Smith, *Social Policies and Population Growth*, 7.

9. African Research Group, "BIOT: Health & Mortality in the Chagos Islands," report, Foreign & Commonwealth Office, London, October 2000, 3, 5.

10. Comité Ilois Organisation Fraternelle, "Paper Prepared by the Comité Ilois Organisation Fraternelle," Port Louis, Mauritius, n.d.: 2–5.

11. Ibid., 3–5.

12. Ibid., 2–3.

13. I. Walker, *Zaffer Pe Sanze*, 14.

14. Martin Walker, "Price on Islanders' Birthright," *Manchester Guardian*, November 4, 1975.

15. Comité Ilois Organisation Fraternelle, "Paper Prepared by the Comité Ilois," 2.

16. See, e.g., Sydney Selvon, *A Comprehensive History of Mauritius* (Mauritius: Mauritius Printing Specialists, 2001), 394.

17. A. Wooler, letter to Eric G. Norris, August 22, 1968, attachment to Eric G. Norris, letter to Mr. Counsell, September 9, 1968, PRO: FCO 31/134.

18. I. Watt, letter to D. A. Scott, L. Monson, and Mr. Kerby, January 26, 1971, PRO: T317/1625, 3.

19. Vine et al., *Dérasiné*, 114.

20. Ottaway, "Islanders Were Evicted for U.S. Base"; See H. Siophe in U.S. Congress, House, "Diego Garcia, 1975," 112–21.

21. Madeley, "Diego Garcia," 5. These reports seem clearly to suggest increased mortality compared with life in Chagos. Yearly average death figures during the last years in Chagos for individuals born there are 0.75 per year in Diego Garcia, 4.75 in Peros Banhos, and 2.33 in Salomon. See "B.I.O.T. Death Peros-Banhos, Solomon Island, Diego-Garcia 1965–1971," death records, SNA.

22. Comité Ilois Organisation Fraternelle, "Paper Prepared by the Comité Ilois," 3.

23. Michael Cernea, "Anthropological and Sociological Research for Policy Development on Population Resettlement," in *Anthropological Approaches to Resettlement: Policy, Practice, and Theory*, ed. Michael M. Cernea and Scott E. Guggenheim (Boulder, CO: Westview Press, 1993), 12. Research in India, for example, has shown that the country's "development" programs have displaced more than 20 million over four decades and that 75 percent have ended up worse off than before their displacement. Cernea writes, "Their livelihoods have not been restored; in fact, the vast majority . . . have become impoverished."

24. Titmuss and Abel-Smith, *Social Policies and Population Growth*.

25. See, e.g., Durbarry; "The Export Processing Zone"; Bowman, *Mauritius*; Kevin Ramkalaon, "Post-Independence Mauritius: An Economic Vision," in *Colouring the Rainbow: Mauritian Society in the Making*, ed. Marina Carter (Port Louis, Mauritius: Centre for Research on Indian Ocean Societies, 1998), 27–32; Berhanu Woldekidan, "Export-led Growth in Mauritius," Indian Ocean Policy Papers 3, Australia, National Center for Development Studies, 1994.

26. Pacific & Indian Ocean Department, "BIOT Working Papers: Paper No. 5—Evacuation and Resettlement of Inhabitants of Chagos Archipelago," 1969, PRO, paras. 6, 8.

27. See, e.g., Marion Benedict and Burton Benedict, *Men, Women and Money in Seychelles* (Berkeley, CA: University of California Press, 1982); Raphael Kaplinsky, "Prospering at the Periphery: A Special Case—The Seychelles," in *African Islands and Enclaves*, ed. Robin Cohen (Beverly Hills: Sage Publications, 1983), 195–215; Ronny Gabbay and Robin Ghosh, "Tourism in Seychelles," in *Tourism and Economic Development: Case Studies from the Indian Ocean Region*, ed. R. N. Ghosh, M. A. B. Siddique, and R. Gabbay (Hampshire, UK: Ashgate Publishing, 2003), 104–27.

28. Benedict and Benedict, *Men, Women and Money in Seychelles*,161.

29. Marcus Franda, *The Seychelles: Unquiet Islands* (Boulder, CO: Westview Press, 1982), 16, 81, 84–85.

30. M. Walker, "Price on Islanders' Birthright."

31. Ranjit Nayak, "Risks Associated with Landlessness: An Exploration toward Socially Friendly Displacement and Resettlement," in Michael Cernea and Christopher McDowell, *Risks and Reconstruction: Experiences of Resettlers and Refugees* (Washington, DC: World Bank, 2000), 103.

32. Jean-Claude Lau Thi Keng, "Intégration/Exclusion," in *Etude pluridisciplinaire sur l'exclusion à Maurice*, ed. Issa Asgarally (Réduit, Mauritius: Présidence de la République, 1997), 17–48.

33. Roland Lamusse, "Macroeconomic Policy and Performance," in Dabee and Greenaway, *The Mauritian Economy*, 41.

34. Rosabelle Boswell, "Views on Creole Culture, Economy and Survival," *Revi Kiltir Kreol* 1 (2002): 15–26.

35. Botte, "The 'Ilois' Community," 27.

36. Herve Sylva, "Report on the Survey on the Conditions of Living of the Ilois Community Displaced from the Chagos Archipelago," report, Mauritius, April 22, 1981, 2–3, 11–13.

37. Prostitution appears as an ongoing employment opportunity of last resort for Chagossians with few other opportunities. Botte's 1980 study of islander women found at least 23 engaged in prostitution (in Chagos, by contrast, "prostitution as a trade did not exist"). Although few were eager to discuss this subject, my research in Mauritius suggested that prostitution remains a source of employment for some. See Botte, "The 'Ilois' Community," 41–42. On prostitution and other illegal activities, see also Madeley, "Diego Garcia," 6; Sylva, "Report on the Survey on the Conditions of Living,"; Comité Ilois Organisation Fraternelle, "Paper Prepared by the Comité Ilois."

38. Chagos Refugees Group, Port Louis, Mauritius; N. C. Aizenman, "New High in U.S. Prison Numbers," *Washington Post*, February 29, 2008. Based on CRG registration statistics, there were around 4,000 Chagossians age 12 and older in 2001; thus the 38 adults incarcerated easily represented more than 1 in 100 adults."

39. Botte, "The 'Ilois' Community," 30–31.

40. Ibid., 30–31; I. Walker, *Zaffer Pe Sanze*, 17.

41. Boswell, "Views on Creole Culture," 19–21.

42. See, e.g., Botte, "The 'Ilois' Community," 47. See also Boswell, "Views on Creole Culture," for more on this phenomenon among the poor of Mauritius generally, and Elizabeth Colson, *The Social Consequences of Resettlement: The Impact of the Kariba Resettlement upon the Gwembe Tonga* (Manchester: Manchester University Press, 1971), on the phenomenon among involuntary displacees as a group.

43. Michael Cernea, "Risks, Safeguards, and Reconstruction: A Model for Population Displacement and Resettlement," in Cernea and McDowell, *Risks and Reconstruction*, 26–27.

Chapter Nine
Death and Double Discrimination

1. This accounts for some of the inspiration behind the adoption of the term *Chagossian*.

2. I. Walker, *Zaffer Pe Sanze*, 24.

3. Nearly two-thirds (65.5 percent) of the first generation and almost half of second-generation respondents (44.7 percent) said they had been a victim of verbal abuse. See Vine et al., *Dérasiné*, 125.

4. Ottaway, "Islanders Were Evicted for U.S. Base."

5. In my 2002–3 survey, half of those surveyed from the generation born in Chagos and one-third of the second generation reported suffering job or other discrimination as a Chagossian. See Vine et al., *Dérasiné*, 125; see also, Botte, "The 'Ilois' Community," 38–39; I. Walker, *Zaffer Pe Sanze,* 21–22; Tania Dræbel, "Evaluation des besoins sociaux de la communauté déplacée de l'Archipel de Chagos, volet un: santé et education, " report, Le Ministère de la Sécurité Sociale et de la Solidarité Nationale, Mauritius, December 1997, 36.

6. Botte, "The 'Ilois' Community," 39, 25; see also I. Walker, *Zaffer Pe Sanze,* 16.

7. For an interesting comparison in another island nation with strikingly similar historical and demographic conditions, see Viranjini Munasinghe's description of the emergence of stereotypical, racialized discourses about peoples of African and Indian descent in Trinidad and Tobago. Viranjini Munasinghe, *Callaloo or Tossed Salad? East Indians and the Cultural Politics of Identity in Trinidad* (Ithaca, NY: Cornell University Press, 2001).

8. Franda, *The Seychelles.*

9. Issa Asgarally, ed., *Étude pluridisciplinaire sur l'exclusion à Maurice* (Réduit, Mauritius: Présidence de la République, 1997).

10. Thomas Hyland Eriksen, "Creole Culture and Social Change," *Journal of Mauritian Studies* 1, no. 2 (1986): 59.

11. Similarly in the Seychelles, most Chagossians are recognized as belonging to a stigmatized darker-complexioned minority.

12. Differences between peoples of Indian, African, and European descent are generally perceived locally in terms of race, as being fixed in biology; to avoid reifying race as a legitimate, scientifically accurate concept based in biological reality, it is useful to introduce the language of ethnicity.

13. Larry W. Bowman and Jeffery A. Lefebvre, "The Indian Ocean and Strategic Perspectives," in *The Indian Ocean: Perspectives on a Strategic Arena*, ed. William L. Dowdy and Russell B. Trood (Durham, NC: Duke University Press, 1985), n. 28; Pranay B. Gupte, "Dispossessed in Mauritius Are Inflamed," *New York Times*, December 14, 1982, A5; *60 Minutes*, "Diego Garcia," CBS Television, prod. Andrew Tkach, June 15, 2003. At least one grandchild of someone born in Chagos has worked on the base in the laundry and in other jobs. His obtaining a job seems to support the claim that Chagossians have been disqualified from employment on the basis of their place of birth or their parents' place of birth.

14. Utterances in italics like this one are quotations where I was not absolutely certain to have recorded every word spoken. These quotations are not reconstructions or paraphrases but instead indicate instances where I could not ensure that I had recorded a direct quotation word for word (although at their least accurate they are missing only few words). All other quoted utterances are direct word-for-word quotations recorded either electronically or by hand during research.

15. Durbarry, "The Export Processing Zone," emphasis added.

16. U.S. Congress, House, "Diego Garcia, 1975," 115–16.

17. Ibid., 118–19.

18. Dræbel, "Evaluation des besoins sociaux"; Sheila Bunwaree, "Education in Mauritius since Independence: More Accessible But Still Inequitable," in *Consolidating the Rainbow: Independent Mauritius, 1968–1998*, ed. Marina Carter (Port Louis, Mauritius: Centre for Research on Indian Ocean Societies, 1998).

19. Text translated from French by the author.

20. Interview with Seychelles government official, September 28, 2004.

21. Elizabeth Colson, "Overview," *Annual Review of Anthropology* 18 (1989): 1–16.

22. Liisa Malkki, *Purity and Exile: Violence, Memory, and National Cosmology among Hutu Refugees in Tanzania* (Chicago: University of Chicago Press, 1995).

23. She is not far off in her estimate: The base area of Diego Garcia resembles, if not the Seychelles, a small town in the United States.

24. Thayer Scudder, "The Human Ecology of Big Projects: River Basin Development and Resettlement," *Annual Review of Anthropology* 12 (1973): 51.

25. Colson, *The Social Consequences of Resettlement*.

26. Botte, "The 'Ilois' Community," 38.

27. Mauritius Legislative Assembly, "Report of the Select Committee on the Excision of the Chagos Archipelago," Port Louis, Mauritius, June 1983, 3–5.

28. Botte, "The 'Ilois' Community," 29, 30; Sylva, "Report on the Survey on the Conditions of Living," 3.

Chapter Ten
Dying of *Sagren*

1. Dræbel, "Evaluation des besoins sociaux"; see also Madeley, "Diego Garcia," 10–11.

2. Vine et al., *Dérasiné*, 174–87.

3. Ibid., 116–19.

4. Dræbel, "Evaluation des besoins sociaux," 15–16.

5. This figure is a revision of an earlier finding after final data cleaning and analysis. See Vine et al., *Dérasiné*, 116–19.

6. Dræbel, "Evaluation des besoins sociaux."

7. Ibid., 18–25, 34.

8. Ibid., 26–35.

9. Vine et al., *Dérasiné*, 213.

10. Ibid., 229.

11. Mindy Thompson Fullilove, *Root Shock: How Tearing Up City Neighborhoods Hurts America, and What We Can Do about It* (New York: One World, 2004), 224.

12. Chagos Refugees Group statistics.

13. Dræbel, "Evaluation des besoins sociaux," 25.

14. Fullilove, *Root Shock,* 11.

15. Nancy Scheper-Hughes, *Death without Weeping: The Violence of Everyday Life in Brazil*, (Berkeley, CA: University of California Press, 1992), 173–87. The

analysis in this chapter was unconsciously influenced by Scheper-Hughes; only after returning to reread *Death without Weeping* did I recognize how her remarkable work shaped my own.

16. Thayer Scudder and Elizabeth Colson, "From Welfare to Development: A Conceptual Framework for the Analysis of Dislocated People," in *Involuntary Migration and Resettlement: The Problems and Responses of Dislocated Peoples*, ed. A. Hansen and A. Oliver-Smith (Boulder, CO: Westview Press, 1982), 269.

17. Ilan S. Wittstein et al., "Neurohumoral Features of Myocardial Stunning Due to Sudden Emotional Stress," *New England Journal of Medicine* 352, no. 6: 539–48; Scott W. Sharsky et al., "Acute and Reversible Cardiomyopathy Provoked by Stress in Women from the United States," *Circulation* 111: 472–79.

18. Anne Fadiman, *The Spirit Catches You and You Fall Down: A Hmong Child, Her American Doctors, and the Collision of Two Cultures* (New York: The Noonday Press, 1997), 188.

19. Nayak, "Risks Associated with Landlessness," 95–96.

20. Scudder, *The Human Ecology of Big Projects*.

21. Saminaden et al., Petition to British Government.

22. Nayak, "Risks Associated with Landlessness," 96.

23. Translation by author.

24. Nayak, "Risks Associated with Landlessness," 96.

25. Mimose Bancoult Furcy, Grup Tambour Chagos, *Grup Tambour Chagos*, Island Music Productions, 2004. Translation by author.

26. Fullilove, *Root Shock*, 12.

27. Arthur Kleinman, Veena Das, and Margaret Lock, eds., *Social Suffering* (Berkeley, CA: University of California Press, 1997).

28. Ibid., xxi–xxiv.

29. See Laura Jeffery, "The Politics of Victimhood among Displaced Chagossians in Mauritius" (Ph.D. diss., University of Cambridge, 2006).

30. The words point to a common narrative of the expulsion and to the injuries experienced in exile. Among other purposes that the shorthand serves is to allow people to allude to the expulsion and other painful experiences of suffering without having to recite the entirety of the narrative or the specifics of their own painful injuries (including rape, hunger, and crime). See Jeffery, "The Politics of Victimhood."

31. Charles Taylor, "A Different Kind of Courage," review of Jonathan Lear, *Radical Hope: Ethics in the Face of Cultural Devastation, New York Review of Books* 54, no. 7 (April 26, 2007).

Chapter Eleven
Daring to Challenge

1. *Le Mauricien*, "150 'Ilois' expulsés refusent de débarquer à P-L," May 4, 1973, 4.

2. *L'Express*, "L'accueil aux îlois: le PM donne des précisions," May 10, 1973, 1. Parts of this chapter draw on David Vine, "Challenging Empires: The Struggle of the People of Diego Garcia," in *Souls: A Critical Journal of Black Culture, Politics, and Society* (forthcoming, 2008), and David Vine and Laura Jeffery, "Give Us Back Diego Garcia: Unity and Division among Activists in the Indian Ocean," in *Undermining the Bases of Empire: Social Movements against U.S. Overseas Military Installations*, ed. Catherine Lutz (Ithaca, NY: Pluto Press, 2008).

3. Saminaden et al., Petition to British Government.

4. U.S. Congress, House, "Diego Garcia, 1975."

5. A.R.G. Prosser, "Visit to Mauritius, From 24 January to 2 February: Mauritius-Resettlement of Persons Transferred from Chagos Archipelago," report, Port Louis, Mauritius, September 1976, p. 6.

6. Madeley, "Diego Garcia," 7.

7. *Le Mauricien*, "Trois des sept grévistes de la faim admiser à l'hôpital Civil," September 21, 1978, 4.

8. Madeley, "Diego Garcia," 7.

9. Ibid., 6, 8, 15.

10. They also asked for recognition as refugees, a demand which was immediately rejected by the Mauritian Government, which considered Chagossians to be Mauritians who could not be refugees on Mauritian soil.

11. *Le Mauricien*, "Nouvelle manifestation des ilois, hier: épreuve de force avec la police," March 17, 1981, 1, 4; Lalit, *Diego Garcia in Times of Globalization* (Port Louis, Mauritius: Ledikasyon pu Travayer, 2002), 113–17.

12. This section draws on Jeffery, "The Politics of Victimhood," 93–97.

13. Lassemillante and the CSC argue that the expulsion and continued exile of the Chagossians is contrary to UN declarations on human and indigenous rights.

14. At the time Gifford worked for the London law firm of Bernard Sheridan, the attorney who represented the islanders' aborted efforts to gain compensation in 1979. Gifford says that part of his inspiration to take up the case was his interest in his firm's role in the Chagossians' saga.

15. Several Mauritian governments have likewise rejected recognition of the Chagossians as an indigenous people or as refugees, concerned about undermining the sovereignty claim.

16. *Regina (on the application of Bancoult) v. Secretary of State for the Foreign and Commonwealth Office* [2006] EWHC 1038 Admin. 4093, para. 27.

17. CRG was joined by islanders in the Seychelles eventually known as the Chagossians Committee Seychelles.

18. Pilger, *Freedom Next Time*, 54.

19. *Bancoult et al. v. McNamara et al.*, 360 F.Supp. 2d (D.D.C. 2004).

20. This analysis draws substantially on Jeffery, "The Politics of Victimhood," 114–17.

21. Laura Jeffery, "'Our Right Is Our Land': The Chagos Archipelago and Discourses on Rights to Land in the Indian Ocean," in *Rights and Development*

in Mauritius—A Reader, ed. S. Bunwaree and R. Kasenally (Reduit: OSSREA Mauritius Chapter /University of Mauritius, 2007), 10.

22. Ibid., 11.

23. Lindsay Collen and Ragini Kitnasamy, "Diego Garcia Visit after Life-time Banishment Due to Bass," press release, Lalit, Port Louis, Mauritius, March 25, 2006. Emphasis in original.

24. Walter H. Annenberg, telegram to the Secretary of State, June 10, 1969, NARA: RG 59/150/64–65, Subject-Numeric Files 1967–1969, Box 1552.

25. See Vine and Jeffery, "Give Us Back Diego Garcia."

26. When Chagossians claimed citizenship, some Mauritians criticized the move as unpatriotic and a threat to the nation's efforts to regain sovereignty over Chagos. Some were angered when CRG members publicly celebrated their new citizenship by waving the Union Jack and pictures of the Queen.

27. In the years following the expulsion, a handful of women had followed Mauritian or Seychellois husbands to Europe or Australia in search of work.

28. *Chagos Islanders v. The Attorney General, Her Majesty's British Indian Ocean Territory Commissioner*, [2003] EWHC 2222. For a discussion of all the major suits, see Christian Nauvel, "A Return from Exile in Sight? The Chagossians and Their Struggle," *Northwestern Journal of International Human Rights* 5, no. 1 (2006):111; *Chagos Islanders v. The Attorney General, her Majesty's British Indian Ocean Territory Commissioner*, [2003] EWHC 222.

29. *Bancoult et al. v. McNamara et al.*

30. Ibid., 117 n.156.

31. Ibid., 120.

32. Pilger, *Freedom Next Time*, 55.

33. Neil Tweedle, "Britain Shamed as Exiles of the Chagos Islands Win the Right to Go Home," *Daily Telegraph*, May 11, 2006, http://www.telegraph.co.uk/news/uknews/1552445/Chagos-Island-exiles-win-right-to-return-home.html.

34. In 2000, the British Government allowed Olivier Bancoult and two other Chagossian leaders to briefly visit the islands.

35. *Regina (on the application of Bancoult) v. Secretary of State* [2006], para. 142.

36. Paul Majendie, "Chagos Islanders Win Right to Go Home," *Reuters*, May 11, 2006.

37. *Secretary of State for the Foreign and Commonwealth Office v. The Queen (Bancoult)* [2007].

38. Richard Gifford, press statement, May 23, 2007.

39. Bill Rammell, Parliamentary Answer, July 12, 2004, http://domain1164221.sites.fasthosts.com/parliamentary%20questions.htm#12jul04.

40. Sean Carey, "Don't Mention the Chagossians," *New Statesman*, November 20, 2007.

41. Regina [2006], para. 96.

42. The CRG also argues that Chagossians are a peaceful people wishing no harm to the United States; that Peros Banhos and Salomon are over 150 miles from

Diego Garcia, raising serious questions about the "security" argument; and that civilians live next to U.S. bases around the world (even "the enemy" in Cuba).

43. The following paragraphs stem from Vine and Jeffery, "Give Us Back Diego Garcia."

44. Louis Olivier Bancoult, Chagos Refugees Group, speech, Working Group on Indigenous Populations, Geneva, July 20, 2004.

Chapter Twelve
The Right to Return and a Humanpolitik

1. CIA Board of National Estimates, "Strategic and Political Interests in the Western Indian Ocean," special memorandum, April 11, 1967, LBJ: NSF, Country File, India, Box 133, India, Indian Ocean Task Force, vol. II. The land area of the BIOT was described as "N/A" for not applicable. A document most like written by Stuart Barber described the population in Peros Banhos and Salomon as "minor" (see Rivero, "Assuring a Future Base Structure").

Race and racism defined two of the main criteria for the selection of Diego Garcia as a base site: First, under the Strategic Island Concept's criteria, islands selected for base development were to have small non-European indigenous populations that, as Horacio Rivero knew well with the Bikinians, the government could easily remove. Second, the Strategic Island Concept held that islands selected for base development had to be controlled by the United States or by a Western ally, like the United Kingdom or Australia; they could not be controlled by a non-Western, non-white government.

It's not unreasonable to think that the World War II island-hopping campaign in the Pacific influenced more than just officials' ideas about the importance of island bases. The island hopping is likely also to have powerfully shaped ideas about race shared by Navy officials in particular. During the campaign, Navy and other forces had what for almost all of them were their first interactions with local tropical island populations. Given popular ideas at the time (for the most part held to this day), it would have been difficult for sailors and soldiers to think of these islanders as anything but the "primitive" natives they were portrayed as by anthropologists and journalists alike. The government's widely publicized deportation of the Bikinians after the war and its paternalistic treatment of islanders elsewhere in the Pacific would have only reinforced these views.

2. Nancy Scheper-Hughes and Philippe Bourgois, "Introduction: Making Sense of Violence," in *Violence in War and Peace: An Anthology*, ed. Nancy Scheper-Hughes and Philippe Bourgois, (Malden, MA: Blackwell Publishing, 2004), 21.

3. Mark Curtis, *Web of Deceit: Britain's Real Role in the World* (London: Vintage, 2003).

4. W.E.B. DuBois, *The World and Africa*, expanded ed. (New York: International Publishers, 1965[1946]); Hannah Arendt, *Imperialism*, part II of *The Origins of Totalitarianism* (New York: Harcourt, Brace & World, 1951).

5. Scheper-Hughes and Bourgois, "Introduction: Making Sense of Violence," 19.

6. Leith Mullings, "Interrogating Racism: Toward an Antiracist Anthropology," *Annual Review of Anthropology* 34 (2005): 684.

7. Gillem, *American Town*, 37.

8. Catherine Lutz, "A U.S. 'Invasion' of Korea," *Boston Globe*, October 8, 2006; KCTP English News, "When You Grow Up, You Must Take the Village Back," http://www.antigizi.or.kr/zboard/zboard.php?id=english_news&page=1&sn1=&divpage=1&sn=off&ss=on&sc=on&select_arrange=headnum&desc=asc&no=204.

9. Kiste, *TheBikinians*, 198.

10. Stuart B. Barber, letter to the editor of the *Washington Post*, unpublished, March 9, 1991.

11. A. M. Jackson, memorandum for the Chief of Naval Operations, December 7, 1964, NHC: 00 Files, 1965, Box 26, 11000/1B, 3–4.

12. The U.S. Government did not, however, grant the islanders' requests for U.S. citizenship, finding them to be Japanese nationals. In 1961, the U.S. Government paid the islanders of Japanese ancestry $6 million in compensation in the (ultimately failed) hope of stemming their repatriation claims. The U.S. Government maintained the policy of refusing repatriation to those of Japanese descent until 1968, when under continued pressure the islands were returned to Japanese sovereignty. See ibid.

At least one similar case exists, on Ascension Island, part of the British territory of Saint Helena in the Atlantic Ocean. There, about 1,000 islanders who are mostly of mixed ancestry, the descendants of English settlers and enslaved Africans, live and work next to a U.S. base in place since World War II. Together the Bonin-Volcanos and Ascension underline how the pattern of base displacement has been shaped to some extent by population size but as importantly by a closely intertwined nexus of one's skin color, status in the colonial hierarchy, and relative wealth and power.

13. Rivero, "Assuring a Future Base Structure"; see also Bezboruah, *U.S. Strategy in the Indian Ocean*, 58.

14. Richard Rhodes has made this argument. See Thompson, "Arsenal of Words," C2.

15. This analysis builds on Cynthia Enloe's critical insistence that scholars make the gender of foreign policy actors a visible part of foreign policy analysis. See, e.g., Enloe, "Bananas, Bases, and Patriarchy."

16. Hochschild, *King Leopold's Ghost*, 123.

17. Halberstam, *TheBest and the Brightest*, 746. A less aggressive solution to ensure long-term base occupancy would have been to adjust U.S. relations with nations hosting bases or the policies affecting such relationships. This was apparently never considered. Even if taking control of Diego Garcia had remained the policy, the expulsion was again the toughest of policy options in privileging the military's interests over the Chagossians' rights and any policy of coexistence (as was explored in the Bonin-Volcano islands and elsewhere).

18. See Bandjunis, *Diego Garcia,* 167–262.

19. C. Johnson, *The Sorrows of Empire,* 253.

20. Gillem, *American Town,* 263, 272, 17.

21. C. Johnson, *Nemesis,* 148–49, quoting Thomas Donnelly and Vance Serchuk of the neoconservative American Enterprise Institute.

22. Ibid., 147–49.

23. During the 1973 Arab-Israeli war, the base served as a runway for surveillance planes.

24. Seeing the ways in which the United States enjoys a significant degree of *de facto* sovereignty over the world's oceanic territory points to the further similarity (albeit a more hidden one) between the U.S. Empire and the European *territorial* empires of the past. This also points to how the ability of the U.S. Navy to provide unchallenged control of the Earth's major bodies of water since World War II has been another underappreciated pillar of U.S. Empire. As Admiral Mahan pointed out, since the beginning of European expansion in the fifteenth century, with few exceptions, empires have been naval powers. Air forces are increasingly playing a parallel role, but navies have been a critical tool for empires to send troops to conquer foreign lands, to dominate the flow of trade, and to exert political and economic influence over other nations by threat or actual attack. While interest in Diego Garcia shifted from spices to oil, the base illustrates the continuing centrality of naval power to empire, linking the naval empires of France and Britain to the naval empire of the United States, which finally built the base its predecessors coveted. Similarly, Diego Garcia shows how the "geopolitical attractiveness" of island bases has resonated across the centuries. Island bases have been attractive as protected oases from which empires can use their navies to defend oceangoing commerce. As Stuart Barber realized, without large populations or hinterlands to govern, small islands generally have little vulnerability to attack, making them a cost-effective way to support a navy. See George H. Quester, ed., *Sea Power in the 1970s,* Conference on Problems of Naval Armaments, Ithaca, NY, 1972 (New York: Kennikat Press, 1975), 162.

25. Foster, "A Warning to Africa."

26. VOAnews.com, "Sao Tome Sparks American Military Interest," http://www.voanews.com, November 12, 2004, http://www.voanews.com/english/archive/2004-11/2004-11-12-voa42.cfm?CFID=134408071&CFTOKEN=70993939.

27. BBC News, "US Naval Base to Protect Sao Tome Oil," August 22, 2002, http://news.bbc.co.uk/2/hi/business/2210571.stm.

28. IRIN, "Sao Tome and Principe: Attorney General Finds 'Serious Flaws' in the Award of Oil Exploration Contracts," November 15, 2005, http://www.irinnews.org/report.aspx?reportid=57579.

29. Cooley, "Base Politics"; Foster, "A Warning to Africa."

30. Scott, *Limuria,* 68.

31. The creation of a base as part of Britain's last colony, the BIOT, itself created through the dismemberment of the colonies of Mauritius and the Seychelles, suggests ways in which the imperial past lives on in the overseas base network as

part of the "imperial present." See Gregory, *The Colonial Present*. (Thanks to Neil Smith for his suggestion of this phrase playing off Gregory's title.) Many other important U.S. bases are located in colonies or what have recently been colonies, including the bases in Thule, Okinawa, and Britain's Ascension island. Several key bases likewise exist in remaining U.S. colonial possessions, including those in Guam, Puerto Rico (until recently in Vieques), and prior to post–World War II statehood, Hawai'i and Alaska.

Elsewhere in the Pacific after World War II, the United States won basing rights and other colonial rights when the UN granted it trusteeship over the Trust Territory of the Pacific Islands, previously "mandated" to Japan after World War I. In the Marshall Islands, the United States conducted its nuclear testing in the Bikinis and retained an important missile testing facility in the Kwajalein Atoll after the islands gained formal independence in 1986 but entered into a protectorate-like "compact of free association" with the United States. Sandars, *America's Overseas Garrisons*, 36.

Other overseas bases exist largely because of relationships between former European powers and their colonies. Bases acquired through lend-lease are a prime example, where the U.S. Government negotiated continued occupation deals after World War II with the help of the still-ruling British. The same is true for post-war French bases in Morocco. In Panama and the Philippines, the United States has benefited from its own neocolonial relationships to maintain important bases near the Panama Canal and in East Asia. The maintenance of U.S. bases in these nations often represents a continuation of colonial relationships in a different form. See Sandars, *America's Overseas Garrisons*, 13.

32. Ho, "Empire through Diasporic Eyes," 232, 238–39. On the privatization of the military, see, e.g., Clifford Rosky, "Force, Inc.: The Privatization of Punishment, Policing, and Military Force in Liberal States," *Connecticut Law Review* 36 (2004): 879–1032.

33. Ho, "Empire through Diasporic Eyes," 230.

34. C. Johnson, *Nemesis*, 171–207. Precedent for this kind of "extraterritoriality" goes back at least to the 1839–1842 Opium War in China. See Ho, "Empire through Diasporic Eyes," 232.

35. Ibid., 230.

36. My thanks to Hugh Gusterson and others for stressing this point.

37. U.S. Congress, House, "Diego Garcia, 1975," 46.

38. The issue of who is a Chagossian should be left to those who self-identify as Chagossians. I would suggest, however, that many long-term Chagos residents who happened, for various reasons, not to have been born in Chagos, but who in some cases were the descendants of people born in Chagos, should be considered eligible for compensation of some kind.

39. Lincoln P. Bloomfield, Jr., letter to Robert N. Culshaw, April 29, 2004.

40. E.g., Gerson, "The Sun Never Sets"; Cynthia Enloe, *Bananas, Beaches and Bases: Making Feminist Sense of International Politics* (Berkeley, CA: University of

California Press, 1990); "Bananas, Bases, and Patriarchy," in *Women, Militarism, and War: Essays in History, Politics, and Social Theory*, ed. Jean B. Elshtain and Sheila Tobias (Savage, MD: Rowman & Littlefield, 1993), 189–206; *The Morning After: Sexual Politics at the End of the Cold War* (Berkeley, CA: University of California Press, 1993); Lutz, *Homefront*; Sandars, *America's Overseas Garrisons*; Baker, *American Soldiers Overseas*; Gillem, *American Town*.

Epilogue

1. Barber, unpublished letter to the editor of the *Washington Post*, March 9, 1991.

2. Madeley, "Diego Garcia."

3. Stuart B. Barber, letter to Aryeh Neier [executive director, Human Rights Watch], February 23, 1993.

4. Barber, letter to Senator Ted Stevens, October 3, 1975.

5. Richard Barber, email, February 24, 2008.

INDEX

Acheson, Dean, 99
Adam, Jean Baptiste, 31, 32, 33
Addu Atoll, 56
Afghan war, 9
Afghanistan, 16, 43, 194
Africa, 21, 23; as a source of oil for the United States, 188–89
"Africa Command" (AFRICOM), 189
Afro-Mauritians (Creoles), 131, 135, 137, 138–39, 140, 143; *ti-kreol* ("little Creole") subset of, 139
Alaska, 246–47n31; displacement of Aleutian islanders, 66
Aldabra Affair, 98
Aldabra Island, 79, 85–86, 96, 99–100, 228n12
Alexis, Charlesia, 168
American Samoa, 48
Andaman Islands, 56
anthropology/anthropologists, and research concerning empire, 210–11n49
Arab-Israeli War (1973), 121, 246n23
Ascension Island, 50, 53, 184, 245n12, 246–47n31
Ashworth, Frederick L., 63
Attu Island, 66
Aust, Anthony, 92
Azores, 50, 53, 121, 184

Bagley, Worth H., 107
Baie du Tombeau, 147
Bahrain, 53, 56, 60
Balad Air Base, 17
Bancoult, Alex, 6, 140, 141, 142, 148, 195; death of his wife by suicide, 153
Bancoult, Eddy, 6, 142, 148, 195
Bancoult, Ivo, 132, 159–60
Bancoult, Julien, 5, 6, 127, 195; death of, from *sagren* (profound sorrow), 149; illness (stroke) of, 132–33
Bancoult, Louis Olivier, 141, 168, 169–70, 175, 177–78, 179, 243n34; on the rights of Chagossians, 191, 195

Bancoult, Marie Rita Elysée, 1, 2, 5–6, 18, 20, 39, 68, 132–33, 141, 167, 168; coconut/copra-processing occupation of, 30–31; on the death of her husband, 149; living conditions of in Cassis, 127–28; social status of, 137
Bancoult, Mimose, 141, 142, 162
Bancoult, Noellie, 5, 39, 127
Bancoult, Rénault, 6, 148, 195
Bandjunis, Vytautas, 42
Barber, Richard, 197–98, 205n5
Barber, Stuart, 4, 18, 59–60, 61, 68, 69, 182, 184, 197–98, 244n1; and the "Strategic Island Concept," 4–5, 41–42, 49, 60
Barksdale Air Force Base (Louisiana), 187
"base displacement," 65-68, 182-83
Benedict, Burton, 134
Benedict, Marion, 134
Bikini Atoll, 16, 63, 246–47n31; compensation paid to the Bikinians by the United States, 221n33; removal of the native Bikinians by the U.S. Navy, 63–64
Bishop, James, 117
Blood, Hilary, 38
Bloomfield, Lincoln P., 177
Bonin-Volcano Islands, 183, 184, 245n12
Boswell, Rosabelle, 135
Botte, Francoise, 136, 138
Bowman, Larry, 21
Boxer Rebellion, 43, 49
Brazil, 50
British East India Company, 23
British Indian Ocean Territory (BIOT), 7, 15, 85, 87, 90–91, 102, 108, 173–74, 178, 180, 244n1; partial payment of its expenses by the United States, 83, 87, 116; refusal of to allow Chagossians back to Diego Garcia, 92–93; ships of (*Nordvær* and *Isle of Farquhar*) used in deportation of Chagossians from Diego Garcia, 109, 113, 114–15, 119–20,

249